ROME'S DESERT
· FRONTIER ·
FROM THE AIR

ROME'S DESERT · FRONTIER ·

FROM THE AIR

David Kennedy & Derrick Riley

B.T. Batsford Limited · London

Typeset by Lasertext,
Thomas Street, Stretford, Manchester M 3 2 0 J T
Printed and bound in Great Britain by
Courier International, Tiptree, Essex

for the publishers
B.T. Batsford Limited,
4 Fitzhardinge Street,
London W 1 H 0 A H

I S B N 0 7134 6262 0

· ACKNOWLEDGEMENTS ·

A work of this sort is dependent on the assistance, co-operation and advice of very many individuals and organizations.

For helpful discussion and advice on specific points, and for general assistance we thank: Jean Ch. Balty, Thomas Bauzou, Alison Betts, Duncan Campbell, Dov Gavish, Michel Gawlikowski, Mordechai Gichon, John Woodhead, Oleg Grabar, Svend Helms, Antonio Invernizzi, Ben Isaac, Geoffrey King, John Larson, Jean Lauffray, Pierre Leriche, Henry MacAdam, Alison McQuitty, Susan Matheson, Avraham Negev, David Oates, Maurice Sartre, Joseph Shereshewski, Yoram Tsafrir, Donald Whitcomb and David Wilson.

For providing or assisting us to obtain illustrations we are specially grateful to: Joseph Aviram, Ghazi Bisheh, Bert DeVries, Philip Freeman, Heinz Gaube, Richard Harper, Jean Batiste Humbert, Alistair Killick, Burton MacDonald, John Matthews, Alastair Northedge, S. Thomas Parker, Michel Piccirillo, Julian Reade, Timothy Rogers, Jim Sauer, Dalya Topel and Francois Villeneuve.

Our colleagues Colin Davies, John Rogerson and Jim Roy have helped with translation.

Various institutions have been generous with their help:
Bodleian Library (Timothy Rogers); British Academy (Jane Woods); British Library, India Office Library and Records (Barry Bloomfield); British Museum (T.C. Mitchell); Institute of Archaeology, London University (John Evans); Library of Congress (George Hobart); Royal Jordanian Geographic Centre (R. Majali); and Yale University Art Gallery (Susan Matheson).

For preparing many of the photographic prints: Peter Morley, David Maddison, John Owens and Bob Wilkins.

Especially deserving of our thanks are: Brenda Cook, Richard Harper and Arthur Segal. Shelagh Gregory kindly read the final draft; Graham Webster also read the entire text – some of it twice – to our considerable benefit. Julie Kennedy laboured for months over the drawings, some of which had to be altered several times.

Finally, we are grateful to the British Academy for generous financial assistance towards the cost of obtaining photographs and preparing drawings.

Figures 35 and 179 have been redrawn and Figures 59 and 75 are reproduced by permission of Wilfrid Laurier University Press from B. MacDonald, 1988.

· CONTENTS ·

PART A
· *Geographical and Historical* ·
Context

PART B
· *Aerial Photography and* ·
Archaeological Prospection

PART C
· *The Sites* ·

CONTENTS

PART D
· Conclusion ·

·ILLUSTRATIONS·

·CHAPTER ELEVEN·
Towers

·CHAPTER TWELVE·
Miscellaneous

·CHAPTER THIRTEEN·
Bones Of The Red Horse

And I saw, and behold a white horse; and he that sat on him had a bow; and a crown was given unto him; and he went forth conquering and to conquer ... And there went out another horse that was red; and power was given to him that sat thereon to take peace from the earth, and that they should kill one another: and there was given unto him a great sword. ... And I beheld, and lo a black horse; and he that sat on him had a pair of balances in his hand. ... And I looked, and behold a pale horse: and his name that sat on him was Death, and Hell followed with him.

THE REVELATION 6.2–8

· PREFACE ·

In the published proceedings of what has proved to be the first of a series of conferences on Roman frontier studies, Sir Mortimer Wheeler began and ended his contribution on 'The Roman frontier in Mesopotamia' by referring to a well-known passage in the *The Revelation*. The first two of these 'Four Horsemen of the Apocalypse' – the white and the red in the book's opening quotation – are commonly interpreted as symbolizing the great empires of Parthia and Rome in the later first century AD, on the eve of a series of destructive wars. With a characteristically dramatic flourish, Wheeler concluded his paper on a hopeful note:

with a jeep and a proper sense of adventure [a young scholar] can sally forth into the desert with the complete assurance of immortal fame. The bones of the red horse and the white await him there, *res vetustate ac raritate notabiles, gigantum ossa et arma heroum.*

(Wheeler, 1952, 128)

Such optimism was well founded when he wrote. The years between the two World Wars had been a period of steady progress in Middle Eastern archaeology, and it was natural in 1949 to assume that this would be resumed. After the end of Ottoman rule in 1918, British and French administrations had opened up Syria, Iraq, Transjordan and Palestine to investigation much more widely. For the Europeans and Americans who then had access, this was a land of enormous interest and excitement: the Holy Land and the neighbouring lands of the Bible. Areas seldom if ever reached by western explorers were penetrated, hundreds of ancient sites were visited and scores were excavated. Several of the excavations were considerable undertakings (Antioch, Gerasa, Palmyra and Hama) and the work at Dura Europos was outstanding. Men then, or soon to be, dominant figures in classical scholarship were involved: Cumont, Rostovtzeff, A.H.M. Jones,

Hopkins, Brown, Kraeling, Welles. And overhead, a passenger in French military aircraft, was the remarkable priest, Père Antoine Poidebard. Flying over regions difficult to reach on the ground and pioneering a technique of the first importance, he found and photographed roads, forts and towns. His classic work, *La Trace de Rome dans le Désert de Syrie*, transformed the map of the Roman frontier in Syria. A few years afterwards, stimulated by Poidebard's achievements, Sir Aurel Stein examined a vast territory and produced complementary maps for Iraq and Transjordan. War intervened, but by 1939 scholars were fully aware of the enormous potential of the region for archaeological exploration and the vital role the aeroplane could play.

By 1949, when the Second World War was four years past, archaeological research in the Middle East could be taken up again. Regrettably, however, the post-war period proved to be an anti-climax, with too little done to match the work of the period between the wars. In particular, as a result of the political situation in the Middle East, the pioneer aerial researches of Poidebard and Stein have not been continued by programmes of aerial reconnaissance comparable to those now in progress in parts of western Europe. The latter have revolutionized knowledge of the ancient landscapes of several European countries and of their ancient remains, especially those below the surface of the ground. One can only speculate on how much could have been achieved in the Middle East in the same period with a fraction of the effort. In this region, where land development has been accelerating rapidly, much has now been lost or damaged. For a generation, scholarship has been the poorer for the diminished level of all fieldwork in the area; the loss of material is a tragedy for the future.

In preparing this book, one of our most revealing discoveries was the extent to which the Roman East was *terra incognita* for even otherwise very well informed scholars. In the field of military studies, only Dura Europos and Masada seemed at all familiar. It is our hope that the book, through its air photographs, will bring at least one part and one phase of the marvellous archaeological heritage of the Middle East to life for a wider audience, evoking the remarkable landscapes and lonely places in which the Roman army was based.

The work has been divided into four parts. In Part A there are chapters on the geography of the region and a brief historical survey of the seven centuries of Roman rule. In Part B, comes a short history of air photography for archaeology in the Middle East and of the men involved, then an examination of the techniques employed by two of these pioneers, Poidebard and Stein. Given the importance of the former in the development of air photography, a large part of his original text describing his methods is provided in translation, and a commentary on it follows. Finally, in Part C, which is the core of the book, some 80 specific sites are illustrated and discussed, beginning with chapters on the Roman infrastructure of these regions – water supply and communications – and continuing to look at individual fortifications under a variety of headings: fortress cities, legionary fortresses, forts of various kinds, towers and miscellaneous military sites. The concluding section, Part D, considers some of the lessons learned and gives some detailed summing up.

David Kennedy   Sheffield, 1988
Derrick Riley

· INTRODUCTION ·

· Background ·

At its greatest extent – under the Emperor Septimius Severus (AD 193-211) – the Roman Empire encompassed some 2 million square miles. Subdivided for administrative purposes into some 50 provinces, its outer limits extended from Central Scotland to the Soviet Republic of Georgia, from the Red Sea to the Atlantic coast of Morocco, a perimeter of some 25,000 km (15,000 miles).

Security was always the primary consideration for the rulers of the Roman Empire. Three-quarters of the perimeter needed to be watched, though some parts more than others, while internally the populace had to be policed and, on occasion, the authority of the emperors had to be maintained against rebellion. By any standard prior to the seventeenth century, the Roman forces for these functions were huge: inclusive of naval forces and the troops in Italy, there were some 400,000 men under arms in the Severan period (cf. Birley, 1981, 39-43; MacMullen, 1980). The financial burden of so large a force was immense: perhaps half the state's income devoted to pay and retirement gratuities (Hopkins, 1980), as well as many of the most able-bodied men largely lost to directly productive activity.

Roman historians have long been fascinated with the forces that maintained the empire. However, their pre-occupation with the period from the first century BC to the collapse of the Western Empire in the early fifth century AD should not obscure the true length of Roman military experience. 'Rome' (in which concept we include the New Rome on the Bosphorus) was involved with questions of population control and territorial defence for over two millenia, from the eighth century BC to AD 1453. Inevitably the numbers, size, organization and character of the army varied considerably during so long a time, but the military history of any period examined within this great span must be seen in context, as a part of a greater whole.

Some of the fundamentals are well established for the major phases of military history. For the Early Empire (27 BC-AD 284), for example, the number of legions and their distribution are well known, and a growing corpus of evidence has given the identity and location of many of the hundreds of provincial auxiliary regiments. The main lines of the frontiers during this period are well established. There is a large body of information about the Roman army, its equipment and facilities, but most readers of this book would do well to remind themselves that their knowledge and perception of the defences of the Roman Empire and to some extent of the Roman army have been conditioned by the immense amount now known about the military zones of Britain and the frontier along the Rhine and Upper Danube. In contrast, the Roman provinces in the East have provided relatively little information so far, though this book will demonstrate how much there is to be learned.

It is instructive to compare the present state of knowledge in these two widely separated zones of the Empire. The military installations of Britain and the frontier provinces as far as the Upper Danube are well known, although the majority have been severely damaged by later exploitation of their sites, particularly by agriculture. This damage has not prevented archaeological surveys, both on the ground and from the air, and excavations from providing copious information about many hundreds of sites, often permitting scholars to develop a detailed and broadly reliable sequence of events, even where literary evidence is slight or lacking. In a local context, archaeologists and historians may think this satisfactory, but the situation will be better understood when reviewed against a wider knowledge of frontier areas elsewhere in the Empire.

The archaeological evidence is much less satisfactory in the eastern and southern provinces of the Empire. Ironically, the remains of Roman structures are often much more imposing; impressive ruins have been revealed in Romania and Bulgaria in recent years, while in parts of North Africa forts are frequently in an astonishingly good state. In the Middle East, the region with which we are here concerned, there is a wealth of little known, though often remarkably well preserved military structures. The area was fought over for centuries and its history was important and complex. The Eastern Empire prospered for two centuries after the end of the Roman Empire in the West. The military sites must preserve a mass of information which would illuminate knowledge of military history. As yet, however, very few sites have been investigated and it may be assumed that many more remain to be discovered. The warfare and political troubles that have plagued the Middle East since the end of the Second World War have caused scholars to lose sight of the importance of the information about the Roman Empire that is waiting to be gathered there.

· The Eastern Frontier ·

The frontier of the Roman Empire in the East ran through a series of 'front line' provinces from the Black Sea to the Red Sea (Figs. 4-7). Great distances were involved; to journey from one extreme of this region to the other, the Roman traveller would have had to cover at least 2000 km (about 1250 miles), even by the most direct route. The political frontier, the land border of the Asiatic Empire, was even longer, probably in the order of 3000 km (nearly 2000 miles) in length. Across this entire region it is still possible to view the remains of Roman military works, the great majority seemingly built between the second and sixth centuries AD. They were constructed to assist in the defence against external dangers – from the great Parthian Empire and its successor Sasanian Persia, and from their mutual neighbours, the peoples of the Caucasus, the Armenians and the Arab nomads – and to police the border areas of the provinces themselves. The frequency of these sites as known at present is, however, very different between the Turkish and the 'Arab' sectors.

From literature and some epigraphic finds, it is known that there were considerable Roman forces in the eastern territory of modern Turkey. Numerous military bases are named in various documents, in particular the *Notitia Dignitatum*, but very few of them have yet been traced along the mountainous Turkish stretch of the 'Euphrates frontier' of the Roman Empire. Here the fertile valleys have long been attractive to settlers, and in consequence ruins have tended to be demolished for their building materials.

In contrast, Roman forts and military works are often well preserved at sites between the Turkish border and the Red Sea, a region where a large proportion of the population has until recently been nomadic. There has been less cultivation of the land and less damage to ancient structures, though things are changing rapidly. Along this 'desert frontier' of the Empire, which ran from the Middle Tigris in northern Iraq, through Syria and Jordan, to the Gulf of Aqaba, relatively few of the many Roman sites have been investigated on the ground, but it was the scene of some of the earliest and most important work by aerial archaeologists.

· Aerial Survey on · the Eastern Frontier

The aeroplane has not been used in Turkey to search for archaeological sites, and air photographs taken there for other purposes are seldom available to scholars. There are clearly great possibilities for aerial survey along the Roman Empire's frontier in that country, but they must await the attention of future archaeologists when current restrictions have been relaxed.

On the desert frontier, however, aerial survey has been one of the main sources of information. Here the Roman military remains have been examined and recorded from the air with great profit. The French scholar, Père Antoine Poidebard, was one of the very first people to realize the possibilities of archaeological work from the air, and his researches in Syria are the foundation of the present book. His work was contemporary with, but independent of, that of Dr O.G.S. Crawford in Britain, the other founder of aerial archaeology (Riley, 1987, 11).

Poidebard and, after him, Sir Aurel Stein were able to take advantage of the presence of the French and British air forces during the period between the two World Wars, when the territories of the former Roman frontier provinces came under the French and British mandates. Between them these two outstanding men reconnoitred a major block of territory which covered some two-thirds of the frontier provinces of the Roman Asiatic East and included the border shared with its great imperial neighbour Parthia, later Sasanian Persia.

· The Desert Frontier ·

The information supplied by air photographs of sites on the desert portion of the eastern frontier of the Roman Empire is the core of this book. There are many gaps in the evidence, but a remarkable picture emerges of the Roman military sites, the importance of which will be seen.

Along the desert frontier, the zone of military installations stretches for about 1200 km (750 miles). The forts and other military works found there stand in territories which are only now beginning to recover from centuries of decay. The prosperity of the Late Roman period continued through the brilliant century of the Muslim Ommayad dynasty (661–750), but this was followed by decline in the later Arab centuries, the disaster of the Mongol invasions and periods of misrule and neglect under the Ottoman Empire. Wholesale abandonment of the land and of many outlying towns and villages took place. From this low point, re-settlement of the more marginal areas recommenced in the nineteenth century (Hütteroth and Abdulfattah, 1977; Lewis, 1986), but it has only been in the last 50 years that the extension of the area of cultivated land and the growth of towns and villages have become rapid.

· The Nature of · the Evidence

Beginning in the second century BC, Roman administration and control was progressively advanced into the Near and Middle East. At first only literary evidence is available to provide knowledge of the wars in the region and the means by which Rome secured and protected her new eastern provinces. From the later first century onwards the range and extent of the evidence widens. The literature continues to be invaluable, and there is archaeological information from the widely distributed remains of forts and roads in the frontier zone.

In the 1920s and 1930s, much of the land surface in the Middle East and the buildings on it were still in a state not very different from hundreds of years before. What would we not give to have pictures equivalent to air photographs of landscapes and sites in western Europe as they were at the end of the Middle Ages? From the Middle East there are air photographs of this kind, because some sites were recorded half a century ago. Figure 56 is a striking record of this nature, a Royal Air Force vertical photograph of the fort at the Azraq Oasis in Jordan, taken in 1927, when the oasis had no regular inhabitants, long before the growth of the town which now covers the land round the fort.

The excellent photographs in Poidebard's first book, *La Trace de Rome dans le Désert de Syrie* (1934), were reproduced by photogravure. In the absence of the original negatives, this process has allowed a selection of his published illustrations to be copied to a high standard in some of the plates below. There is no doubt that Poidebard took many more pictures of archaeological sites than he published, but there is uncertainty about the present whereabouts of the archive he left (below, p. 63). Stein's air photographs are very important, but only those of Iraq are available. Those taken in Jordan cannot be traced (Kennedy, 1982, 201).

Relatively few are left of the vertical photographs taken by the Royal Air Force during their long stay in the Middle East from the end of the First World War till 1955. Several thousand frames are still held by the Royal Air Force but far more have been destroyed, partly because of the difficulty of storing the cellulose nitrate-based negatives standard for much of that period. A selection from the surviving material is given below. Some good pre-war (1925–35) French vertical surveys of parts of Syria are still extant (Villeneuve, 1985, 65), though they are not readily available to British scholars at present. Old air photographs are therefore much less numerous than might have been the case and are correspondingly valuable.

For the time being, the only new sources of information to supplement the pre-war air photographs are prints from air surveys made on the order of current government agencies or from practice photographs made by their air forces. While these can be of immense interest, there are problems and limitations. First, they are hard to obtain in some countries and unobtainable in others. Nor, of course, were they (or the British and French air force surveys) taken with archaeology in mind. The vertical surveys from which they come are normally made at much smaller scales than Poidebard's verticals (e.g. Figs 24 and 68) or the obliques taken by present day archaeologists working in western Europe and North America. It has therefore been necessary to illustrate some sites at rather small scales (e.g. Figs. 47 and 144).

Field work and excavation are still in an early stage in the region. This is a particularly serious problem in Syria and Iraq, where there is a special need to investigate the sites shown by the existing stock of air photographs and to widen knowledge about Roman sites in general. It is unfortunate that less is known than might have been the case about those sites which were investigated between the wars, before the humbler forms of evidence could be exploited to the full. It is frustrating to realize that during the famous and highly productive Franco-American excavations between 1928 and 1938 in the city of Dura Europos (Figs. 58-60) little stratigraphy was observed, so that comparatively few of the coarse wares preserved could be dated (Dyson, 1968, vii-ix, 1; cf. Hassall, 1972). Lack of knowledge about pottery types meant that very little information about the dates of occupation of supposed Roman forts was brought back by Poidebard from the sondages he made (e.g. Fig. 132), by Stein from his observations on surface sherds (see for example Gregory and Kennedy (Stein), 1985, 107; 121), or by other archaeologists who visited the sites in the zone of the former Roman frontier in Syria and Iraq between the wars. It is now encouraging to know, however, that the current work on Roman military sites in Jordan is producing much carefully recorded data and providing a better foundation for Roman studies there (e.g. Parker, 1976; cf. 1986, 10ff).

The results of having no immediate if crude dating medium are apparent when considering many of the air photographs of eastern forts. In north-western Europe most military sites of the Roman period stand out because they are peculiar in plan to the centuries of Roman rule. Parts that were re-used, even reconstructed, in later periods, are relatively easily differentiated from the generally better executed Roman work. The East, in contrast, enjoyed a long tradition of technical excellence in construction techniques, architecture and planning. Not only is it less easy to isolate Roman sites in the East from those of older or more recent periods – or even from contemporary Parthian and Persian – but indigenous influences clearly played a part in the development of Roman military architecture. It is particularly difficult to understand certain forts built in the Roman period, but later remodelled under Islam (below, p. 140).

When reading the works of Poidebard and Stein, it is necessary to remember their tendency to attribute forts to the Roman period because of a regular plan or square shape. There is no proof of the Roman date of many of their sites on the *limes* in north-eastern Syria and in Iraq. The present political situation makes it unlikely that the problem will be resolved quickly. In selecting photographs for this book it has therefore seemed best to accept some of the more plausible of Poidebard's and Stein's unsupported identifications of sites. Sooner or later, however, it must be hoped that there will be the much larger scale work on the ground that is necessary to tackle the question.

Finally, it must be stressed that in selecting photographs for inclusion, the authors could not put together a fully representative sample of the known sites. Rather the choice had to be made from the *available* photographs, which, given the gaps in the photographic coverage, must inevitably result in some unevenness in this survey.

· *Objectives Of* · *this Book*

The pioneering work in aerial archaeology during the 1920s and 1930s by Crawford in Britain and Poidebard in Syria has been followed up very differently in the two countries. In Britain it took root, and later spread to various countries of western Europe, where archaeological air photographers have since found and recorded ancient sites by the thousand, including large numbers of Roman military stations.

How different has been the course of events in the Middle East. Poidebard's surveys were the direct stimulus to Stein's explorations in 1938-9, and also to those by Jean Baradez in North Africa immediately after the Second World War (Baradez, 1949). Unfortunately, however, these men have had no successors because of the very restrictive policies towards aviation by the authorities of the modern states in the regions they explored from the air.

It is regrettable that aerial reconnaissance and photography are not being used widely and systematically to record the antiquities of these states, where parts of the archaeological heritage are now being damaged seriously or even destroyed by the rapid pace of modern developments. Even the most extensive and best-preserved Roman structures will succumb to modern machinery and to population pressure, and if more is not soon done to record and study the ancient sites, further major losses to knowledge will result. There have been encouraging developments in Jordan and Israel, but the slowness of the authorities in other countries of the region to adopt a more open policy continues to contribute to the progressive erosion of remains whose loss they may soon lament.

An important objective of this book is therefore to draw attention to the need to take the following steps: for the results of the great air photographers of the past, Poidebard and Stein, to be reviewed and continued by ground surveys; for the authorities of all Middle Eastern states to release for archaeological study (of all periods) the sets of vertical photographs covering large areas that have been made for government agencies since the Second World War; and for air reconnaissance and photography by archaeologists to be resumed and for the results to be mapped and later followed up by surveys on the ground.

This book will begin the first task, reviewing the work of the great pioneer aerial archaeologists. In support of the second proposal, the release of the vertical air surveys for study, it must be pointed out that many of them are too old to record any sensitive military information, while their very age makes them especially valuable to the archaeologist as records of ancient landscapes which have been damaged in recent years.

Another objective is, by collection of photographs and information, to draw the attention of archaeologists to the remains of structures built by or connected with the Roman army in the Middle East and to encourage more work on them. This book will have served an important purpose if it stimulates enthusiasm for the wider archaeological potential of a fascinating and extensive part of the Roman Empire.

Beyond these objectives, the reader will want to know what wider conclusions may be drawn. The military works illustrated here form a substantial and fairly representative part of what is known in total. As such, they offer the opportunity to summarize the salient points of the information now available and to begin a classification of the Roman military works in this part of the East. In Part C – the main part of the book – is a series of chapters describing various classes of structures. Each chapter is introduced with what can safely be deduced at this juncture about the class of site described. The whole is drawn together in a concluding chapter, but it is important to stress at the outset that this book is not a history of the eastern frontier – nor even the desert frontier; present knowledge is so slight, so few sites have been properly investigated and, as mentioned above, even the Roman date of some forts is not proven. To look for the sort of detailed discussion of tactics and strategy possible with better-known frontiers is to misunderstand what is known of the East. This book should be regarded rather as an important step towards the eventual understanding of the events, trends and policies that make up the history of the frontier and the Roman army in the Middle East.

It is hoped that this work will serve to bring a

greater balance to Roman frontier studies. Though far less well known, the eastern frontier was hardly less vital to Rome than her frontiers on the Rhine and Danube and much more so than the still longer frontier in North Africa. Judged by the relative output of scholars on various sectors of the Roman frontier one would not readily guess that it was in the East alone that Rome confronted the only other great power on her borders.

· TERMINOLOGY AND CLASSIFICATION ·

At the present embryonic stage of classification of the military works of the Roman army in the eastern desert, an agreed terminology has yet to be developed by archaeologists. This is an important but difficult subject, which cannot be ignored in a book that describes a selection of the structures recorded from the air. The terms 'fortress', 'fort', 'watch tower' have varied meanings to archaeologists working in different parts of the Empire and even to those considering different periods. Inevitably, various authors have felt obliged to produce their own definitions. For example, the current standard treatment, *Roman Forts of the 1st and 2nd Centuries AD in Britain and the German Provinces* (A. Johnson, 1983), offered as a generalized definition that:

a fort is ... a permanent fortification ranging in size from c.1 to 5 hectares in internal area, which normally housed a unit of auxiliary infantry or cavalry of 500 or 1000 men, or very occasionally a combined auxiliary and legionary force, whilst a legionary fortress of some 20 hectares was designed to house a full legion of between 5000 and 6000 men.

For the purpose of the present study, such a definition is too limited. It does not cover the small forts of less than one hectare nor various anomalous sites, and was not intended to accommodate the longer time-span of the Eastern Empire and the rather different character and location of garrisons in the East, especially in the later centuries. Consequently, over half the forts illustrated below are less than 1 ha. (2.47 acres) in size, and a majority of those which can be dated closely belong to the Late Empire, a period which extends in the East by over two centuries beyond the latest Roman fortifications in the West.

For the eastern frontier a general classification must be quite wide-ranging to accommodate all the various types of military station. Within this, it may be expected that a refined typology will eventually be developed for each of a number of broad categories. Taking as a first example the most extensive sites, the fortress cities, only about Dura Europos (Figs. 58 and 60) are we well informed. Although, in the West, there were certainly fortress cities in the third and fourth centuries, there was nothing to parallel the major garrisons that were probably established inside towns in the urbanized East as early as the first centuries BC and AD. As a second example, the smallest defended structures, the watch towers, may be cited. Although many are known in the Middle East, few have been examined closely. Between these extremes, however, simply dividing fortifications into fairly arbitrary categories begins to make things clearer.

In this study, many of the fortified sites have been divided very crudely into 'fortresses', i.e. those which are known or suspected to have housed legions, and 'forts'. The important point here is the distinction between those sites intended for a legion (or large legionary force) and those for one or more auxiliary regiments, whatever numerical strength those terms actually meant at different times.

It is essential to take cognizance of the reduced manning of legions and auxiliary units in the Later Empire. Both declined dramatically in size and required far less space than in the Early Empire. The legionary base at Lejjun (Fig. 76), occupying only 4.6 ha. (11.4 acres), and the auxiliary fort of Khan el-Hallabat (Fig. 151), 0.22 ha. (0.55 acres) in area, have only some 20 per cent and 10 per cent respectively of the areas of typical Early Empire fortresses and forts in the West. Khan el-Hallabat would be no more than a 'fortlet' in the classification of Roman military sites in the north-western empire of the first to third centuries (cf. Collingwood and Richmond, 1969, 68ff). Archaeologists working in the West have customarily defined a 'fortlet' as the base of an outposted detachment, reserving 'fort' for the base of the administrative parent unit. The small units of the Late Empire, not necessarily even broadly uniform in size, make this a meaningless distinction.

The forts have been grouped into those with projecting towers and those without, and then subdivided according to ground area into 'large' and 'small' sub-groups. The 'small' forts include some which occupy only 0.17, 0.19 and 0.22 ha (0.42, 0.47 and 0.54 acres) (Figs. 151, 153 and 155), but which, nevertheless, were apparently occupied by discrete Late Empire auxiliary units. This classification is no more than a preliminary attempt to put the material in order, but it has the advantage of allowing us to categorize the often imprecise information from a long time period.

There are anomalies that raise many problems. Thus, the fort at Ertaje has an irregular 'promontory-fort' appearance (Fig. 180), and, ironically, one of the best-known forts, Ain Sinu I (Fig. 167), is unusually large (10.7 ha. or 26.5 acres in area), but cannot be treated − as it might be in the West − as a legionary 'vexillation fortress'. Moreover, its internal layout appears to belong to a type so far identified only in the East.

Poidebard produced his own typology based exclusively on the forts in Syria (Poidebard, 1934, 51-6), but it contains little that is still of value today. Lander (1984) has much more usefully re-examined some of these sites in the context of Roman stone fortifications empire-wide. Some reference will be made to his conclusions, which are a major area of study, but no systematic attempt can be made here to follow up Lander's detailed classification of features such as the plans of towers.

The English terms fortress, fort, camp, tower are normally used in this book. The Romans themselves employed various terms to describe their military bases. Unfortunately, literary requirements led classical writers to strive for elegant variations in vocabulary with often misleading consequences for us. On the relatively infrequent occasions when Latin terms are used below, we have followed the common but by no means universal custom in employing *castra* for a legionary fortress, *castrum* for an auxiliary fort of the Early Empire, and *castellum*, the diminutive, for its Late Empire successor. These and other such terms are listed in the Glossary.

The most difficult terms of all are 'frontier' and '*limes*'. Frontier, *frontière, frontiera, Grenze*, etc. is readily understood as a precise line marking the division between the territories of adjoining states. Its character on the ground can have enormous variations; contrast the frontiers of the United States with its Canadian and Mexican neighbours or, more striking still, those of West Germany with East Germany on one side and the Netherlands on the other. Roman frontiers too varied considerably in character. There is, however, also a problem even about the point at which a 'frontier' province ended. The governor of, say, Syria, would know perfectly well where his province ended. He would also know, however, that his *provincia*, the responsibility with which he had been charged, was more extensive than merely the region under his direct administration. The situation varied of course, but in the Early Empire the province of Syria had 'external' frontiers with friendly states such as Herodian Judaea and Emesa, with hostile states such as Osrhoene, and with desert nomads with whom relations may not have been at all regulated or consistent. All of these nevertheless formed part of the governor's *provincia*, and involved a variety of military responses. No military control was required on the boundary between province and the first type of neighbour, a measure of military preparedness would be required in the case of the second, and a military policing force for the third. Circumstances altered. As friendly neighbours were brought under direct administration, Rome came increasingly to have only potentially hostile neighbours or, with the elimination of such neighbours as the Nabataean kingdom, direct responsibility for policing nomads seeking to pass back and forth between the province and the non-administered desert.

The frontier with which we are here concerned was seldom ever like some ancient Maginot Line. In Mesopotamia in the Late Roman period, there were frontier fortresses such as Dara (Roman) and Nisibis (Sasanian) facing each other across a frontier line in a fashion more familiar in Europe since the time of Louis XIV. Across the desert to the south over which no great army would seek an invasion route, such defences would have been meaningless, as there was no line to be manned or patrolled; indeed, there may well have been a broad no man's land in places.

There is another problem in interpreting the distribution of defended sites identifiable in a frontier region. Most of the military installations illustrated and discussed below were intended to provide security against an external threat, whether a major power such as Parthia or Sasanian Persia, or the more modest danger from nomads who had to be policed. On the other hand, troops were stationed in *all* Roman provinces for purposes other than defence: as guards for the governor or some of the senior provincial officials and for other public duties (as Pliny describes for Bithynia: *Ep.* X.19-22); the protection of major inter-provincial strategic highways (as in Galatia); to collect customs dues; to control turbulent populations (Judaea, renamed Syria Palaestina under Hadrian) or difficult terrain suited to banditry (Cilicia). The numbers could vary considerably but could require quite substantial forces on a long-term basis. Most striking was Judaea. For most of the period in question, the province had no external frontier but there was nevertheless a huge army: in the second century, two entire legions and some 4500 auxiliaries. For the other provinces under discussion, because there was an external threat and the need to police the nomads, additional troops had to be allocated. In consequence the functions of the garrisons could be very varied, even in the desert region from which most of our evidence comes. In addition, the location at which units were stationed was governed not only by strategic factors, but also by the need to be able to supply them with water and food. To some extent troops had to be located near areas of food surplus or in places where food could be got to them without excessive difficulty. The vital water supply, if not readily available, could be obtained by tapping ground water or by collecting such rainfall as there was. A pattern of forts extending back behind a frontier line need not be defence in depth, simply a sensible solution to a logistical problem.

It is precisely because of the potentially misleading picture conjured up by our word 'frontier' that the term '*limes*' has been extensively employed in modern discussions of Rome's frontiers. This is a term which in origin referred to tracks and roads defining boundaries between land holdings. Close study (Isaac, 1988) of the use of the term reveals that its meaning varied over the centuries of its use in Roman sources. In the early first century AD it was applied to military roads, later it was used of administrative borders, and finally, from the fourth century, applied to frontier districts. The term does not imply the presence of military structures as such. Indeed, for the East it comes to refer loosely to the eastern desert. For present purposes, we employ both 'frontier' and '*limes*' but the reader has to bear in mind the varied nature of the military dispositions in any province and that there probably never was at any given time a single uniform procedure along the entire desert frontier, much less the eastern frontier as a whole, or all the frontiers of the empire.

Finally, there are also problems with chronological terms and geographical labels. With no consensus internationally as to where one divides 'Roman' from 'Byzantine', or even about subdivisions, it is intended to impose the term 'Roman' on the entire period down to the Islamic conquests, with 'Byzantine' reserved for the centuries which follow. 'Roman' is divided into: Roman Republic (down to 27 BC), Early Empire (27 BC-AD 284) and Late Empire (284-637). Since many of the dates we have to work with are derived from relatively undeveloped archaeological typologies and are imprecise, even the above broad bands must often be used loosely at the boundaries between them.

Finding a concise name for the area with which we are concerned has been a problem, as has determining how to name the wider region. For the Romans, there was not only a province named Syria but also the whole area encompassed by their four provinces of Syria, Mesopotamia, Arabia and Palaestina was traditionally known loosely as Syria. To avoid confusion with the province of Syria and the modern country of the same name but different boundaries, it has been necessary to avoid use of what would otherwise have been the most suitable ancient name. The modern name of the region is also imprecise because of confusion between what is meant by the terms Near East and Middle East. The latter is the most commonly used and best understood, although it often encompasses a wide region from Turkey to Iran to Morocco. For our purposes we have confined its meaning to the lands of Anatolia, greater Syria and the Arabian peninsula.

· *A N o t e   o n   t h e   T e x t* ·

Various technical points about the text should be mentioned. No detailed and reliable map of the desert frontier exists. The best available until recently was that produced by Poidebard in 1934. This has been combined with sheets for Iraq and Transjordan prepared by Stein in 1938-9 to give a comprehensive, though out of date, map of the desert frontier from the Red Sea to the Tigris as it was known to those men. The new map is too large to be included here, but it may be consulted in a recently published book (Gregory and Kennedy, 1985). It has been the source of the latitudes and longitudes of sites given in the captions of figures in the present book, but its small scale has meant that co-ordinates of sites are often no more than close approximations. To assist the reader who may wish to trace a site, we have presented the information in captions uniformly: site name,

district, country, co-ordinates. However, a large number of small maps and plans have been provided because of the relative unfamiliarity of the region for most readers and the inaccessibility of many of the drawings in periodicals often not readily obtainable. All place names mentioned in the area studied are shown on Figs. 9 a – c.

We have followed the good practice of orienting vertical air photographs with the shadows nearer the viewer and presenting the accompanying plans with the same orientation. Likewise, plans accompanying certain oblique views (e.g. Fig. 82) have been turned from their traditional orientation to match the direction of view of the photograph.

Dimensions are metric with the imperial equivalent in parenthesis; the sole exception is flying heights which, following standard usage in aviation, are given in feet (to which we have added the metric equivalent). In many cases no thicknesses are known for external walls; in the circumstances, therefore, measurements given for sites are for *external* dimensions.

· PART A ·

Geographical and Historical Context

· CHAPTER ONE ·

Physical And Human Geography

The region with which we are here concerned comprises the Roman provinces of Syria, Mesopotamia, Judaea (or Syria Palaestina) and Arabia. In modern terms, these represent Syria, Iraq, Lebanon, Israel and Jordan, together with neighbouring parts of Turkey, Saudi Arabia (the Hedjaz) and Egypt (Sinai) (Fig. 1). In antiquity, this broad sweep of land between the rugged mountain terrain of eastern Anatolia and the barren desert of the Arabian Peninsula was often referred to loosely as 'Syria'.

· *Physical Geography* ·

Geographically the region is zoned from west to east (Fig. 2). A narrow strip along the Mediterranean coast offers useful agricultural land and ports, a number of which are on islands. Most

FIGURE 1 Modern political geography of the Middle East.

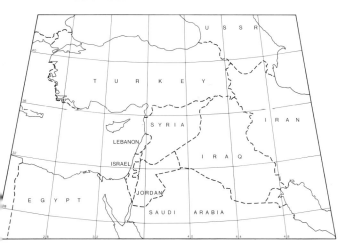

rivers begin in the chain of mountains which rise steeply behind the coast and form the next zone. The mountain ranges fall into five sections, which are, proceeding from the north to the south: the Amanus Mountains, the Ansariyeh Mountains, the towering Lebanon and Anti-Lebanon, which rise to over 2500 m. (c.8000 ft), the rather lower hills of Judaea and Samaria, and finally the Negev Desert and the hills along its eastern fringe. Passes cut through or between these ranges. Beyond them runs a chain of three major rivers: the Orontes, the Litani and the Jordan (Figs. 9a, 9c). The first two of these, rising within a few miles of each other west of Baalbek (Heliopolis), run respectively north and south for considerable distances before turning through gaps between the mountains and flowing into the Mediterranean at Seleucia and just north of Tyre, respectively. The ever-deepening valley of the Jordan, running south through the Sea of Galilee to flow into the Dead Sea, is extended by the dry Wadi Araba down to the Red Sea. Beyond these coastal mountain ranges the land remains high, usually over 500 m. (1500 ft), until it eventually falls to low levels in southern Mesopotamia.

Not that the inland region is featureless. Starting north-east of Damascus, the Jebel Rawaq, rises up and runs north-eastwards to Palmyra. Beyond Palmyra, the squat range of the Jebel Rijmen, north and north-east of the city, extends half way to the Euphrates. Further still to the north-east is the Jebel Cembeh, extending eastwards from Tunainir (Fig. 68) and then rising steeply to become the more formidable Jebel Sinjar which reaches to within 60 km (c. 35 miles) of the Tigris. No mountains lie between the Jebel Rijmen and the Jebel Cembeh.

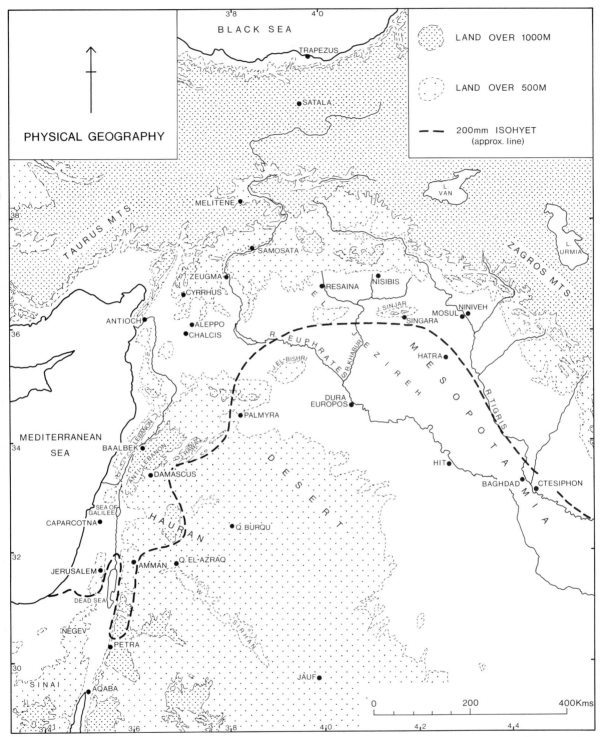

FIGURE 2 Physical geography of the Middle East.

Some distance south of the Jebel Cembeh, and extending for about 150 km (95 miles) southwards towards Anqa (Fig. 9b) on the Euphrates, is a series of wide salt marshes, which formed a natural barrier. From the Tigris to Damascus, and then southwards to the Red Sea, the typical land surface is a gravel desert (*hamada*), but this is interrupted by silts in the river valleys, and by the lava desert in the region south and south-east of Damascus, where the ground is covered by the black basalt of ancient volcanic eruptions, in the form either of lava flow or thickly strewn rocks (Fig. 28).

The land on both sides of the coastal mountains, the coastal zone and the eastern slopes, is well watered and fertile – the valley of the Orontes in particular supported a series of great cities. Further inland, with the exception of the area in the north towards the Euphrates bend, and the Hauran, south of Damascus, this fertile belt soon gives way to regions of steppe and desert extending eastwards to the Zagros Mountains of Iran and south-east to the Arabian Peninsula. Most of the inland region is insufficiently watered to allow dry farming, the limit of which is marked by the 200 mm. (8 in.) isohyet (Fig. 2), though in the steppe area limited agriculture is possible if rainfall is 'harvested' and utilized for irrigation. There are major oases at Palmyra and Azraq, but elsewhere the desert south of the 200 mm. (8 in.) isohyet offers only sparse grazing for the nomad's flocks of goats and camel herds, which were watered at occasional, in places seasonal, wells, water-holes, or streams in wadis. However, the 'desert line', i.e. the boundary or transition between the desert and the region regularly cultivated by village-dwelling farmers (Lewis, 1987, 15), was not always the same. Fluctuations in local security or in rainfall could move it back and forth even over short periods. In the far east of the region are the valleys of the Euphrates and Tigris, and those of their tributaries, especially the Balikh and Khabur. There the ribbon of land near the river, as well as adjacent irrigable land, was settled and farmed intensively.

·*Human Geography*·

Settlement within the region was at its densest in the area of great cities. Antioch at its height, with perhaps a quarter of a million people, was one of the three great cities of the Roman Empire (alongside Alexandria and Carthage). There were many other great urban centres: Laodicea, Berytus, Tyre, Sidon, Jerusalem, Apamaea, Damascus and Palmyra, all but the last on the coast or within 80 km (50 miles) of it. Rural populations could be large; in the time of the Emperor Augustus, a census recorded 117,000 citizens in the city and territory of Apamaea, while Galilee was renowned for its large population. Beyond this fertile strip, good arable land *and* the availability of water were the crucial factors determining the location of population. In the semi-desert and desert, as noted above, these favourable conditions were found in the valleys of the Euphrates, Tigris and their major tributaries on the eastern side of our region, and on the steppe areas of the desert margins on the western side.

The population of the region was overwhelmingly Semitic: Arabs in the steppe and desert regions, including Hatra (Fig. 53) and much of Mesopotamia, Palmyra (Fig. 82), Emesa, Ituraea, the Hauran and Arabia Petraea; Jews in not only the province of Judaea (or Syria Palaestina), but also in the adjoining parts of Syria and as major elements in the great cities throughout the region; Phoenicians along the central and northern Levantine coast; and throughout, a sub-stratum of the older Aramaic population. There were also Greek, or rather semi-Greek, populations in many cities, especially the great Hellenistic foundations of the north – Antioch, Laodicea, Seleucia and Apamaea; a small number of Italians, some who had arrived as traders and administrators, and others among the veteran colonists who settled at Berytus, Heliopolis and Ptolemais. Other subject peoples of the Empire, most notably Gauls, Thracians, Spaniards, Egyptians and Moors, appeared as soldiers, many of whom subsequently settled, and here and there were to be found Parthians, mainly refugees and their descendants.

This heterogeneous population was reflected in the range of languages in use. Latin would have been little heard outside the army camps and the governor's administrative staff; even in the veteran colonies Latin soon disappeared. Greek was the dominant language amongst the bulk of the urban populations, used by immigrant and Hellenized native alike, though many must have been bilingual. Both urban and especially rural people also spoke various dialects of

Aramaic and proto-Arabic – Hatrene, Syriac, Palmyrene, Nabataean and Safaitic, all of which were written languages, surviving on inscriptions and occasionally on documents.

· *E c o n o m i c   F a c t o r s* ·

Economically, this was an important region. To a substantial population and good agricultural lands, one could add a rich transit traffic. The great cities of the Roman Mediterranean received their luxury items from the Orient (silk, spices, ivory, furs, carpets and embroideries), as well as 'Syrian' exports (glass, textiles, cotton, figs, dates, wines and slaves), through the succession of ports which marked the Levantine coast from Cilicia to Alexandria. Beyond, passes through the mountain chain linked these coastal cities to the communities of the interior, and beyond again, there were routes which could be followed across the steppe and desert. Natural routes across northern Mesopotamia, along the Euphrates, across the central and southern Syrian Desert, into the interior of the Arabian Peninsula, through the Red Sea and up the Gulf of Aqaba, brought importance and commercial prosperity to a host of cities. These included (Figs. 9a–c) first, such centres as Hatra, Nisibis, Batnae, Samosata and Zeugma, the last naming a crossing point of the Euphrates; then, Ana, Dura Europos, Beroea, Palmyra, Apamaea, Hama, Emesa, Damascus, Bostra, Gerasa, Petra and Aila; and finally, the ports of Seleucia, Laodicea, Aradus, Tripolis, Berytus, Sidon, Tyre, Ptolemais, Caesarea and Gaza. These and other ports were also, of course, the entry points of much merchandise from elsewhere in the Empire; in particular, some, such as Seleucia, had a vital role to play in the supply of the armies of the region.

The deserts were not the sole preserve of caravan traffic. Nomads lived there, the *Scenitae*, 'tent-dwellers', of the Roman writers. Then, as until very recently, they led a spartan existence, dependent on rare perennial springs and seasonal water courses for themselves and their animals. Consequently, their life was one of constant transhumance with the flocks of goats and herds of camels which were the basis of their primitive economy. Nomad and farmer interacted to some extent. There was some modest trading and the animals could be grazed on the stubble of the farmer's fields, which they simultaneously manured. The relationship between Arab nomad, and Arab semi-pastoralist and farmer varied not only across time but from region to region. Kinship was not always a guarantee of harmony and on occasion nomads preyed on merchants or settlements on the desert's edge.

The settled parts of this great region form what old books on ancient history called the 'fertile crescent', with its western tip in Palestine, now Israel, and the occupied territories, and its eastern tip on the Gulf. The Roman Empire had a firm hold on the western end of this 'crescent' and its central part in Northern Syria. Beyond this, towards the River Tigris, lay debatable lands, and in the far east of the zone was the sphere of Parthia and later the Sasanian Empire. The concave side of the 'crescent' was on the south, roughly outlined on the map by the 200 mm. (8 in.) isohyet; beyond lay the desert.

Since the Roman desert *limes* has been little studied until recently and since some readers may be unfamiliar with the line it followed, it may be useful here briefly to describe its course. Very approximately, the western part of the *limes* coincided with the 200 mm. (8 in.) isohyet (Fig. 2). Commencing at the head of the Gulf of Aqaba, it ran north through the modern country of Jordan, with an offshoot through southern Israel. Near Damascus in Syria it turned northeast towards the Euphrates, taking advantage where possible of the line of mountain ranges and incorporating the oasis of Palmyra. After reaching the Euphrates, it followed the river south-eastwards for some distance, and here it may be said to have reached the debatable lands. From the confluence of the Euphrates with the Khabur the *limes* went north and north-eastwards to cut through the 'crescent', taking advantage first of a river line and then a mountain range.

Behind the *limes* lay densely populated regions, some of the most important parts of the Empire. Beyond its southern part there was quite different terrain – desert, with nomad peoples. After it had turned north to cut through the 'crescent', there was again desert beyond it in places, but there were also areas which had carried large populations from the earliest times.

· CHAPTER TWO ·

Historical Survey

Roman rule over the Semitic provinces of the Middle East extended across some seven centuries. In 64/3 BC Pompey the Great entered the area and, refusing to restore the former Seleucid Hellenistic dynasty, which had declined into warring factions, organized what was left of their kingdom as the Roman province of Syria (Fig. 3). At the other extreme, the annihilation of the field army of the Emperor Heraclius at the Battle of the Yarmuk in AD 636 ended forever Roman rule over the lands south of the Taurus Mountains.

The military requirements of the region varied greatly with the changing political and economic background. There were, however, at all times two main considerations determining the size of garrisons and their distribution: the need to secure and police the population – particularly those of the great urban centres and in the mountainous areas and desert fringes, and the need to protect from external threat the sources of wealth – the cities and their rural populations, and various important natural resources. A limiting factor to the routine implementation of a policy was the need to place major units where they could be sustained with food and supplies. Ancient agricultural surpluses were low and troops had to be located where either they would not be competing with some existing major population centre or food could be brought in. In practice the dispositions made for either of these could overlap with those required for the other.

· Internal Security ·

As noted above (p. 26), most of the great cities were within 80 km (50 miles) of the coast, some of the largest being in the north. The concentration of so many people in a single centre such as Antioch raised the danger of disturbance amongst what was a racially mixed and, on occasion, volatile population. In the south, Jerusalem was not only a large city but also the political and religious centre of a numerous people. The Jews became increasingly alienated from Rome in the Early Principate. Sporadic insurrections were followed by bloody rebellions in the time of Nero and Hadrian. There may have been an uprising of some sort as late as the reign of Septimius Severus (193-211) and the Caesar Gallus (351-4) certainly had to put down a rebellion in Galilee. Clearly, however, the wholesale slaughter and dispersal of the Jewish population of Syria Palaestina in the first and second centuries ended the major revolts. By the late third century the two legions which had been based there since the early second century had both gone.

Outside of the Jewish heartland, rebellion was rare in the East. Banditry, however, was another matter. Indeed, it was clearly a major policing problem in certain areas: Judaea and Ituraea are the most notorious (Isaac, 1984), and there and in other intractable regions, Rome for long avoided direct responsibility for the problem. Instead, native dynasts were recognized as allied rulers, and were expected to maintain order with their own military forces. The result was that in the Late Republic and Early Empire, the directly administered Roman 'province' of Syria consisted of a fairly limited area, mainly in the northeast and along the coast of the Levant, controlled by an imperial governor and his troops. The rest of the region was a patchwork of native states of varying sizes, ruled by kings, tetrarchs or ethnarchs, who administered their own territories and were in treaty relationship with Rome (Fig. 4). The large number of such states in the time of Augustus was gradually reduced in the succeeding generations, as dynasties died out or were removed and their territories brought under direct administration. Thus, Pompey's new province of Syria was surrounded by the states of allied rulers in Commagene, Emesa, Arabia Petraea and Judaea. In the years that followed, some smaller states were simply absorbed into Syria itself – as Commagene and Emesa were to be in the later first century AD. On the other hand, the annexation of Judaea and the Nabataean kingdom (Arabia Petraea), led to the creation of the provinces of Judaea (AD 6) and Arabia (106).

In the succeeding five centuries, new, and usually smaller, provinces were created. Some were the outcome of acquiring additional lands (principally in northern Mesopotamia); more commonly they arose by division of existing provinces. Names too changed or were modified. Thus the three provinces in the region by the time of Hadrian (Fig. 5), had become six under the Severi, twelve by c.395 (Fig. 6), and thirteen by the middle of the sixth century (Fig. 7).

· The External Threat ·
Parthia

External threats came from two directions: on the one hand, the Parthians and their Persian successors, and on the other, the Arab nomads of the Syrian Desert. When a Roman army first arrived on the Upper Euphrates in eastern Anatolia in, probably, 96 BC (Keaveney, 1980), much of the great sweep of land from Mesopotamia across Iran to Afghanistan, was subject, directly or through subordinate kings, to the Parthian Arsacid dynasty (Fig. 8). Formerly, until conquered by Alexander the Great, this region had been the heartland of the Achaemenid Empire (550–330 BC) of Cyrus, Darius and Xerxes. Alexander's successors, the Seleucid kings, had ruled over it from their twin capitals of Antioch on the Orontes and Seleucia on the Lower Tigris.

However, in the generation before the arrival of Rome on the Euphrates, Iran and even the eastern capital at Seleucia, had gradually been lost to the Parthians. For the next six centuries, first the Arsacid dynasty of Parthia, then their neo-Persian Sasanian successors, were to represent the single most potent threat to Rome on her eastern frontier, the only power comparable to herself in size or power she faced on any of her frontiers.

Not that the threat was unremitting. Far from it. Although early amicable contacts between representatives of the two empires (L. Cornelius Sulla and a Parthian envoy in c.96 BC) soon deteriorated, wars were in fact uncommon before the third century. The reasonable Parthian expectation that the boundary between the two empires might be the Euphrates, was soon to be dashed by Pompey whose forces in the mid-60s BC crossed the river and drove deep into Armenia and the Caucasus. Indeed, they even crossed the Upper Tigris and one Pompeian general returned to Syria across the breadth of northern Mesopotamia.

A major reversal came a decade later when the Triumvir, M. Licinius Crassus, for reasons of personal ambition, provoked a war with Parthia

FIGURE 3 Map to illustrate the political shape of the Middle East in 133 BC. C = Commagene.

and invaded Mesopotamia. His disastrous defeat and death at the Battle of Carrhae in 53 BC opened Syria to the first Parthian invasion. Raids took place in 52, and in 51 came a major invasion. Though Cassius, the *de facto* governor of Syria after Crassus' death, inflicted a defeat, a Parthian army wintered in northern Syria and the province remained in turmoil. Internal dissension within the Parthian royal family, however, ended the invasion and the Parthian threat faded for a few years.

Pompey negotiated with Parthia for support in 49 BC at the outset of his civil war against Caesar. It was not till 45, however, that a Parthian force appeared in Syria and was able to raise the siege by a Caesarian army of a Pompeian army inside Apamaea. In 44 some of this force was found with Cassius, who sent them home to seek more extensive support for him in the new round of civil wars. Once again their support was too late; the decisive battle was fought at Philippi a few months later. However, in 40, soon after the victor of that battle, Mark Antony, had passed

FIGURE 4 Map to illustrate the political shape of the Middle East in the time of Augustus (30 BC–AD 14). P = Pamphylia; CT = Cilicia Tracheia; KT = Kingdom of Tarcondimotus; C = Commagene; HT = Herodian Tetrarchies.

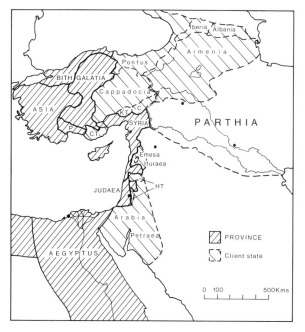

through Syria to Egypt, a major Parthian invasion of Syria took place. Alienated by widespread Roman corruption and extortion, many cities opened their gates to the Parthian prince, Pacorus, and all but Tyre fell into his hands. The occupation was short-lived. Antony's general P. Ventidius Bassus soon drove them out in a succession of victories – the second resulting in the death of Pacorus—in 38 and 39. It was to be two centuries before a Parthian army again appeared in Syria.

The wars, however, were not over. Antony's attempted revenge for Roman defeats and loss of prestige nearly ended in disaster when he led an army through Armenia into Media in 36 BC. That, however, was to be the last direct clash of Roman and Parthian for nearly a century.

There had been important lessons for both. By the end of the 30s each had tasted victory as well as defeat. Rome was to remain the more aggressive, but there was now an undoubted wariness of the military ability of a state which had seized much of the former Achaemenid and Seleucid empires, and inflicted signal defeats on major Roman armies.

It was now clear that though Roman expeditions could take many months to prepare, Parthia's lack of a standing professional army revealed a great weakness already evidenced by her slowness in responding to the appeals of Pompey and Cassius. However, if the feudal nature of her organization made her slow to gather her strength for aggressive warfare, the reaction time for countering a Roman invasion of her territory was rather faster. More important for Syria was that the scene of likely and actual warfare moved northwards. The mountains of Armenia not only offered Roman armies some protection against the formidable Parthian cavalry, but geographically the region became a bone of contention until Rome gained a more lasting advantage in the second century. At that point the war zone moved south to Mesopotamia. However, the Roman planners did not enjoy our hindsight. Even if *Roman* expeditions until the time of Trajan were in practice to be across the Cappadocian rather than the Syrian frontier, the *Parthian* threat to Roman territory was long perceived to be towards Syria. The Syrian Euphrates was literally and figuratively the direct point of contact between the two empires.

The Emperor Augustus threatened war with armies on both the Cappadocian and Syrian frontiers, but ultimately achieved his ends – the recovery of the lost eagles of Roman legions and a dominant role in Armenia – by diplomatic means. Disputes arose over Armenia, but it was not to be until the reign of Nero (54-68) that a great war broke out in that region. Even then, and only on one occasion, and in Armenia not Syria, did Roman and Parthian forces clash. Not that Syria did not seem threatened. The historian Tacitus explicitly tells us how in AD 62 the governor of Syria, C. Domitius Corbulo, fortified the Euphrates' bend in the face of a possible Parthian attempt to break into his province. None of his forts has yet been identified (but cf. Stucky, 1973; 1975, and p. 138).

The next major war – the first extended warfare between the two – came half a century later. Trajan's Parthian War of 113-17 saw Roman armies, for the first time since Crassus, thrusting across Mesopotamia. His forces advanced down the Tigris and Euphrates. Ctesiphon, the Parthian capital, fell and new provinces were declared: Mesopotamia (northern Mesopotamia) and Assyria (Babylonia), as well as Armenia to the north. These were short-lived; rebellion and Trajan's death gave his successor Hadrian his pretext to abandon them. Trajan's reign, however, marks something of a watershed in the history of the desert frontier. The Parthian War itself was a great aggressive adventure aiming permanently to cripple, if not fragment, Parthia. Not only did Trajan aim at seizing large new territories which would have needed garrisons, but, as noted above, he completed the process of annexing allied native states west of the Euphrates and the desert. Thus Arabia Petraea was annexed in 106 and a garrison established, including a legion at Bostra, which became the capital of the new province.

Trajan's war was to be the first of several thrusting deep into Parthian territory. Half a century later, in the wake of initial defeat in Armenia and a Parthian invasion of northern Syria, Roman armies struck back. Ctesiphon was sacked once more and Roman direct control was again pushed beyond the Euphrates. This Parthian War (162-5) in the reign of Marcus Aurelius was, however, rather more modest in its territorial

ambitions than had been that of Trajan. Roman garrisons were pushed further down the Euphrates and occupied Dura-Europos (Figs. 58, 60), while others appeared on the River Khabur, effectively turning the former Parthian vassal kingdom of Osrhoene in north-western Mesopotamia, into a Roman vassal. By 165, Rome ruled, directly or indirectly, the whole sweep of territory from the headwaters of the River Khabur to the Gulf of Aqaba.

Intervals between warfare had shortened and with the Severan period wars were to come in swift succession, foreshadowing a very different situation in the third and subsequent centuries. Septimius Severus' First Parthian War of 195-6 took Roman armies across northern Mesopotamia against Parthian allies and vassals on the Middle Tigris, and resulted in the annexation of part of Osrhoene as a province of that name. The Second Parthian War of 198-9 followed the paths of Trajan and Marcus Aurelius: Ctesiphon was captured, and new territory seized. A province of Mesopotamia was created, extending to the Middle Tigris and with two legions in garrison. Control may even have been pushed further

FIGURE 5 Map to illustrate the political shape of the Middle East in the time of Hadrian (AD 117–38). SP = Syria Palaestina.

down the Euphrates. Less than 20 years later, in 216, Septimius' son and successor Caracalla, launched another aggressive war, cut short by his own assassination. The next emperor, Macrinus, fared badly and peace was made in 218. It was to be the last war with Parthia.

· The External Threat · Persia

By the close of the second century, Parthia had been in gradual decline for several generations. The extensive Arsacid family clung to royal power, but it had suffered from civil wars and too powerful vassals. The expeditions of Severus had further weakened the dynasty and, at the time of Caracalla's assault on Parthia in 216, his opponent Artabanus was already distracted by war with an internal rival. More to the point, the ruler of Persis, nominally a vassal kingdom, rebelled about this time and began extending his power over adjacent lands. In *c.* 224 this 'Neo-Persian' king, Ardashir, a descendant of one Sasan, defeated and killed Artabanus and proceeded to establish his control over what henceforth is traditionally called the Sasanian Persian Empire (Fig. 8).

Conditions changed almost immediately. The new empire was much more tightly controlled, and its rulers, fired by religious zeal, laid claim to all the lands of their Achaemenid Persian predecessors. In the west, that meant lands which now formed the eastern provinces of the Roman Empire from the Aegean to the Nile. The new rulers themselves were also aggressive and able men who, in contrast to their Arsacid predecessors, whose claims to the region were rather half-hearted, rapidly and vigorously took the offensive against Rome.

Septimius Severus had claimed that his new province of Mesopotamia was to be a bulwark for Syria. Cassius Dio was to write, however, that even within his own lifetime (he died post-229), it was proving to be a cause of new war and a drain on resources. And Dio may not even have lived to see the first of the major wars of the region.

In 230 Ardashir invaded Mesopotamia and besieged Nisibis; raids were mounted against Syria. The consequent war when the Emperor Severus Alexander came east with an army in 232, is little understood. The outcome, however, after mixed success for both protagonists, seems to have been the retreat of the Persians. Ardashir was undeterred and returned to the attack, probably in 238, with the capture of Carrhae and Nisibis in Mesopotamia; probably then or soon after, his armies also captured Hatra (Fig. 53). Increasingly pre-occupied in the west by civil upheaval and barbarian attack, the Roman response was again slow and it was not till 243 that the Emperor Gordian III arrived to drive them back, subsequently losing his life in the course of his advance. With Ardashir now dead, Gordian's opponent had been his son, Shapur I, a man of enormous energy and ability and, unfortunately for Rome, great longevity – he was to rule for some 30 years. As such, his reign spanned very closely the period of Rome's greatest weakness, his actions indeed being a major contributor to it.

The murder of Severus Alexander in 235 had ushered in a period of short-lived emperors and civil wars which were to persist for half a century. Bad enough in itself, it was unfortunately only part of a calamitous cycle also involving extensive external war which was in large part responsible for the internal upheavals and for their continuance. Faced with repeated barbarian assaults along the European frontiers and their deep penetration within the Empire, emperors were unable to tackle vigorously the mounting crisis in the East.

Gordian's successor Philip made peace with Shapur in 244, but the latter returned to the offensive in 252 or soon after with a catastrophic assault. Roman fortresses and cities all along the Euphrates were captured (cf. Figs. 58, 60), a Roman army was annihilated at Barbalissus on the Euphrates opposite Antioch, and Antioch itself was amongst many great cities captured and sacked in Syria and beyond. A few years later, probably in 258 or 259, the Emperor Valerian himself was defeated and captured by Shapur near Edessa. Once again the Roman lands were overrun, cities and forts sacked but not held. Order was restored over most of the region only by the rallying of some scattered Roman forces and the vigorous counter-attack of the Palmyrene prince Odenathus. Subsequently, however, Zenobia, Odenathus' widow and regent for their son, tried to assert her independence of the embattled emperors in Europe, and rule the East – further parts of which she proceeded to overrun. When eventually the Emperor Aurelian came east in 271-2, Zenobia's 'Palmyrene Empire' was rapidly overthrown and the emperor set about the huge task both of restoring and reorganizing the frontier and re-asserting Roman dominion. Fortunately, it was at this juncture, in 270 or 273, that Shapur I died; his immediate successors, were lesser men – and shorter lived.

Odenathus had reputedly invaded Babylonia and assaulted Ctesiphon following his defeat of Shapur in 259/60; two decades later the Emperor Carus was certainly to do so in 283, though dying in the course of the campaign. The subsequent peace involved, probably, the restoration of the Roman province of Mesopotamia and, in the aftermath, Rome entered on a renewed period of stability under first the Emperor Diocletian (284-305) and his associates in the Tetrarchy, then the first part of the dynasty of Constantine the Great (324-63). The period of relative weakness in Persia ended temporarily in 293 when Narseh, a son of Shapur, came to the throne (293–302). Initially his efforts to recover Mesopotamia went smoothly; Galerius, Diocletian's junior colleague, his 'Caesar', in the East, was defeated in 297 by Narseh. The very next year, however, Galerius inflicted a crushing defeat on the Sasanians and not only recovered Mesopotamia once more, but acquired new territories beyond the Tigris. It was an important victory, bringing stability to the region and ending warfare for 40 years. Diocletian took the opportunity to overhaul and reorganize the eastern defences, with a large number of new forts (Figs. 76, 79, 82, 122, 126, 130, 151, 153 and 155 show sites which are probably of this period) and the reconstruction of great strategic highways (Figs. 151-60). Significantly, it seems to have been at about this same period that the Persians too began to construct in the region their own system of fortifications against Rome. One consequence was to be the tendency for wars to be fought out in the same relatively restricted area of Mesopotamia, and deep invasions of each other's provinces became rarer.

In part, peace was lasting because of the death of Narseh in 302, the short reign of Hurmazd II (302-9), and the accession of the infant Shapur II. This last, however, was to prove every bit as much a thorn to Rome as his great namesake and predecessor. Shapur II reigned for 60 years (309-79). Coming of age, he rapidly displayed his ambition to recover Sasanian control of Armenia and, in particular, Mesopotamia. It was in the latter that most of the warfare took place and, an indication of changed conditions after the great programme of fortification and a reliance on static defences, wars became largely campaigns of sieges of the great fortress cities. The pages of the history of Ammianus Marcellinus record graphically the sieges of Amida, Bezabde, Nisibis and Singara. Only with the reign of Julian do we again find an aggressive Rome taking the initiative. Julian's expedition in 363 took him to Babylonia and a victory before the gates of Ctesiphon. His return up the Tigris, however, was a catastrophe in which the emperor himself perished. The outcome was disastrous for Rome. The Emperor Jovian concluded a most unfavourable peace by the terms of which Rome abandoned Armenia, and not only gave up the Transtigritan territory gained by Galerius but ceded Roman Mesopotamia east of the River Khabur. The real measure of Roman weakness, however, is that Nisibis, the strategic key to northern Mesopotamia, which had been defended so often, was also ceded.

During the century and a third which followed, Roman-Persian wars were rare. More to the point for Syria and Mesopotamia, they were more often fought out further north in Armenia and the Caucasus. Thus, for example, the war of Valens of 370-8, though directed by him from his headquarters in Antioch. A few years later, *c.* 386, even in this region peace was established by the partition of Armenia, which removed a bone of contention. Not until 421/2 did Rome and Persia again clash in Mesopotamia. Rome was victorious, attacking Nisibis in 421 and, after inflicting a defeat the next year, making peace. A brief period of hostility in the north followed again in 439, but was soon settled and a peace made in 442. It was as well that it should have been so, for Rome was heavily distracted in this period by the barbarian pressure and invasions in

FIGURE 6 Map to illustrate the political shape of the Middle East in AD 395. IS = Isauria; EUPH = Euphratensis; MES = Mesopotamia; OSRH = Osrhoene.

Europe. Even within the eastern half of the Empire, the power of German generals in Roman employ, rebellions and civil war remained a preoccupation throughout most of the fifth century, but relations with Persia were not difficult. The explanation for this relative stability on the eastern frontier seems to lie in a parallel Persian pre-occupation with both internal problems and assaults on her own frontiers in the Caucasus and in the north-east. A measure of the introversion of both states during this period can be seen in the failure of Rome to act when, in 483, Persia refused to return Nisibis, which had been ceded for 120 years by the treaty signed by Jovian in 363; conversely, the Persians let pass for almost 20 years the Roman retaliatory refusal of an agreed payment to support the defence of the Caucasian passes against their common Sarmatian foes to the north.

The early years of the sixth century saw a renewal of warfare in the East, for an account of which we are indebted to Procopius, who records not only the wars themselves but, in his *Buildings*, the detailed account of the fortification or refortification of cities and forts (Figs. 63-8). War was initiated in 502 by Persia which seized fortresses in Armenia as well as taking Amida in Mesopotamia. The Roman counter-attack re-took Amida and led to the construction of a great new fortress at Dara, confronting Nisibis. A seven-years peace was made in 506 which lasted in fact until the last year (527) of the next reign. Ironically, the new war was in large part the outcome of the refusal of Justin to adopt the heir-apparent of the Persian king, Kavad; in anger, the latter initiated the new war (in the north again) but it was to be the spurned son, Khusrau I, who was to be the main protagonist over the course of a long reign (531-79).

In the war which began in 527, Justinian's generals had mixed fortune. In the north-east, victories were won by Sittas in 530, while in the Syrian region, Belisarius, who had been engaged on fort building, first won a victory at Dara in 530, then was heavily defeated the next year at Callinicum, at the confluence of the River Balikh and the Euphrates. In the event, however, it suited both empires to conclude, in 532, a Treaty of Eternal Peace: it lasted eight years.

Khusrau's assaults on the Roman defences began in 540 and continued through to a five-year truce in 545. He made significant advances in this period, not just in the Caucasus, where he seized territory (and which was not covered by the truce), but in Mesopotamia and along the Euphrates, where his armies sacked fortress-cities or allowed themselves to be bought off (Figs. 63, 65-7). Once again, Antioch was sacked. In 551, the truce was renewed for the Mesopotamian area, though again the two empires continued to fight in the Caucasus; indeed, fighting dragged on there until 557 and then in 561, a comprehensive 50-years peace was agreed. By the terms of this latter, the existence of the great fortress city of Dara was accepted by the Persians, but no new forts were to be built by the Romans near the Persian frontier.

A new round of fighting broke out a decade later in the time of the Emperor Justin II. It went badly for Rome: they failed to seize Nisibis in 572 but the Persian counter-attack took Dara and then went on to ravage parts of Syria – including the sack of Apamaea – forcing Justin to make peace. Once again the peace only covered the Syria-Mesopotamia region, and war continued vigorously in Armenia. Khusrau's death in 579 failed to end the fighting which again flared up in Mesopotamia.

Peace was not in fact finally restored until 591, by which time both sides had been debilitated by two decades of warfare. Even then, its achievement was due to a quite unforeseen piece of good fortune for the Romans. Hurmazd IV died in 590 and a consequent civil war not only distracted Persia from further thoughts of warfare but actually worked very much to Roman advantage. One protagonist, Khusrau II obtained the help of Roman troops to regain his throne, granting in return, by a treaty of 591, territory which included Dara. While the Emperor Maurice lived, Khusrau was content to remain at peace; Maurice's overthrow by Phocas in 602, however, provoked a Persian invasion of Mesopotamia. Their victory in battle was followed swiftly by the fall of Edessa and Dara, and, in 606, the capture of Amida and Resaina led to raids into Syria. Phocas was overthrown in 610 but his successor, Heraclius, was to face on his eastern frontier one of the greatest threats of any emperor for centuries.

Khusrau II was not content, as many of his predecessors had been, with simple expeditions into Syria for booty. In rapid succession after 610 his armies struck through the Roman defences: in the north, they reached Chalcedon opposite Constantinople itself; in the south, Syria was overrun, and armies passed into Egypt, which they occupied in 619. The long-standing Persian claim to the lands of the eastern Roman Empire seemed to have been made good at last. Heraclius' counter-attack was equally dramatic. Beginning from a base in north-west Armenia, he gradually turned the tide through a series of victories, ultimately forcing Khusrau to recall his troops from Chalcedon. The climax came in 627/8 when Heraclius led an army down into Mesopotamia, defeated a Persian army at Niniveh on the Tigris, then marched on to the capture and sack of Khusrau's palace at Dastagird in Iran, over 300 km (almost 200 miles) to the south-east.

The disaster soon led to the death of Khusrau in 628 and a period of internal strife and a whole succession of short-lived monarchs. In 632 when Yazdgird II became King of Kings, Heraclius was already re-established in his eastern possessions,

FIGURE 7 Map to illustrate the political shape of the Middle East in the time of Justinian (AD 527-65).

returned by treaty after Khusrau's death.

This final great series of campaigns in which the frontier defences of each side were swept aside as bold thrusts were made into the empire of the other, were in fact to prove just wasted energy. Both empires, debilitated by the effects of this and earlier wars, civil strife and wars on other frontiers, were too weak to resist the Arab forces of Islam. In 636, at the Battle of the Yarmuk in north-west Jordan, an Arab army annihilated the main Roman army in the region and went on to overrun all of Syria; in the same year, at Qadisiyya, the Persian army was soundly defeated and in 642, after a period of resistance, the army of Yazdgird was destroyed at the Battle of Nihavand in Iran. The outcome of centuries of war was, ironically, to be the destruction of Persia and the uniting of the entire region of the Persian Empire and the former Roman eastern provinces up to the Taurus Mountains under the rule of a new Moslem Arab empire.

· *The External Threat* ·
The Nomads

It will be clear from the above that only on rare occasions were sectors of the desert frontier other than those of Mesopotamia and northern Syria threatened by Parthia or Persia. Nevertheless, the semi-desert and desert from the Euphrates to the Red Sea and the Negev are studded with Roman forts. Here, however, the perceived threat could not have been the powerful army of Parthia or Persia; it has been traditional to explain these forts in terms of the threat posed by the desert's nomadic tribes.

Arabs could be found in the entire region from Mesopotamia to the Sinai Desert and Arabian peninsula. Some had settled in great cities such as Hatra, Palmyra and Petra, but most retained their traditional way of life as nomads – *Scenitae*, 'Tent-dwellers'. For such tribes in a difficult environment, a crucial factor in their simple and

FIGURE 8 The Roman, Parthian and Sasanian Empires.

precarious economy was the availability of water, which led to their regular transhumance between winter and summer pasturage with their flocks of goats and herds of camels.

The presence of these nomads in the desert regions from an early stage is evident not only from the widespread physical traces of their simple structures at camp sites and from 'kites' (probable animal traps; cf. Fig. 28), but from the thousands of graffiti left scratched on rocks by the southern, 'Safaitic', tribes. Most of the literary evidence for them is, however, late in date.

In the first and second centuries there is a handful of epigraphic references mainly from the region of the Hauran to individuals described as 'General' (*strategos*) or 'Tribal Chief (*phylarchos*) of the Nomads'. This is a period, however, when much of the land along the desert fringe was under the control, not of Roman troops, but those of various allied rulers. Thus, relations with the tribes and the task, if necessary, of policing their movements, fell to states whose populations were themselves often Arab. The removal during the first century of most of these native rulers, brought Rome directly into contact with some

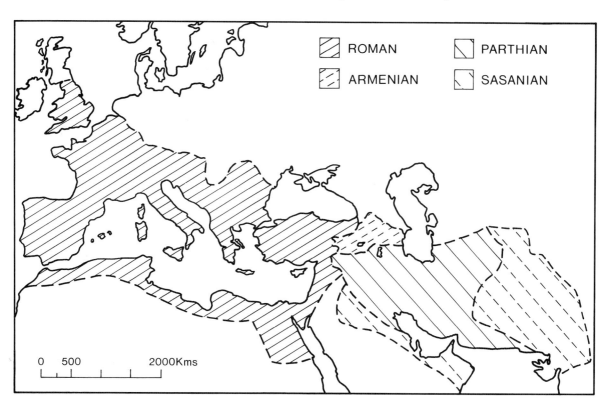

ROMAN   PARTHIAN

ARMENIAN   SASANIAN

0   500   2000Kms

of the tribes. These direct responsibilities increased in the second century with the annexation of the Nabataean kingdom in 106. There was a brief confrontation with the Arabs east of the Euphrates at the time of Trajan's Parthian War and, half a century later, Rome extended her control into north-western Mesopotamia. Significantly, it is then, in the middle of the second century, that the first clear evidence emerges for a Roman garrison at Palmyra, a city which had hitherto provided its own troops to police the desert caravan routes. The corollary to this is that there is virtually no clear evidence for Roman military installations in the desert regions before the end of the second century. There are few such traces anywhere in the region in this period, but in the desert areas where structures are well preserved, their near absence may be regarded as significant and not merely the consequence of later building or agricultural activity.

There is a little evidence for the possible trouble the nomads could cause. Inscriptions from Palmyra honouring various caravan leaders allude to trouble with the nomads: one of 132 speaks of the deliverance of a recently arrived caravan from Vologesias 'from the grave danger that surrounded it'; another of 199 honours a man 'for the continuous expeditions he has raised against the nomads'; and a third, of about the same period, shows us a *strategos* who received imperial approval for his work of pacification in the desert (Matthews, 1984, 167ff). A Nabataean inscription from the Sinai with the date 190/1 speaks of that as being the year 'during which the Arabs [?] ravaged the land' (*CIS* II: 964). But these were almost certainly modest affairs, the nomads posing no threat to major settlements, much less any of the cities of the region.

In the first and second centuries, in the absence of forts there is little information about the Roman forces only at Hegra, with some graffiti scratched by Roman auxiliary soldiers on a cliff face, and an inscription dedicated by a legionary of the *III Cyrenaica*, do we get some hint of where troops were. Perhaps, as Sartre has suggested (1982, 131), the Roman military presence was like that of the nomads—seasonal and in tents. However, physical evidence for Roman military presence becomes more abundant towards the end of the second century, as at Qasr

el-Hallabat (Fig. 147) and around the Azraq Oasis (Fig. 28).

There seems however to have been a change taking place in tribal nomadic society in this period which may have had serious consequences for Rome. This is the process of 'bedouinization'. It is suggested that in the early Principate there took place in the region of north Arabia a breakdown of such modest urbanism as had developed. Instead of a nomadic society influenced and controlled by a town-based aristocracy, there appeared one dominated by those already adapted to desert life. Typical bedouin society emerged with the characteristic blood feuds and raids (Caskel, 1954). The case is difficult to prove. It is a fact, however, that the desert tribes begin to appear in the records from the Severan period as a troublesome element on the frontiers, looming ever larger over the next four centuries and playing a growing role in the developing contest between Rome and Persia.

The danger posed by nomads should not be overestimated. Undoubtedly, hostile if relatively small nomadic tribes could cause extensive disruption and tie down a disproportionate number of soldiers. The evidence that they did so and are the explanation for many of the forts which first appear along the desert fringe of Syria and Arabia in the third and fourth centuries, is at best thin. An interesting alternative explanation which draws on the evidence for upheaval in the Arab population of the provinces in the aftermath of the collapse of Palmyrene power in the late third century (p. 33), envisages many of the forts as built to guard communications against uprooted dissident provincials operating in the difficult fringes of the province itself (Graf, 1988b).

Nevertheless, nomads seem to have been more significant in Roman military thinking from the third century. There is evidence of a changed relationship; it is in this period that we begin to find the literary sources preserving the names of nomad chiefs and the names of tribal confederations become common. Thus there was Jadhima, king of the Tanukh, who fought for Rome against the Palmyrenes. It would seem that this confederation had once been localized in the vicinity of the north-west shore of the Persian Gulf, but had subsequently removed to the Roman frontier; more precisely, Jadhima is named on an inscription from Umm el-Jemal (Fig. 130). We can hardly doubt that the downfall of Palmyra and its subsequent inability to police the desert (we hear of no more caravans through Palmyra after that of 269) gave far greater power to nomad chiefs especially one such as Jadhima who had assisted the Romans. Not that we need believe Jadhima motivated by loyalty to Rome. Rather, hostility to Palmyra seems the key.

The appearance of larger tribal groupings is notable and helps explain the growing potency of Arab chiefs in the subsequent centuries. Bedouinization need not have led to such a development. Rather, we should perhaps see it as a response to the very success of Rome. It is surely no coincidence that all round her frontiers tribes were coalescing in this period to form powerful confederations: the Maeatae who appear in northern Britain in the Severan period, the Alammani on the Rhine (and later the Franks), and now in the East, the Tanukh, responding to Roman and Palmyrene power in the same way. Indeed, it seems that the very name 'Saracen' is derived from a word meaning 'confederation' (Graf and O'Connor, 1977).

More was to come. Within a generation, the Tanukh itself was absorbed into the new powerful Lakhmid confederation ruled over by Imru'lqais, 'king of all the Arabs', and whose power stretched from the Arabian peninsula to the Persian Gulf to the Hauran. Imru'lqais is said to have offered the service of his troops to both Rome and Persia, but it may be indicative of a closer relationship with Rome that in 328 he was buried at Nemara in the Hauran, near a former Roman military post.

The wide power of the Lakhmid kingdom seems not to have survived Imru'lqais. The confederation itself survived, based henceforth on the Sasanian frontier at el-Hira and closely allied to Persia. Indeed, for the next three centuries the desert tribes were to be largely divided between the pro-Persian Lakhmids and the pro-Roman Ghassanids who were soon to emerge on the Roman frontier (below, p. 34). It would be misleading to present this development as simply a return to the Early Empire system of client-rulers being left in charge of difficult areas or peoples. In the Early Empire Rome was acting from a position of strength, *choosing* to administer

some regions in this manner; in the Late Empire it is clear that these Arab phylarchs were powerful and independent. Many were keen to obtain recognition in their role by Rome or Persia but they were plainly far less reliable than were the one-time rulers of Commagene or Arabia Petraea.

In the pages of Ammianus Marcellinus there is a description of the Saracens as fighters. They appear in the Emperor Julian's campaign as raiders and guerrilla fighters, well-adapted to desert conditions; in battle with the Goths it is their ferocity and barbaric appearance which arrests the attention of even their opponents (Amm. Marc. XXXI.16.6).

What the appearance of such allied tribes or confederations might mean for the Roman defences begins to become clear both from literary references as to where these nomads were operating and from the archaeological evidence. Some of the more distant frontier forts such as Qasr el-Azraq (Fig. 126) in the desert itself or on its fringes began to be given up from the later fourth century, security being vested instead in the hands of individual tribal chiefs who entered into formal alliances with Rome and probably undertook the protection of travellers previously secured by the forts.

Throughout this period there are references to Saracen raids: on the hermits on Mount Sinai in *c.*373; another attack on those of Palestine in the early fifth century; widespread raids in Palestine, Phoenicia and Syria in 410; an attack on north western Syria in the mid fifth century; in 473, after a period of raiding, the Emperor Leo was asked to recognize a tribal chief in the Hedjaz, Imru'lqais (= Amorcesos), as phylarch; and at the close of the century, St Sobas asked the Emperor Anastasius for a fort and garrison to protect his new monastery in Palestine, this coming at about the same time as the raids of 491-2 which struck in northern Syria as deep as Emesa. In other respects, the fifth century was, however, apparently one without any great upheavals, perhaps because of the power and influence of a new confederation, the Salih, based in central Syria.

With the sixth century there was a resurgence amongst the Arab tribes. The period saw various major developments, above all, the appearance of the Ghassanid confederation. This, according to Procopius, was the outcome of a policy decision by the Emperor Justinian to transform one of his Arab Phylarchs, al-Harith (= Aretas), son of Jabalah, into a paramount chief with the title of *patricius*, probably interpreted by his followers as king. In doing so, he was evidently concerned to create on the Roman side an organized counterpoise to the powerful pro-Persian Lakhmids at Hira near the Lower Euphrates, whose raids into Roman territory were proving disruptive. Al-Harith first appeared alongside the Roman forces in 531 at the Battle of Callinicum (above, p. 34) but was prominent thereafter throughout the *c.*40 years of his reign. Ghassanid troops not only assisted as allies in Roman armies, but also conducted a war of their own against the Lakhmids *c.*544. Al-Harith appeared too as a more traditional king, responsible for building and the patronage of art. The Ghassanid kingship did not long survive his death: the Emperor Maurice early in his reign, ended the patriciate, retaining the Ghassanid successors as phylarchs only. The period of some half a century is significant both as reflecting the important role being played by Arab tribes on both the Roman and Persian side, the dominance nevertheless of the emperor who could apparently make and unmake a kingship, and the extent to which the defences of the eastern frontier in desert and steppe were placed in the hands of Arab allies.

Both in the time of the patriciate and later under the rule of the fragmented Ghassanid family and other Arab phylarchs, we find extensive tracts of eastern Syria under their authority. Not just the desert and semi-desert, but settled, urbanized areas from Resafa (Fig. 64) through Damascus and Bostra to the vicinity of Jericho. In short, many of the forts of the desert frontier, previously garrisoned by Roman troops, were now in regions under the authority of Arab phylarchs. The building inscription of 529 from Qasr el-Hallabat (Fig. 147) is the latest piece of certain evidence of direct Roman military involvement in Arabia. The peasant militia into which the *limitanei* had sunk, had long since ceased to have any serious military function. Imperial forces now only garrisoned the major towns to the west and along the Euphrates, towns whose populations sheltered behind massive and imposing walls (e.g. Fig 67).

The great tragedy of Heraclius' remarkable recovery of his eastern provinces from the Persians after a titanic struggle, was that they were now weakened and disorganized by years of war and recent Persian occupation. Further, they were divided from the imperial court by religious differences. When the first Muslim assault on southern Palestine came in 629 – the only one directed by Muhammad before his death– it would have been seen as of no great significance; another Arabian tribe thrusting out of the desert as the tribal constituents of the Tanukh, Lakhmids, Kindites and Ghassanids, and many others had done before, and in due course to be assimilated as *foederati*, their chief recognized as *phylarchus*. Besides, this was the moment at which Heraclius, having freed Syria the preceding year from more than 14 years of Persian rule, was triumphantly replacing in Jerusalem the fragment of the True Cross. Muhammad's death and the internal struggle which took place in Arabia, resulted in the dramatic outburst of Arab armies in 633 which led to the overthrow of Sasanian Persia and to a series of Roman defeats culminating in the Battle of the Yarmuk in 636 and the loss of Syria to the Roman Empire (above, p. 36).

· *The Army* ·

From the earliest days of Rome's recorded history, her forces had evolved to meet changed circumstances and different opponents. In the East they had to adapt to climate, geography and the military situation. The military needs of the region naturally varied over several centuries. The elimination of allied rulers and the extension of Roman territory brought additional military responsibilities. New conditions were created by political and social developments amongst the peoples beyond the frontiers outlined above and changes within the Roman Empire itself. As a survey of the evidence shows, changes appeared in the character of the Roman forces and in the tactics and strategy employed.

Throughout the Roman period, the province

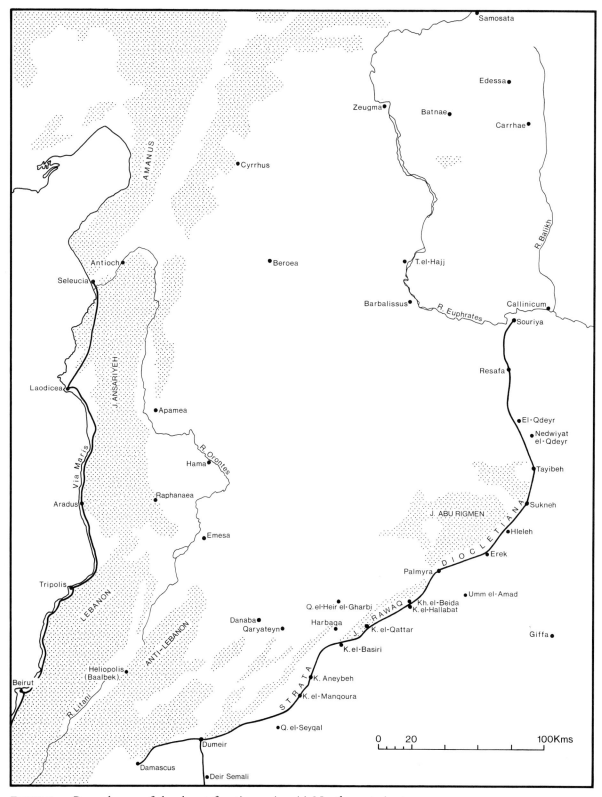

FIGURE 9 General map of the desert frontier region (a) North–west sheet

Bezabde

Dara

Amida

Nisibis

R. Tigris

Resaina

W. Jaghjagh

T. Bati

T. Brak

T. Zenbil

Bir Haidar

Eski Mosul

Gartulah

Dulalyah

Niniveh

Tunainir

Lake Khatuniyeh

Kh. Hassan Aga

J. CEMBEH

J. SINJAR

Ain Sinu

T. Afar

Amostae

El-Han

Singara

Sheikh Ibrahim

Araban

T. Sufuq

M
E
S
O
P
O
T
A
M
I
A

T. el-Hamda

T. el-Ghail

Jaddalah

Fadgami

Marqada

R. Khabur

Hatra

R. Euphrates

Halebiyeh

Qreiyeh

Deir ez-Zor

Apatna

Circesium

Dura Europos

Ertaje

Ana

Gamla

Kifrin

Anqa

W. Khidr

Umm es-Selabikh

Q. es-Swab

EL-QA'ARA

0   20   100Kms

Hit

Q. Amij

Q. Khabbaz

(b) North-east sheet

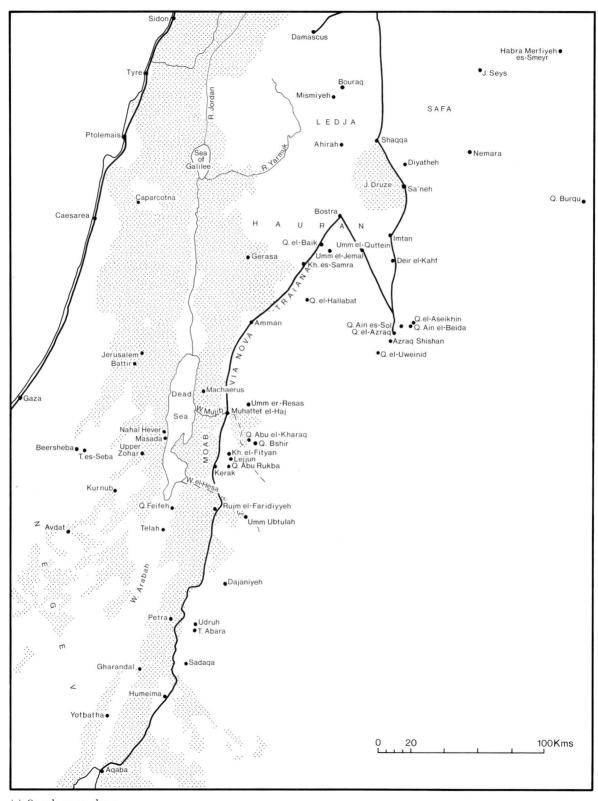

(c) South-west sheet.

of Syria had the principal military force in the entire East. Consequently, its governors exercised a general responsibility over not just the province of Syria, but the adjacent provinces too, from the Black Sea to the Red, and even, on occasion, to the Nile. Even when additional major military provinces were created in neighbouring Cappadocia, Judaea, Arabia and Mesopotamia, Syria remained the largest and most important. Because of the military interdependence of all the provinces in the region, it is more apt to look at the forces not just in the provinces of the central and southern areas of the eastern frontier with which we are concerned, but of the Asiatic East as a whole. Much of the East was technically 'unarmed', though all governors had some troops at their disposal.

In the Late Republic, the governors of Syria were generally allowed only two legions of citizen soldiers (approximately 10,000 men), although the civil wars had often seen many more there. With the establishment of the Principate the number increased. Much of the evidence can be conveniently presented in tabular form. Table I shows the position for the legions. It is generally accepted that the normal legionary establishment of the Asiatic East was 4 legions from Augustus to the early 70s, though with, perhaps, 5 or 6 for about a generation under Augustus. By the close of Vespasian's reign the number had increased to 6; under Hadrian to 8; 10 under Septimius Severus; and 16 in the time of Diocletian (as reflected in the *Notitia Dignitatum*). The same Table shows the broad distribution. For the first century of the Principate, with the possible exception of a legionary province of Galatia under Augustus (*c.* 25 BC – AD 6), the entire Asiatic East from Sinai to Hellespont had only four legions, all of them in the single province of Syria. Three imperial provinces – Cappadocia, Syria and Judaea – emerge in the Flavian period (69-96), a fourth under Trajan with the annexation of Arabia Petraea, while with Septimius Severus, Syria was divided into Syria Coele and Syria Phoenice, and a new legionary province of Mesopotamia was created. Finally, in the Diocletianic period, legions are strung out through nine provinces from the Black Sea to the Red (Table I; cf. Fig. 6).

TABLE I
Legions in the Asiatic East from Augustus to Diocletian

	Julio-Claudians	Flavians	Trajan	Severus	Diocletian
Pontus					1
Galatia (Augustus – 1/2?)					
Cappadocia/Armenia		2	2	2	2
Isauria					2
Mesopotamia				2	2
Osrhoene					2
Syria	4	3	3	2	2
Phoenicia				1	2
Arabia			1	1	2
Judaea/Palaestina		1	2	2	1
TOTAL	4	6	8	10	16

The legions are of course only part of the story. Unfortunately, we cannot produce a picture of the auxiliary forces (largely recruited amongst non-citizen provincials) with anything like the same confidence. Nevertheless, from Tacitus' observation (*Annals* IV.5 referring to AD 23) that overall within the Empire auxiliary forces were broadly equal in strength to the legions, we may tentatively infer some 20,000 under Augustus and the early Julio-Claudian emperors. By the time of Nero our information has improved somewhat: the army mustered by Vespasian at Ptolemais in 67 for the Jewish War is said (Josephus *Bellum Judaicum* II.66) to have included over 22,000 auxiliaries to which would have to be added the units retained by Mucianus in Syria, and the units in Cappadocia and in the so-called 'Unarmed Provinces' of Asia Minor. However, it is for the mid second century that our best estimates are available. These are presented in Table II. Including the 'Unarmed Provinces', there would have been in total some 35,000 auxiliaries; adding on the legions gives 75-80,000. This latter figure may have risen to perhaps 90,000 by the death of Severus.

TABLE II
*Approximate Sizes of
the Provincial Armies in
the Asiatic East c.150.*

	Legions	Auxilia	Total
Cappadocia	10,000	8,000	18,000
Syria	15,000	14,500	29,500
Palaestina	10,000	4,500	14,500
Arabia	5,000	5,000	10,000
TOTAL	40,000	32,000	72,000

The third element is that of the armies of the allied kings and princes in the region. These had their own role to play in providing internal security, but could be called upon in time of major warfare. The evidence for these armies is even more fragmentary than for the auxiliaries. Occasional references give us some idea of the order of magnitude, but it is again from the passage of Josephus just cited that we get our most comprehensive insight: Vespasian's army at Ptolemais was augmented by some 15,000 troops from four allied kings. The forces of allied kings were not, of course, a constant. The annexation of allied states eliminated the royal armies which then often appeared amongst the local auxiliary forces or were exchanged for existing units elsewhere. Thus, the annexation of the Nabataean kingdom led to the appearance in the Roman army lists of six *Cohortes Ulpiae Petraeorum*, some 4500 men. By the early second century, there were no longer any allied states west of the Euphrates to contribute to Roman campaigns.

The evidence for the tactical distribution of legions and *auxilia* within any province of the Asiatic East is patchy even when the evidence is at its best. For the Julio-Claudian period we have precise locations for legions on only two occasions (Cyrrhus and Raphanaea; Zeugma may be inferred). From a passage in Tacitus (*Histories* II.80), we may infer that some at least of the legions of the East in 69 were based amongst or close to the urban populations of the province. Little can be said about the location of auxiliary units except in Judaea, where cities such as Caesarea, Ascalon and Jerusalem had garrisons, as well as the border fortress palaces at Masada and Machaerus (Figs. 44, 47).

After 70 the information improves, especially all that showing legions now firmly located on the Euphrates itself (Melitene, Samosata and Zeugma) and auxiliary units likewise pushed out onto the Euphrates and into the desert further south. Vexillations ('detachments') of legions appear more frequently, two at least at apparently temporary outposts in distant locations: Baku on the Caspian Sea under Domitian, and another at Hegra in the Hedjaz in, perhaps, the mid second century.

No new province was created under Marcus Aurelius but the army was thrust further eastwards again. Troops appear at Dura-Europos and a reasonable inference from the report in Dio (LXXV.1.2) of Roman troops being attacked in 193 by the Osrhoeni and Adiabeni – Nisibis is explicitly mentioned – is that units were in central North Mesopotamia. With Severus one must suppose that auxiliary units were firmly established east of the Euphrates but only one – on the Lower River Khabur – can be located. *Legio I Parthica* is now known to have been at Singara in his reign (cf. Fig. 73); the other legion assigned to the province was probably at Nisibis. Legionary detachments again appear operating far from the parent unit. Dura, for example, has them from three different legions. A few years later, under Severus Alexander and Gordian III, an auxiliary cohort is attested inside Hatra far to the east (Fig. 53).

With the upheavals in the East in the mid third century, our evidence becomes very scarce and it is not until the end of the century that we can again see something of what is going on. Then the *Notitia Dignitatum* gives a list of units which nominally reflects the situation *c.* 400 but is commonly believed to have changed little since the reforms of Diocletian and Constantine. Under these emperors, the entire structure of the Roman army altered. Diocletian is conventionally – though, perhaps, erroneously – credited with massively increasing the size of the Roman army after the near collapse of the third century. The restored units and new regiments were, however, distributed along the frontiers again, rather as they had been in former times – albeit now rather more numerous. It is to Constantine that historians traditionally attribute the change which resulted in a major mobile field army developed out of the nucleus of one which had first begun to take shape in the time of Septimius Severus. To do so, however, was to some extent a matter of withdrawing some units from the frontier forces. Although initially held centrally by the emperor, this field army was later divided to provide a few regional field armies, one of which was assigned to the East. Thus, from the late fourth century through to the time of Justinian, the arrangement in the East consisted of this field army, the *comitatus*, held as a strategic reserve, below which came the *limitanei* who actually garrisoned the forts and frontier cities, then the federate tribes.

There was also a reversal of status. Legions – or rather their much smaller Late Empire successors (Figs. 76, 79) – were no longer the elite troops, but were now largely part of the static, relatively low-grade frontier forces, the *limitanei* who garrisoned most of the sites with which we are concerned here. Ancient references make it clear that increasingly the quality of these was often poor, their morale low, and, in times of monetary shortage, it was not uncommon for their pay and equipment to have been neglected; they tended too to become more farmers than soldiers and less useful even as garrison troops. The units became smaller as may be seen not just from the documentary evidence, but from the size of the forts entire units now garrisoned (e.g. Figs. 151, 153, 155). From time to time too, elements of this frontier force were drawn off to join the field army; in short, the trend over the three centuries to Heraclius was for the first line of defence to decline in numbers and quality and for the real defence to depend ever more on the field army. Both the *comitatus* and the *limitanei* declined in numbers. Jones (1964, Table XV) has calculated that at the time of the compilation of the *Notitia Dignitatum* in *c.* 400, on paper at least, the former in the eastern half of the Empire numbered some 104,000; the latter in the same region, 248,000. We have no way of estimating the decline in numbers of the *limitanei*, but it comes as something of a shock to be told that when Justinian reinforced the *comitatus* in the East, he brought its strength up to 25,000!

These changes in the make up of the army reflect an altered strategy and new tactics. No longer was it possible, as in the Early Principate, to concentrate the bulk of the garrison of the region behind the frontier and leave much of the everyday policing to the armies of allied rulers. Rome was now responsible for the protection of a frontier often under threat *and* for providing a field army in time of major war. The character of the army also changed. Cavalry was more prominent, the field army as a whole being more mobile. Rome had always been willing to adopt and adapt the weapons and tactics of her opponents. Thus the huge numbers of auxiliary troops included not only infantry but the cavalry in which the Roman armies were deficient, and the archers and the *dromedarii* one increasingly finds in the East from an early date. Significantly in the great wars in the East, it was Rome which adopted major features of the armies of her opponents, not vice versa. Only the technique of siege war seems to have been taken up by any of Rome's enemies. Where the Parthians had been notably deficient, the Sasanians became adept. Hence the very different character of Roman-Sasanian campaigns, settling down in the third century into a series of sieges, usually of Mesopotamian fortresses, and the increasing emphasis placed by both sides on fortifications and heavily garrisoned strong points (Figs. 60, 63–5, 68).

Barbarian troops become more prominent not just as *foederati* but in the field army and *limitanei*. Thus, after the defeat of Valens by the Goths in 375, it was felt necessary as a precaution to carry out a surprise massacre of all the Gothic troops in the East before they could think to rebel. In the aftermath, as Theodosius attempted to fill the gap created by the annihilation of Valen's army, many regiments were drawn westwards and new regiments introduced to the East. Since these latter, unusually, have no ethnic title, it has been proposed that they were pure barbarian units, the name being omitted to disguise their numbers. The *Notitia Dignitatum* also refers to several units of Arabs, some of whom were probably recruited from amongst the allied nomads. The practice continued, and a century and half later, we hear of five regiments of Vandals brought by Belisarius from Africa being sent to the eastern frontier.

In the final battles for Syria against the forces of Islam, the Byzantine armies seem modest. Even for the last battle, at the River Yarmuk, the field army is said to have been only 50,000.

By that time of course, the troops of the *limitanei* were no longer a meaningful force in any area and many of their forts will have been either abandoned or become the homes of the peasantry into which the former frontier army had disintegrated.

· PART B ·
Aerial Photography and Archaeological Prospection

CHAPTER THREE

History of Archaeological Air Reconnaissance and Photography in the Middle East

Air photography first became important in the great expansion of aviation that took place during the First World War on the Western Front in France and Belgium, though no ancient remains are known to have been recorded there from the air on those devastated battlefields. The first significant archaeological use of the aerial camera took place in the countries of the Middle East and the eastern Mediterranean, where fighting was on a smaller scale and less destructive. There, aviators often had to fly over ancient remains so clear that they could hardly be missed. Remembering his flight as an artillery observer for the fleet during the Gallipoli campaign in 1916, Sir John Myers later wrote, 'What distracted me all the time was the unexpected view of the villas and gardens of Roman Branchidae [Didyma in modern Turkey]. I would never willingly dig again without aerial reconnaissance,' (Dunbabin, 1955, 357).

The British, French and German air forces all played a part. In 1917, near the Sinai Front, Oberleutnant Falke photographed the ruins of Byzantine towns in the Negev on behalf of the distinguished German archaeologist Dr Theodor Wiegand, leader of the *Deutsch-Türkisches Denkmalschutzkommando* (Unit for the Protection of Monuments) (Wiegand, 1920; Crawford, 1954, 206). At another eastern theatre of war, the Salonika Front in northern Greece, French air photographs of ancient sites were collected by the *Service Archéologique de l'Armée de l'Orient* and used by Leon Rey to illustrate the book later published to report the numerous ancient sites which had been recorded (Rey, 1921). The French photographs, some of which date from as early as November 1915, are less striking than

those taken by the Germans but both are evidence of an enlightened approach at the time. One cannot fail to be impressed by the fact that the French and Germans set up these organizations 70 years ago, in the middle of the desperate conflict of 1914-18. The British contribution, characteristically, was the work of an individual officer, Lt.-Col. G. A. Beazeley, who was in charge of a small survey party, making maps of the Mesopotamian Front in 1917 and early 1918. He became interested in the ancient cities and canals recorded by air photographs, some of which he took personally while attached to the Royal Flying Corps. In May 1918 his aircraft was shot down and he and the pilot were captured. Fortunately he survived the experience, and after the war was able to publish in the *Geographical Journal* reports of his results, which included both photographs and detailed maps of the vast ruins of the early Islamic city of Samarra (Beazeley, 1919 and 1920).

The potential of the aerial view was well appreciated by Beazeley, who was apparently the only one of these pioneers who actually flew himself. Describing the maps of Samarra, he wrote:

Had I not been in possession of these air photographs the city would probably have been merely shown by meaningless low mounds scattered here and there, for much of the detail was not recognisable on the ground but was well shown up on the photographs, as the slight differences in the colour of the soil came out with marked effect on the sensitive film, and the larger properties of the nobles and rich merchants could be plainly made out along the banks of the Tigris.

FIGURE 10 The Royal Air Force R.E.8 aircraft in which Professor James Henry Breasted flew during 1920 to examine the plain between Abu Kemal, Syria (from where the aircraft took off) and the confluence of the Rivers Khabur and Euphrates. *Photograph: Oriental Institute, University of Chicago (P.7346/N.3786 D.D.L. no.418).*

The cameras in use at this time were cumbersome and used slow emulsions, but the large size of the glass plate negatives ensured that the photographs were good records, as may be verified by taking prints of them on visits to the sites (cf. Riley, 1982).

After the war little happened for a few years, but the seed had been sown and the circumstances were propitious for archaeological research from the air to begin. The Ottoman Empire had gone and in its place were the French and British Mandates of Syria (including Lebanon) on the one hand, and Iraq, Transjordan and Palestine on the other. Their air forces were important in the peace-keeping forces (Iraq and Transjordan were Air Commands rather than Army), gradually bringing stability and order to the region.

One of the first archaeologists to enter the field in the Middle East was Professor James Henry Breasted of the Oriental Institute of the University of Chicago, a leading figure of his time. The potential of the aerial view was plainly at the forefront of his mind from the outset. He records how on 13 January 1920, by the instructions of Lord Allenby, who had accompanied him to the pyramids of Abu Roash, he was taken on a two-hour flight in a Royal Air Force aircraft to view and photograph sites along a 60-mile tract from Abu Roash to the mouth of the Fayyum (Breasted, 1933, 39 and Fig. II). The files of the Oriental Institute contain a handful of these photographs, which are apparently the first known air photographs taken after the war for archaeological purposes. There are fewer than might have been expected – Breasted was later to confess that because of the roar of the engine, he did not realize that for three-quarters of the time the shutter was not working! From Egypt he moved on to Iraq, and then to Syria, where important excavations were taking place on the site of the fortress city of Dura Europos, the modern Salihiyeh on the Euphrates (Figs. 58–

60). Again Breasted sought an aerial view. He managed to secure a reconnaissance flight in a British aircraft (Fig. 10) over the region above Abu Kemal (i.e. just inside what was to become part of the French Mandate of Syria) (Breasted, 1924, 64, Fig. 37). In 1922, at his request, a vertical photograph – a record of Dura before excavations began – was taken by the French forces in Syria and later published (Breasted, 1924, 3, 93, Fig. 55). Vertical photographs of parts of north-west Syria, also taken in 1922, but for other purposes, were later found to show ancient sites, for example, the fort at Tell al-Ghail (Fig. 139) (Poidebard, 1934, 128).

In 1923-4 aerial surveys by 14 Squadron, RAF, formed part of the work carried out at Petra by Sir Alexander Kennedy's expedition. The published results (Kennedy, A., 1925) include four oblique photographs and two mosaics which covered large areas. The better of the mosaics (op. cit., plate opp. p. 18), made from parts of at least 16 vertical photographs, showed the city site at a scale of about 1 in 7300.

· Père Antoine ·
Poidebard

It was not until May 1925 that the really important figure, Père Antoine Poidebard, came on to the scene. He was clearly a man of unusual character and experience, and a short account of the background to his work in the air must first be given, remembering that flying was then something new and revolutionary.

He was born in 1878 at Lyon, France, entered the Society of Jesus in 1897 and was ordained in 1910, after which he was sent to the Middle East to work in Armenia. In the course of the First World War his knowledge of languages was valuable and he served as a liaison officer to units of the French army in the Middle East. During his service he was in 1918 attached to the British military staff in the north-west of Iran, where he was trained in aerial observation by the Royal Air Force, a significant event for archaeology in the region in later years, though of minor importance at the time. His character and background evidently made him remarkably well-

suited to fill important roles at this time in the Middle East, because in 1919 he became the French military representative in the short-lived Republic of Armenia, a position of responsibility and delicacy in the war-torn lands on the borders of Turkey and Russia. At one stage this unusual priest and the British military representative, Colonel Plowden, arranged a cease-fire between the Armenian and Turkish forces (Hovannisian, 1982, vol. 2, 75).

After the end of hostilities Père Poidebard moved to Syria. In 1925 he was making use of aerial reconnaissance in an investigation of the sources of water available in arid regions of north-eastern Syria, and from this his archaeological work in the air developed, as explained in his book *La Trace de Rome dans le Désert de Syrie* (Poidebard, 1934, 4ff and below, p. XX). He was then an officer of the reserve, attached to *l'Armée de l'Air, 39ème régiment d'Aviation* (Mouterde, 1955-56, 319), and the qualities he had displayed in the war must have enabled him to maintain the good relations with the officers of the regiment which were essential for the successful prosecution of his aerial researches. The portrait given in Figure 11 must date from this period.

His first work in archaeological air reconnaissance took place over the Syrian Jezireh, that is, north-eastern Syria, and the results were published soon afterwards in the journal *Syria* (Poidebard, 1927b). Further papers in *Syria* mention surveys of the Roman frontier defences in the area south and south-east of Damascus in May 1927, in the Jezireh again in the autumns of 1927 and 1928, and between Bosra and the River Euphrates in autumn 1930 (Poidebard, 1927, 1928a and b, 1930 and 1931). In 1929 his objective became the exploration of the entire course of the *limes* in Syria and of the routes and stations beyond the *limes* towards the Gulf, a very big project. Further campaigns, not reported in *Syria*, in 1929, 1931 and 1932, are mentioned in *La Trace de Rome*, which was published in 1934. His flying appears to have been done in Potez 25 general purpose biplanes piloted at different times by various officers, the most important of whom was Commandant de Boysson. Poidebard's aerial surveys were supplemented by visits to sites on the ground made with the help of the French army (Fig. 13). The *méharistes* (camel corps) and

FIGURE 11 Père Antoine Poidebard, S.J. portrait, wearing flying helmet, inscribed '*A Sir Aurel Stein, fidèlement. AP*'. *Photograph: (n.d.). Stein Archive (Bodleian Library, Ms. Stein 450, fol.5).*

other troops acted as protectors and guides and provided labour if excavation was carried out. This *vérification au sol* must have been essential in the interpretation of the photographs and important in getting to know the country across which the *limes* ran.

The parts of *La Trace de Rome* that are now most valuable include the photographs themselves, a number of which are reproduced here, and a large map that summarizes Poidebard's knowledge of the fortifications and roads of the Roman frontier defences in the modern country of Syria, that is, in the central part of the *limes*. The book was very well received. Its great virtue was that it enabled scholars to begin to see a coherent scheme in the remains of the frontier defences, which had previously seemed a series of unconnected sites. To quote from a review by Sir George Macdonald: it was 'one of the most important and illuminating contributions ever made to the unwritten history of the Roman Empire', that is, history derived from the physical remains of the Empire rather than from classical authors (Macdonald, 1934, 373; cf. Stein, 1936).

After the completion of this major work, Poidebard transferred his attention to an important area in Syria lying behind the Roman frontier. His flying in 1934-7 provided data for another book (jointly with R. Mouterde), *Le limes de Chalcis*, publication of which was delayed until 1945. Although there is an overlap, this survey covered territory outside the scope of the present book. In the introduction to this second work, Poidebard, perhaps with some satisfaction, noted two scholars, Deschamps and Schlumberger, who had employed the aeroplane in their archaeological research and credited his own pioneering efforts in the field (cf. Figs. 17, 171; Mouterde and Poidebard, 1945, VIII; cf. Schlumberger, 1939, 198 and n.3; 1986).

· O.G.S. Crawford and · the Royal Air Force

Among the principal sources of information utilized by Poidebard in his search for the sites of forts and roads were vegetation marks and slight earthworks shown by the shadows of the low sun. In Britain during the 1920s another scholar, O.G.S. Crawford, became aware of the importance of exactly the same factors (Crawford and Keiller, 1928, 5ff). According to Poidebard (1934, 16) it was in 1927 that the two men first made contact, but curiously there is no mention of Poidebard in Crawford's report of the visit that he made to the Middle East in 1928 (Crawford, 1929; cf. Crawford, 1955, 189-200). He visited and flew with Royal Air Force units in Iraq, Transjordan and Palestine (now broadly modern Jordan and Israel respectively) and Egypt with the object of finding photographs showing ancient sites taken on training flights and arranging for their despatch to England regularly in later years (cf. Engelbach, 1929). The Crawford collections at the Institutes of Archaeology in Oxford and, in particular, London include interesting photographs brought back on that visit, for example Figure 56, but the proposed arrangement for regular despatch unfortunately was never put into effect.

There must have been a connection between Crawford's Middle East visit and three articles published in the volumes of *Antiquity* by Royal Air Force officers then serving in Transjordan, Fl.Lt. (later Air Vice Marshal) P.E. Maitland (1927) and Group Captain L.W.B. Rees (1929a; 1929b; cf. Williams, 1989). An article on Masada by C.F.C. Hawkes (1929) may also have been connected. These articles included photographs of the Roman forts at Azraq and Uweinid, which are used again here (Figs. 28, 105). The Azraq picture is an excellent mosaic, one of several now in the Institute of Archaeology, London which were made by the Royal Air Force at about this time.

A few years later, in 1936, Sq.Ldr. Traill, commanding officer of 14 Squadron RAF, which was stationed at Amman, Transjordan, undertook a long flight over archaeological sites east of the Jordan with the American archaeologist Nelson Glueck, who afterwards commended his knowledge of, and interest in, the ancient remains (Glueck, 1937). Similarly, the 'Notes and photographs of Roman remains in Transjordan' prepared by the Royal Air Force in Transjordan for Sir Aurel Stein in 1939, were the work of an informed and intelligent commentator, perhaps showing the influence of Traill again (Kennedy, 1982, 204).

Although it was not realized at the time, the period between the two World Wars was a time of exceptional opportunity for archaeological exploration in the Middle East. Before the First World War the lawless conditions endemic in much of the Ottoman Empire made travel difficult and sometimes dangerous. The books of the traveller and archaeologist, Professor A. Musil,

mention a number of unpleasant encounters with armed bedouin tribesmen when, for example, he was exploring the Roman forts between Damascus and the Euphrates (Musil, 1928, 180-1; cf. 1927, 24-33). Between the wars most of the Middle East was under French and British control, which established far better security and more stable living conditions. This period came to an end in 1939 with the outbreak of the Second World War.

Two interesting episodes in the early 1930s illustrate how much easier flying and aerial archaeological work was then than it is at present. At intervals between October 1931 and November 1933, the Jerusalem-based Swedish photographer Matson chartered an aircraft and took photographs of various sites in Egypt, Palestine, Transjordan, Syria and Iraq. The originals of these are now in the Library of Congress in Washington; one is reproduced here (Fig. 172). Shortly afterwards, in 1932-3, James Henry Breasted Jr returned to his father's interest in the excavations at Dura Europos and was flown over the site, which he photographed with his new 35 mm format Leica camera. With their chartered aircraft, the opportunity was taken by the Breasted party to photograph other sites in the Middle East, and several hundred frames taken from the air are preserved in the Oriental Institute, Chicago. The quality varies considerably both through blurring of the image and from views not being taken from the best height or direction.

· Sir Aurel Stein ·

Just before the Second World War, another outstanding man, Sir Aurel Stein, began a major programme of aerial research on the Roman desert frontier. Marc Aurel Stein was born in Budapest, Hungary in 1862. Although his family was Jewish, he was baptized in the Protestant church by ambitious parents, who wished him to escape the handicaps then imposed on Jews. His education culminated in a degree at the University of Tübingen (Baden Württemberg, Germany), where he studied Sanskrit and Persian.

After a period of postgraduate work in Britain, he was appointed in 1887 to a position at the

Punjab University, Lahore, in what is now Pakistan. Research on Sanskrit manuscripts led to archaeology, and by degrees his name became known. He appears to have been a tremendous worker, very persistent and with the capacity to impress leading figures in the Government of India. After long efforts to persuade the authorities to back his plans, he was able to make a series of expeditions beyond the Himalayas to remote areas of Sinkiang in Eastern China. His fame rests mainly on the three expeditions he made in 1900-1, 1906-8 and 1913-16.

The scene of his work in Central Asia was a remote territory, 1600 km (1000 miles) in length west to east, ringed by high mountains, and with the Taklamakan Desert at its centre. Stein, the only European in these expeditions, must have inspired the confidence of his Indian and Chinese assistants to an unusual degree, and in consequence his parties enjoyed great success in the tasks of exploration, surveying (the good maps they made were undoubtedly valuable to the Indian Government) and excavation. The arid soil of the desert margins preserved perishable material, including the remains of wooden buildings and furniture, and, importantly, numerous inscribed wooden tablets. Frescoes were found in many ruined temples. The most celebrated haul came in 1907 from a great deposit of Chinese and Tibetan manuscripts and painted and embroidered textiles that had been walled up in about AD 1000 in a hidden chamber of the 'Caves of the Ten Thousand Bhuddas'. Much of this was purchased by Stein from their single guardian, a Bhuddist priest. It was sent on the 2250 km (1400 mile) journey back to India in boxes loaded on camels, and thence by sea to the British Museum in London. He published his results in some splendid books, of which *Ancient Khotan* (Oxford, 1907; 2 vols) and *Serindia* (Oxford, 1921; 5 vols) are the premier. In this brief account we must pass over Stein's explorations in the high mountains and much more; suffice it to say that his work was widely acclaimed and that he was knighted in 1912 – a wonderful achievement for the Hungarian boy of 40 years before (cf. Mirsky, 1977; Oldham, 1943; Andrews, 1944).

After retirement in 1927 he continued archaeological exploration, but in the Middle East. As early as 1919 he had signalled his interest in air

reconnaissance and photography by a letter to the *Geographical Journal*, commenting on the importance of Beazeley's work in Iraq (Stein, 1919). He realized the importance of Poidebard's work in Syria, and, as early as 1929 (Kennedy, 1982, 199), aspired to emulate it in the British mandated territories of Iraq, Transjordan and Palestine. After many delays, he was able to 'pull the right strings' and gain the support of the Royal Air Force in the air and the Iraq Petroleum Co. on the ground for his survey of the Roman *limes*. In preparation for this work, he conferred with Poidebard at Beirut in January 1938, later mentioning in a letter that 'P. is a man of much humour and knowledge of the world' (Mirsky, 1977, 510). The surveys were made in 1938-9, and while the autumn 1938 campaign was in progress he reached his 76th birthday.

Sir Aurel Stein's two long campaigns of flying and photography in 1938 and 1939 must represent the most ambitious and extensive archaeological air survey ever completed. We can use the word completed, because although the effects of the war and, later, his death in 1943, caused his photographs to be scattered and often lost and led to a long delay before the appearance of the report he left, most of the material has now been collected together again and his *Limes Report* published (Gregory and Kennedy (Stein), 1985). In addition to this long report, the published material about his expeditions includes three preliminary reports (Stein, 1938, 1940 and 1941), and in the Bodleian Library, Oxford are many letters to friends worldwide and the typescript of his *Personal Narrative* for this period (Stein, n.d.), an informal account which supplements the more technical *Limes Report*. Only a very brief selection from this mass of material can be given here.

His first campaign in March, April and May 1938 was spent in northern Iraq, immediately to the east of the territories covered by Poidebard in north-eastern Syria. It would be inappropriate to comment here on the long and complicated itinerary, but the organization of the expedition must be touched on in order to suggest the scale of the undertaking. A Vickers Vincent general-purpose biplane was allotted by 55 Squadron of the Royal Air Force and Stein was evidently well pleased by its suitability for the work in hand and by the enthusiasm and competence of

FIGURE 12 Sir Aurel Stein (centre) and his Royal Air Force party, probably at Habaniyyah, Iraq in 1938. P.O. Leslie Hunt is the tall figure on Stein's left. The third man in a flying suit is probably the photographer. In the background is the Vincent aircraft they used. *Photograph: (1938). Stein Archive (India Office Library and Records).*

Pilot Officer L.H. Hunt, who flew it. The rest of the Royal Air Force party, which is seen in Figure 12, standing in front of the Vincent, included a photographic detachment and a team to man the wireless tender from which radio communication was maintained with the aircraft. A car and lorry, presumably accompanied by their drivers, were provided by the Iraq Petro-leum Company, which also seconded the services of the expedition's surveyor, Iltifat Husain, late of the Survey of India. He was an important member of the team because the air reconnaissance was systematically complemented by exploration and site visits on the ground, during which measured surveys were made.

The second campaign from November 1938 to May 1939 again started in northern Iraq, but at the end of November the expedition moved south to the Middle Euphrates and the desert of western Iraq. By mid-February the *limes* in Iraq had been covered and it was time to carry the work across the border into Transjordan. This was a move into the territory of a different Royal Air Force command. With many regrets the

Vincent aircraft was left behind.

In Transjordan a period of difficulty started. Because of the beginnings of trouble in Palestine at that time, aircraft convenient for close examination of the ground were all required there. The only type which could be allocated to Stein was the Wellesley, a newly introduced monoplane bomber, about which he wrote that it 'being a very fast machine, could not offer me the same facilities for a lookout as I had enjoyed when standing in the cockpit of the Vincent, immediately behind the pilot' (Gregory and Kennedy (Stein), 1985, 234). Evidently the positions for the crew, together with the higher speed and larger turning circle of this aircraft made observation of features on the ground more difficult (Riley, 1986, 667). It says much about the great prestige of Sir Aurel Stein that he was given so much flying time in these circumstances. A further problem was that the pilots changed frequently, so the previous close co-operation with P.O. Hunt could not be repeated. The surveys now had to be based mainly on the ground, aided by the transport still provided by the Iraq Petroleum Company. Fortunately, on 28 April 1939 a Vincent again became available, and the campaign was finished with a period of intensive photography which ended in mid-May 1939. This was the close of a remarkably extensive reconnaissance from the air and on the ground, and Stein ends his *Personal Narrative* of the expedition by writing '*finis longae chartaeque viaeque*' – appropriate words.

· *Recent Work* ·

Aerial exploration by archaeologists has never been resumed in the Middle East, though photographs of sites in Israel and Jordan have been taken from the air as illustrations for the ever-popular books on the Bible or biblical archaeology. A set of slides of archaeological sites in Jordan prepared by the former President of the American Schools of Oriental Research, Dr James Sauer, includes a number of aerial views, two of which are reproduced on the covers of this book. The principal activity, however, embracing both these two countries and Egypt – though mainly Israel – has been by a British photographer, Dr Richard Cleave. Jerusalem-based like Matson, he is the founder of a large collection of air views of the Holy Land; his high quality colour transparencies of sites and landscapes form a splendid series of views, many of relevance to Roman military work (cf. Negev, 1983, 63, 69; Rogerson, 1985, *passim*, esp. 212f).

Vertical photography has continued for military and cartographic purposes in many areas. It is normally difficult to get access to this material, but several archaeologists have been able to examine the photographic cover of large areas and do important work. The researches of van Lière and Lauffray (1954-5) in the Syrian Jezireh, Adams (1981) in Iraq, and Villeneuve (1985) in the Syrian Hauran have been of especial importance for the study of the ancient landscape. In Jordan, by the enlightened policy of the Royal Jordanian Geographic Centre, scholars have been allowed some access to the surveys of that country made by the Royal Air Force during and after the Second World War, by Hunting Air Survey in 1953 (Figs. 20, 31, 79, 86, 89, 130, 144) and recently by the Jordanian Air Force and the Institut Géographique National (Figs. 47, 76, 135).

CHAPTER FOUR

Reconnaissance and Photography from the Air in Arid Regions of the Middle East

To make the best use of the results of Poidebard's and Stein's systematic aerial explorations, we must try to understand their methods of work, and how the archaeological sites they found were identified from the air. Fortunately they both left not only collections of photographs, but also books describing their work. It is therefore possible to make well informed interpretations of their photographs and to apply the knowledge so gained to photographs from other sources, such as recent vertical cover made for survey purposes, which show archaeological sites only incidentally.

· Poidebard's Research · Methods

La Trace de Rome begins with a chapter headed 'Aerial Research Methods in Historical Geography', in which Poidebard reviewed the subject in the light of his experience. He included a section on the origins of the method (mentioning the names of Rey, Wiegand and Beazeley), some general information about aviation, aerial mapping techniques and geography, and a detailed description of his methods and techniques in the air. This is a source document of great interest, describing much that is still the common currency of present day aerial archaeologists, such as the detection of sites by the shadows cast by the low sun – and also much that is certainly not now standard practice, such as landing near a site to make an immediate ground reconnaissance. A translation of part of this chapter follows, giving the section in which he described his methods and techniques (Poidebard, 1934, 4-11).

ARCHAEOLOGICAL RESEARCH METHODS ON THE STEPPE

I EXPERIMENTS AND TECHNIQUE

Aerial Reconnaissance (1925-29)

In 1925, working for the *Société Géographique de France*, I was studying the economic possibilities of the Syrian Jezireh and the mountain ranges crossing the desert between the Anti-Lebanon and the Jebel Sinjar. During these geographical surveys, the aeroplane proved to have an unsuspected value in the archaeological examination of Roman Upper Mesopotamia. To the north of the Euphrates, in the Khabur basin, the network of ancient roads became apparent to me, clearly marked out by the ancient tells of the steppe. Viewed from ground level, the innumerable tells (or artificial mounds) are strewn over the plain of the Jezireh like a scattered flock of sheep. Seen from 1500 m. [5000 ft], they were strictly aligned. A glance at a map giving the positions of the ancient Assyrian and Roman towns convinced me that I had beneath my eyes the whole network of ancient communications, marked out by these remains of ancient agricultural communities or fortified posts. Descending by slow spirals to very low heights above the ancient tells, I noted that under a low oblique light many details appeared on their platforms or on their slopes, though on the ground the turf covering them seemed quite uniform. Was aerial observation going to give precise details of the exact courses of the historic routes that join the markets of the Far East with the Mediterranean ports, problems which had troubled me since my first flight in the spring of 1918 over the Persian plateau?

An aerial sketch map of the ancient road network

of the Syrian Jezireh and a summary of the observations made during the flights were presented to the *Congrès archéologique de Syria et de Palestine* (Beirut, April, 1926) (Poidebard, 1927a) at the request of M. Dussaud. The *Académie des Inscription et Belles-Lettres* then instructed me to verify my results by a ground survey. The autumn 1926 campaign, made in collaboration with M. Maurice Dunand, demonstrated to us, as it had to previous explorers, how unrewarding the Jezireh could be to archaeologists. Between the Tigris and the Euphrates almost all traces of the ancient Assyrian and Roman civilisations have been levelled by successive destructions and the Persian, Arab and Mongol invasions. Through the millenia, wind-blown dust has covered the steppe with a uniform layer through which no ruins can be seen, even in places where good evidence of ancient sites is visible from the air.

Faced with this basic difficulty in fulfilling the allotted task, I could not admit defeat. It was necessary to find a method of locating the ruins hidden under the soil by using the aeroplane. This was two years' work, from autumn 1926 to autumn 1928. A long and thorough study of the climate and the terrain, patiently made with the assistance of specialists from the *Aviation Française du Levant*, led me to firm conclusions. Since the end of 1926, thanks to the collaboration of Commandant Ruby, the officer in charge of the *Groupe de l'Aviation de l'Euphrate*, I have been confident in broad outline of the main principles of aerial observation for the investigation of ancient remains hidden below the surface of the Syrian steppe.

The Jezireh, like all the Syrian desert, is a steppe region, with clayey or alluvial soil, where sand only occurs in very limited areas. Grass and wild plants prevent the formation of dunes. The layer of silt that has been deposited by the wind in the course of millennia rarely exceeds 30 or 40 cm. [12 to 15 in.] in thickness. Buried ruins therefore necessarily produce slight undulations of the surface. Often invisible at ground level, these slight irregularities show clearly to the aerial observer who makes use of the low light of the early and late hours [e.g. Fig. 100].

The oblique rays of light, skimming the surface of the ground at morning and evening, bring out and exaggerate the least unevenness of the ground.

We may compare the way in which a road appears flat and uniform during the hours when the sun is high, and very uneven at night time, when seen by the almost parallel pencils of light from the headlights of a car.

After the first rains of autumn, the steppe quickly becomes green again, but in different shades, depending on the permeability of the soil and the depressions in its surface. It is lighter toned where a subterranean ruin is hidden, because of its reduced permeability or because of the appearance of plants which had been adversely affected by the stone of the old walls. It assumes a darker shade in the depressions of an old road or an old ditch, in which a hollow a few centimetres deep is enough to retain more moisture. As soon as hot weather returns in the spring, when the fierce heat of the sun dries up the vegetation in a few weeks, the same effect is produced on the colours of the steppe [Figs. 13 and 101]. (For the photography of the sites of buried ruins completely invisible to the eye, it seems necessary to raise the possibility of different actinity of the ground in such places. Plates with normal emulsion or, better, with special emulsion bring out details which the eye does not see, even from an aeroplane.)

The next stages were the application of these principles in the air as the main means of finding ruins hidden under the steppe, and then checking the information gained by field work and excavation. This was done during the 1927 and 1928 campaigns [Poidebard, 1928a and 1930a].

In autumn 1926, with the help of Commandant Ruby, I had recognized several camps on the Romano-Byzantine frontier south of Nisibis, near Tell Brak. These enclosures were almost invisible at ground level, but were clearly marked on air photographs taken at a height of 600 m. [2000 ft] with a very oblique light – forgotten entrenchments, far from modern roads and revealed from a distance by the evening shadows.

In autumn 1927 during a flight piloted by Commandant Pitault I completed the investigation of the camps on the outer defences of the Roman strong point of Tell Brak. The flight took place some hours after the first rains of autumn. At the corners of a platform of earth, itself apparently without interest, a lighter tint in the vegetation clearly re-vealed the towers of a *castellum* buried a metre [$3\frac{1}{4}$ ft] below the surface [Fig. 132]. The excavation of the site, decided on the very next day after the flight and begun by trial trenching, took place in 1928. It was continually guided and checked, and amplified in its conclusions, by observation and photography from the air. In both exploratory trenching and full excavation, the guidance given by air photographs was crucial.

The map made from the autumn 1928 results, produced with the help of officers of the cartographic unit of the *39e Régiment d'Aviation*, was presented on 31 May 1929 to the *Académie des Inscriptions*. It gave us:

1.   120 km. [75 miles] of the Romano-Byzantine frontier of the 4th century between Tunainir and Dara, with all the defensive *castella* spaced at ten Roman miles (X M.P.) and the intermediate signal posts;
2.   60 km. [37.5 miles] of the Roman frontier of the first four centuries, between the Upper River Khabur and the Jebel Sinjar;
3.   The Roman defences and the lay-out of fortified towns extending along the Khabur up to Ras el-Ain. Their positions were mapped using data from a photographic survey made in 1922 by *l'Aviation Militaire du Levant*;
4.   The identification of the marching camps [cf. p. 103 below] and the fortified towns along the great Roman road joining Nisibis and Sinjar, stages of the Peutinger Table itinerary *Nisibis – Singara*.

During our work many other ancient sites were identified and photographed: remains of roads, camps, forts, irrigation canals.

Much experience was gained in 1927 in the aerial examination of the steppe and basalt terrain in the volcanic region south of Damascus: the Ledja, the Safa and Diret et-Touloul. A flight on 10 May, piloted by Captain Tourre, enabled us to survey the road leaving the *castellum* of Jebel Seys towards Palmyra, a Roman road invisible at ground level [Fig. 26]. The work was continued for the whole of the year by Commandant de Boysson and Captain de Castet during the cartographic reconnaissances made by the group of squadrons at Damascus. They were invaluable collaborators, who supplied me with a photographic study of the ancient Roman road over the Ledja, vertical and oblique views giving the line, the method of construction and the watch towers of the great military road from Bosra

to Damascus and a detailed plan of the Roman ruins of Jebel Seys. From the geographic aspect, they confirmed my aerial observations of the faults in the Damascus plain, marked out by the lines of craters of the Diret et-Touloul [Poidebard, 1928a; 1929c].

The results of this work were presented to the *Académie des Inscriptions* in May 1929. The aerial method of archaeological research in the steppe region was confirmed as based on sound principles. I was then requested to review the map of the Roman *limes* in the whole of the Syrian desert, both south and north of the Euphrates in order to test the new technique thoroughly. This was the task of the campaigns of 1929 to 1932.

Technique

In practice it is not possible to establish a general technique. 'Exploration', Gabriel Bonvalot once said to me, 'depends on the minute preparation of details.' Each region has its own peculiarities, and, above all, each explorer has his own methods, based on his personal experience. The direction and the advice of aviators with specialist knowledge of the region under study are the only practical guides for successful archaeological research.

I will note only a few essential points of the technique... Lengthy and detailed preparations must be made if aerial reconnaissance is to be fruitful. The minds of both the archaeologist and his pilot must be alerted to all the points that may have to be watched during the flight. Sketches or maps at a suitable scale should be prepared, ready for details observed to be pencilled in. Several flying heights corresponding to the scale of the sketches and the maps should be agreed in advance with the pilot.

The main decision is the choice of pilot. The ideal is clearly to be able oneself to pilot, observe, sketch, write and photograph. Such topographical acrobatics are only for the exceptionally talented. Further, they are difficult to keep up consistently in the course of a long survey, during which attention must not be relaxed. In practice, the ideal is to train in the method of work an aviator who knows the region well and is at the same time a competent and bold pilot, an excellent observer, and as keen as his passenger in the task of recording. In research on historical geography and archaeology it is not enough for a pilot to be familiar with the air; he must also know the landscape and know the light. He must cooperate in seeking a site and, once it has been found, in presenting it under favourable illumination.

After landing, the observer must check his notes against those of the pilot and indicate to him the places to photograph, deciding the direction and the scale of the pictures to be taken. Then, in a later flight, taking as passenger a photographer used to the region and the method of research, preferably always the same man, the pilot must ensure that the sites discovered are recorded from the best height and with the right light.

The employment as photographer of someone other than the archaeologist is a check on the recording. With his mind concentrated on the objective, the researcher may often be tempted to record a point of view or a detail which suits his theories, rather than to produce a direct and unbiased representation of the subject. Experience shows that this method of a team of three, i.e. two pairs sharing the same pilot, gives valuable results.

Whenever possible, flying must be followed by surveys on the ground. Observation from the air prepares the way for reconnaissance on the surface, which it directs and checks, facilitating preliminary investigations and making a considerable saving of time and money. It cannot, however, be a substitute for the surveys on the ground... essential... to determine the age of the features studied... In cases where the explorer thinks that he will be unable to return on the ground to examine the site, the field work may be done by landing in the course of a flight, provided that the terrain is suitable. Measuring equipment and pickaxes for rapid excavations ought therefore always to be carried in the aircraft. On the other hand, when it is possible to visit a site on foot, one does this with the air photograph in hand.

If the aeroplane is to be truly an elevated and mobile observatory, from which the ground can be studied like a relief map seen under the best lighting, the fundamental principle of the technique must be for the pilot to be able to help the archaeologist to see with precision, and the photographer to record the same view on his plate or film. The eye of the archaeologist and the lens of the camera must become one with the eye of the pilot. During the aerial search, the rear-view mirror in the pilot's cockpit provides the intimate link between the archaeologist and his guide that will be the result of long experience gained during many flights together. The development of a research team is thus the essential basis of the technique.

2 DEVELOPMENTS AND RESULTS
During many flights, followed by checking on the ground, made in the autumns of the years 1929 to 1932 to produce the map of the Roman *limes* in the Syrian desert, we were able to use the aerial method boldly and push it to its limits, thanks to the technical ability of the pilots and photographers trained by four years of the method of research (Poidebard, 1931a; 1932a; Mouterde and Poidebard, 1931; Mouterde, 1930). Certain points were resolved and certain improvements were made in the methods.

Height Of Observation

The original principles were greatly modified. The high altitudes (1000 and 1500 m. [about 3000 to 5000 ft]), usual before 1929, were only retained for general reconnaissance flights intended to study the geographical conditions in part of the *limes,* take an overall view of a strategic scheme, make a quick comparison of distant points, or make general revisions.

Flights at low altitude, that is 300 m. [1000 ft] and below have proved since the autumn of 1929 to be much more fruitful in the observation of detail, and we regularly made them. Thus a reconnaissance of water supply points and watch towers on the ancient caravan route between Damascus and Jebel Seys was done in autumn 1929 at a height of 25 m. [80 ft] for a distance of 250 km [160 miles]. The examination of the road-marking monument at Umm el-Amad, on the ancient route from Palmyra to Hit, where we found an inscription of the second century, dating the road and fixing its destination, had been made a little previously, when surveying the site from a height of 5 m. [16 ft], with the propeller just turning over [see below, p. 62 for a comment on this man-oeuvre, which sounds rather alarming].

Apart from the extremes to which we went in the course of these trials, which I wished to be as complete as possible, I can say that a good height for reconnaissance flights is from 300 to 400 m. [1000 to 1300 ft]. Lower heights are often necessary for the observation of details. Accustomed to landing in open country during flights made to watch the bedouin tribes, the desert pilots can put the archaeologist down near any site, except in the basalt areas [where the surface is strewn with boulders]. The low passes above the ground made when selecting a landing place are precious moments for observation while just skimming the surface.

At places where it would be dangerous to descend too low, a ride with the camel corps [méharistes] provides an excellent low-level observatory. Camels are immune to the whirlwinds of the torrid air and the atmospheric turbulence of the hot season, and are a great help to the explorer who wishes to spend a whole day at 3.50 m. [11½ ft] above the surface [Fig. 13].

Vegetius has already noted their natural ability to recognise ancient tracks obscured by the desert sands. 'Certain nations in former times fought on camel-back, as the Ursulians and Macetae still do today. It is said that this animal, made for the sands, knows instinctively how to identify dust-covered roads' (*Epitoma rei militaris* III.23). The importance of the part which the *Méharistes du Levant* take in the checking of aerial research on the ground is therefore well founded. The *méhariste* guides are well-informed critics of the results of the archaeological aviator in desert regions.

Flight Under A Screen Of Clouds

To obtain a light almost parallel to the ground, trials were made in autumn 1929 with Captain Dunand, flying in late afternoon under low-level cloud cover immediately after the heavy November rains. The last rays of the sun, kept in a beam parallel to the soil by this artificial screen, caused the slightest ridges to stand out on the tells of the steppe beside the River Khabur. It was possible to take a photograph illustrating this procedure at Deir es-Zor in autumn 1930. On the ground were seen traces of an ancient track invisible during the day.

Looking Into The Sun (Contre-Jour)

A flight in July 1931, piloted by Captain Almy, enabled a trial to be made in atmospheric conditions previously thought impossible for archaeological observation: excessive brightness, absolute drought on the steppe and turbulence in the torrid air near the ground. Looking straight towards the sun [*plein contre-jour*], screened by the shade of the upper wing, and with the aircraft flying low at about 100 m. [300 ft], I was able to see below us for 40 km [25 miles] the traces of the old road leaving Tell Hmedeh (a post on the Byzantine *limes* of the Wadi Jaghjagh) towards the Tigris area. Invisible at ground level, this important road had escaped all our previous aerial searches, although the tells on the plain had given us its stages (cf. Poidebard, 1934, 168).

The flight took place at nine in the morning, with the sun already high and at full strength. The full *contre-jour* viewpoint and the closeness to the ground allowed the narrowest shadows to be seen distinctly, black on white. As the sun rose, the oblique lighting needed to reveal the details of the site was maintained by proportionately lowering the height. *Contre-jour* lighting emphasizes the least unevenness of the ground.

Trials of the use of *contre-jour* were repeated and taken to the limit between June and August 1932 under the intense light of the hot season and in air with a slight sandy haze. Some distant views, taken without using special filters, demonstrated that by photographing almost directly into the sun at a low height it was possible to prevent fogging the plates and to avoid reflections from the ground or the sandy haze [Fig. 163].

· Comments on · Poidebard's And Stein's Methods

The information left by both the great pioneers will be valuable when the time comes to resume archaeological air reconnaissance and photography in the Middle East. Many of Poidebard's procedures need no comment other than an appreciation of his quick recognition of two phenomena of great importance: the long shadows cast by the sun when low in the sky and the vegetation marks that appear under certain conditions. The air photographers who have been so active in Europe in recent years have made

FIGURE 13 Field work on the ground with the camel corps (*verification au sol avec les méharistes*) in the desert at Segri about 100 km (60 miles) south-east of Palmyra. *Photograph: A. Poidebard (n.d.). From Poidebard, 1934, Pl.VI.2.*

great use of similar phenomena when recording ancient sites (e.g. Bradford, 1957, 13-41; Wilson, 1982, 27-33, 53-70; Christlein and Braasch, 1982, 26-38; Riley, 1987, 19-21, 27-40).

In contrast, modern archaeologists are surprised by Poidebard's flights at low height and by his practice of landing in the desert to visit sites on the ground; such flying is unheard of in the disciplined conditions of present day aviation in Europe. Further, none of those active at present would wish to copy Poidebard's method of sending up the photographer on a subsequent flight without him. The different conditions under which Poidebard operated in Syria explain

many of the differences between his procedures and those customary at present, though some points remain unanswered. The matter is discussed below.

Stein did not leave a description of his methods comparable with the long account by Poidebard given in the preceding pages, but much can be deduced by reading his *Limes Report* and *Personal Narrative* (Gregory and Kennedy (Stein), 1985 and Stein, n.d.), and by examining the negatives of his photographs of Iraq now preserved in the Institute of Archaeology, London.

PÈRE A. POIDEBARD

Some of the forts of the Syrian *limes* had already been described before the First World War in the reports of travellers such as Professor Alois Musil, but the difficulties of travel in the Ottoman Empire caused many gaps and limitations in his reports. Even when conditions became better in the period of the French Mandate between the World Wars it was not easy to reach the more remote parts of the Roman frontier. By making use of the aerial view and the mobility conferred by the aeroplane, Poidebard began a new stage in the study of the *limes*.

Many of the things that now seem unusual in Poidebard's methods may be assumed to have resulted from the design of the Potez 25 biplane in which he customarily flew, to judge from the plates in *La Trace de Rome* (e.g. Fig. 15), and from the skills of the French military pilots of the day. Considering first the heights at which he was flown, it is easy to understand the reason for the choice of about 1000 to 3000 ft (300 to 400 m.), which is similar to the level adopted by many present-day operators for archaeological reconnaissance and photography (Riley, 1987, 45). However, an explanation is needed for the occasions when his pilots flew very much lower in order to permit a close view of the ground. Low flying has disadvantages, the most serious of which is the reduced safety margin in the event of a forced landing caused by engine trouble, when the pilot might have to attempt to put the aircraft down on ground with obstructions. The French military pilots were accustomed in the course of their duties to landing in remote places on the flat surface of many parts of the Syrian steppe, though Poidebard mentions that they first made low passes over the ground to check that the surface was suitable, as good airmanship would have required. These landings enabled aerial discoveries to be followed immediately by a visit on foot – though how often Poidebard does not say. Using a pickaxe carried in the aircraft, a little digging was also possible on such occasions! The descent to a few metres above the ground to look at the inscribed dedication set up on the caravan route at Umm el-Amad (above, pp. 59) must have been a glide, with the engine throttled back as if to make a landing, and it may be assumed that the pilot quickly opened up to full power to climb away.

Flying must have been great fun in these conditions, though there were certain risks, and an accompanying aircraft would have been an advantage, so that there was a machine in reserve in case of difficulty. There were evidently two aircraft present when the Roman road shown on Figure 15 was photographed. When necessary, British practice was similar. It is on record that G. Capt. Insall (the discoverer of Woodhenge), when stationed in Egypt, was at one time in the habit of landing in the Sinai desert to look for antiquities, and that another British aircraft accompanied him to provide safety cover (Mole, 1984, 81). Again, the aircraft each carried a spade and pickaxe.

It is less easy to understand fully Poidebard's technique of *contre jour* photography at low level in the hot summer months, with visibility reduced by haze, though the main points are comprehensible. When the sun is high, shadows are short and are likely only to be visible from the air when looking towards the shadowed side of a feature, i.e. towards the sun. Also, in conditions of reduced visibility the ground is seen distinctly only by reducing the thickness of hazy air it is necessary to look through, i.e. from an aircraft flying low. With the camera facing nearly towards the sun and shaded by the upper wing, it was therefore possible for some types of 'shadow sites' to be photographed successfully in the heat of the day during the Syrian summer.

One of Poidebard's illustrations of the technique (Fig. 163) seems to demonstrate this clearly, but two others (1934, Pls. XCI.1 and 2) are confusing. They show, not a near view, but a distant panorama, which is distinct when looking towards the sun (Pl. XCI.2) and obscured by haze when looking away from it (Pl. XCI.1). This is the exact opposite of general experience in Europe, where the distant view in hazy conditions is obscured when looking towards the sun, but is seen much more distinctly when looking away from it. An article by Poidebard on the subject of *contre jour* air photography makes the question raised by these examples no clearer (Poidebard, 1933).

The photographs reproduced in *La Trace de Rome* are generally of a high standard. Only in a few cases can faults be detected, e.g. the blurring of Fig. 40, which was probably caused by the use of too low a shutter speed. The large plate cameras then in use produced good negatives, and the French Air Force was no doubt well experienced in their use. The plates in *La Trace de Rome* include many excellent vertical views (e.g. Figs. 100, 128, 151, 153, 155), under which the name of the pilot is given. It must be presumed that these photographs were taken by a vertical camera, fixed to the aircraft and operated by the photographer, under the direction of the pilot (for the Royal Flying Corps practice in Palestine in 1917-18 when photographing cities for mapping see Gavish and Biger, 1983, 85). This is not the end of the matter, however, because there are also oblique views, under which either the pilot's name or Poidebard's initials (A.P.) are given. The probable explanation is that only the photographer could operate the vertical camera, but that both he and Poidebard could take oblique photographs, using hand-held cameras. It is evident from some of these obliques (e.g. a view of Dura Europos, 1934, Pl. LXXXVIII), that Poidebard was able himself to take this type of photograph successfully. In his later campaigns the photographic arrangements must have been modified, because in *Le Limes de Chalcis* (Mouterde and Poidebard, 1945) are published many obliques, with the initials A.P. below, and few verticals.

The part of the photographic procedure that now seems surprising – the pilot and photographer flying without Poidebard to record sites he had seen on a previous flight – was probably caused by limited space in the Potez 25, which only had room for the pilot and one other person, in two open cockpits, one behind the other. The photographer and archaeologist therefore could not fly together. This procedure resulted in many good representations of ancient forts, other buildings, towns and lengths of road. It would have been unsuitable for the study of the many minor sites which are to be seen in a region so rich in ancient remains as Syria, but it is evident that this type of investigation was not included in Poidebard's programme of work..

As with all pioneer work, those who review it years afterwards can see many ways in which it could be followed up and expanded. The descriptions of the component parts of the *limes* in *La Trace de Rome* have many gaps. On the map of the *limes*, one of the most useful items in the book, are marked many sites, particularly in the far north-east of Syria (see Fig. 188), which are illustrated neither by photographs nor plans and which receive only the most cursory descrip-

tion in the text, or are not mentioned. As noted above (p. 15), it is probable that the photographs included by Poidebard in his books represent only a small part of those actually taken. Unfortunately, because of the present troubles at Beirut no enquiries have produced a satisfactory report about the current location or condition of the archive of photographs. All the more fortunate that the photogravure plates in *La Trace de Rome* are of such good quality.

Finally, Poidebard's field work on the ground must be mentioned. He published many measured plans, which were valuable additions to the archaeological knowledge of the Roman *limes*. It is impressive to find that at this time, in the 1920s, when air photography was a completely new archaeological technique, he was not content just to take photographs, but also followed up his aerial discoveries by field surveys. His work had great originality, was very thorough and was completed by the publication of his discoveries. Few today can match this achievement.

SIR AUREL STEIN

There is no doubt that Stein was greatly influenced by Poidebard, of whose work he was aware as early as 1929 (Poidebard, 1929f, 319; Kennedy, 1982, 199; cf. above, p. xxx). His review of *La Trace de Rome* (Stein, 1936), was enthusiastic, and they evidently got on well at their meeting at Beirut in January, 1938 (Mirsky, 1977, 510, 519). They both gave most of their attention to roads and forts, and Stein followed lines of investigation suggested by Poidebard, for example in parts of northern Iraq which border north-eastern Syria. However, while searching for forts, Stein appears to have devoted all his attention to upstanding walls and banks and does not mention the sites with buried remains, to which Poidebard attached considerable importance. He evidently concentrated on the observation and recording of sites which were clearly visible to the naked eye under normal conditions, a sensible policy in view of the huge territory that had to be searched.

Once seen, most of the ancient features he found must have been unmistakable, though unfortunately their Roman date may not always have been as certain as he seems to have assumed.

In Iraq, much help came from vegetation marks, pale toned on banks, dark in ditches (Figs. 103, 109, 139, 164), 'the wide fosse... as seen from the air shows up clearly on all sides by the dark colour of the denser vegetation' (Gregory and Kennedy (Stein), 1985, 57 referring to Fig. 103), but it is surprising that Stein does not mention the use of shadows.

Because of its higher rainfall, the Tigris valley north-west of Mosul is more fertile than the arid steppe to the south. Stein made many references to sites in this region which were overgrown by vegetation (e.g. Fig. 110). In such conditions only banks or ruins of a fair height would have been seen and it was probably easier to miss them than on the bare ground of the desert margins. The land is no doubt now under cultivation, and if archaeological flying takes place here in the future it will be interesting to see if crop marks occur. Stein remarked that the site of one fort was covered by a crop of wheat, but said no more (Gregory and Kennedy (Stein), 1985, 111).

In Iraq, Stein did a great deal of flying, though the actual number of flying hours was never recorded in his typescript. The great forts at Ain Sinu (Figs. 113, 167), for example, were only located after 'repeated enquiries and air reconnaissances'. Again, 'on frequent reconnaissance flights ... the hills along the right bank of the Tigris and the course of the river itself from Mosul up to Fesh-Khabur were repeatedly searched' (ibid. 113) and 'after a long flight in zig-zags over the plateaux... stretching down to the Tigris below Fesh-Khabur... the pilot's keen eye noticed a "square"... one mile to the north of the Yazidi village of Qabaq' (ibid. 121). Pilot Officer L.H. Hunt, the officer detailed to pilot the aircraft for most of the time in Iraq, was clearly more than just a 'bus driver'. Stein makes frequent appreciative references to his help, which was evidently not only the good airmanship expected of a Royal Air Force pilot, but also a keen interest in spotting the square earthworks that Stein expected to prove to be Roman forts. Posted to Egypt, Hunt later wrote to Stein telling him that he was now noticing sites in the Egyptian Desert. There were few airfields in much of the great territory which Stein surveyed and the aircraft often had to be based on landing grounds chosen on suitable spots in the desert. It is interesting to see an aircraft on the ground in the background of a photograph of Qasr Khabbaz, in the desert of southern Iraq. It may be noted that they relied on a single aircraft, in spite of the remoteness of the ground they covered.

The Vincent aircraft flown in Iraq had three open cockpits (Riley, 1986, pl.37.2). The pilot was in the front cockpit and Stein was in the middle one, from which he and the pilot could communicate by speaking tube. The photographer occupied the rear position. This was a much better arrangement than in the Potez aircraft used by Poidebard, who could not fly at the same time as his photographer. Stein's reports mention the names of several Leading Aircraftsmen and a Corporal who acted as photographers.

The surviving negatives are on 140 mm. (5.5 in.) wide cut roll film. They are nearly all oblique views, but a few verticals (e.g. Fig. 62) are included. Although they record the sites well, many of the oblique views would have been rather better if the sites had not been photographed from too flat an angle and too far away, faults often found in archaeological photographs taken by those new to this kind of work. In general the standard of photography is lower than that of Poidebard's photographs given in *La Trace de Rome*, though it is probable that the latter were selected from a much larger number and that we only see the best.

Stein's ground field work was at least as thorough as Poidebard's and he was well aware of the importance of following up discoveries made from the air by visits to the sites, during which his knowledge of languages must have been a boon. He spoke Turkish and some Arabic (as well as eight other ancient and modern languages: Mirsky, 1977, 6), and had improved the latter by six weeks of study at Beirut before his first expedition. His practice was clearly very thorough in making site visits and taking measurements. It is unfortunate, as said before, that evidence of date of occupation of sites was not obtained by the systematic collection and analysis of sherds of pottery, but this was not possible because knowledge about Roman pottery in the East was then extremely limited. Some of the measured surveys were of a high standard, for example six drawings of sites, a number contoured, all made by the surveyor Iltifat Husain

(Figs. 19, 37, 75), which were identified in the British Museum in 1986 by Julian Reade.

·The Identification of· Ancient Sites

Many of the the Roman forts and towns in the Middle East, though damaged by stone robbing and long centuries of decay, are in a relatively good state of preservation, and they were in an even better state when photographed in the period between the two World Wars. Recently, the spread of cultivation and the growth of villages and towns has caused much damage at some of the sites, but others are in areas that are still hardly touched by modern changes. The air photographs, whether taken between the World Wars or in recent years, often show remains of buildings standing to a good height, either as ruined stone walls or as the earthworks formed by the collapse of buildings made of sun-dried brick. Less conspicuous remains also occur, for example, the forts in north-eastern Syria where the surface is covered by wind blown silt (Figs. 132-3).

In studying the desert *limes*, we are concerned with landscapes very different from those of the Roman frontier in Britain or Germany, where cultivation is much more extensive. In these countries the most important service given by aerial archaeologists has been the discovery and recording of sites shown by crop marks. Such discoveries can usually be fitted into a framework already established by the study of previously known sites with upstanding remains. The investigation of the desert frontier is at a far less advanced stage. Few even of the standing ruins of forts have received much attention, and often there is no reliable evidence of their date. There are imposing structures, for example Figures 151, 153 and 155, about which the only information is the brief notes of visitors, a plan and some photographs. In these circumstances archaeological air photography in the Middle East has been directed primarily towards the discovery and recording of standing remains which would have been found years before by field work on the ground in better explored countries. Poidebard

also examined features concealed beneath the surface or shown only by low earthworks, but, although his pioneer work in this field had some important results, they were not numerous.

The ruins of stone buildings standing to a good height, nearly all of which are in the central or western parts of our region, are illustrated by numerous photographs (Figs. 122, 124, 147, 151, 153, 155, 165, 184). The best pictures were taken with the sun high in the sky in a position that gave short shadows to outline walls; when recording high walls long shadows are undesirable because they obscure small features on the ground, though Poidebard reproduced a striking picture of Palmyra with towers emphasized by long shadows (1934, Pl. LXVI). Oblique pictures of standing ruins are most effective when taken looking towards the sun, i.e. towards the shadowed side and, to judge from their photographs, Poidebard and Stein were both aware of this (e.g. Figs. 64, 165). Fallen buildings at such sites may be recognizable by the rough 'texture' of a mass of fallen stones (e.g. Fig. 137). 'Texture', the repetition of many small features close together, is a useful concept to have in mind when examining air photographs. This property of the surface is, however, only noticeable when the site is shown at a fairly large scale. Not all of the pictures reproduced here satisfy this condition. The scale of survey photographs taken for non-archaeological purposes is usually too small to show texture (e.g. Fig. 89).

Some idea of the heights of structures can be formed from the examination of single photographs. A sharp outline and shadows suggest walls still standing to a fair height (Figs. 153, 155), while a 'rough' texture and the absence of shadows suggest the ruins of walls, such as those at the Masada camps (Fig. 45). The broad, textured dark marks round the fort at Sa'neh (Fig. 135) suggest the collapsed remains of a high stone wall.

On desert land, vegetation growing along the base of a wall may outline it and help to show its position. The photograph of the fort at Nedwiyat al-Qdeyr (Fig. 92) provides an example of vegetation marks which clearly show the positions of walls, though there is a little doubt about the exact interpretation of some parts of the photograph.

Poidebard published an air photograph of the

FIGURE 14 Vegetation mark in the Jebel Cembeh, Hasakeh, Syria (36°25′N 41°15′E). *Photograph: A. Poidebard (1928–29). From Poidebard, 1934, Pl.IV.2. The line of a ditch is given by a remarkably clear dark toned (positive) vegetation mark. According to Poidebard's text (1934, 6), this mark appeared after the first hot weather of spring. It is probably best to ignore the seemingly contradictory statement in the caption of Pl.IV, 2 that it appeared after the rains of spring.*

fort at Hlehleh (Fig. 98) to illustrate how buried walls might be revealed by pale-toned (i.e. negative) vegetation marks, and a ground photo of the better growth of plants in a ditch in the Jebel Cembeh to illustrate dark-toned (positive) vegetation marks (Fig. 14) (made memorable by

the inclusion of a fierce-looking Arab soldier).

In the north-eastern part of the region sun-dried brick was the main building material. Exposed brickwork of this kind weathered badly, with the result that after the passing of time the walls of forts became broad banks (e.g. Fig. 139), and individual buildings subsided into mounds (Fig. 53), though their general layout might remain visible (Fig. 167). Vegetation marks are important aids to recognition of the 'earthworks' formed in this way. As already mentioned, they are seen on many of Stein's photographs of sites in Iraq (Figs. 103, 109, 139, 164, 169). The earthworks may also be shown up by the shadows cast by the low sun. Poidebard's excellent oblique of Dura Europos (1934, Pl. LXXXVIII) demonstrates this, showing the street plan, though not the individual buildings made of sun-dried brick, which the excavator said had 'collapsed into a fairly flat desert surface two to six feet [0.6 to 1.8 m] deep' (Hopkins, 1979, 50). The excavated buildings also show up very well on this photograph.

Poidebard remarks on the layer of wind blown dust which masked many sites in the Jezireh, and made it difficult to find ancient remains, though the great tells could not be hidden. He located, and later excavated, a fort near Tell Brak, which was shown only as a low, square earthwork, revealed by shadow and by pale-toned (negative) vegetation marks above walls (p. 188). A photograph of the excavations (Fig. 133) demonstrates the way in which the remains of the stone walls of the fort had been buried by silt.

Soil colour as an indicator of ancient features is illustrated in the ditch or *vallum* at Jebel Cembeh (Fig. 42). The vegetation marks in the same area, mentioned above (Fig. 14), were perhaps photographed at a different season.

Nearly all the 'site indicators' mentioned above also help to show the lines of Roman roads. On the remarkable picture of the lava waste of the Ledja, the road is clearly shown by texture and shadow (Fig. 24). At some other places the necessary information is given by differences in the colour or tone of the road and the ground across which it runs (Figs. 26, 28). Both Poidebard and Stein mentioned that the two lines that revealed the Palmyra-Hit road (Figs. 15, 27) were low ridges of stones cleared from the surface and piled on each side. They also wrote that some roads were made visible by vegetation marks caused by the accumulation of moisture in the shallow depression worn by traffic.

· Future Work ·

Sets of vertical photographs, preferably not less in scale than 1: 10,000, and overlapping so that they can be examined in stereo pairs, will give much new information to the careful interpreter. They should be particularly useful on the desert margins, where remains of structures should be less damaged than on intensively cultivated land. As mentioned earlier (p. 55), good work has already been done with vertical photographic cover, but this is only the beginning of a great

FIGURE 15 Roman road from Palmyra to Hit: oblique view of the Roman road in the region Giffa – es-Swab looking south.
A Potez 25 aircraft has landed and taxied on to the road (note the marks on the ground caused by its tail skid) in order to act as a standard of measurement by which the width of the road (about 15 m.) could be estimated. Photograph: de Boysson (09.45; 3 March 1930). From Poidebard, 1934, Pl.VIII.1. Cf. Figure 27.

task. Such photographs (e.g. Fig. 89) should record ruined walls and stony banks, though not shadows, as they are usually taken with the sun at a good height. If taken at the right time of the year, they may also record vegetation marks.

The detection of ancient sites shown on vertical photographs will need somewhat different visual skills from those of the observer in an aeroplane, but the problems are the same and the signs to look for are already familiar to those who make use of the work of the air photographers of the 1920s and 1930s.

The resumption of aerial reconnaissance is naturally the hope of the authors of this book. There has been a long interval since Sir Aurel Stein climbed out of his Vincent aircraft for the last time in 1939. It is unlikely that there will be a general abatement of restrictions on aviation for many years, but when openings come every opportunity of resuming work in the air should be taken. Future aviators will probably wish to look at the whole landscape, not to search only for Roman features. This will be a departure from Poidebard's practice of only photographing selected sites. Modern experience suggests that complete surveys are more valuable than selective surveys, though the time required to carry out a complete survey is likely to be much greater. However, it may well prove possible to combine aerial reconnaissance with research on photographs taken during previous vertical surveys of the same area, and thus ease the load. The magnitude of the task must not be underestimated, but neither should the probable benefits. How much more complete and cost effective could good aerial survey make the otherwise laudable national survey of Saudi Arabia, currently in progress (see, for example, Adams *et al.,* 1977, 24, 32)?

Although future reconnaissance and photography will be able to take advantage of the improved techniques developed in Europe since 1945, methods of work will have to be adapted to the very different climate and landscape of the Middle East. It will be necessary to proceed carefully, taking note of the records left by Poidebard and Stein. Assuming that a suitable aircraft and pilot become available, one of the first problems will be to know when to start.

Fortunately, both the great pioneers left good records of the dates of their campaigns. Poidebard is known to have worked in April or May in 1925, 1934, 1938 and 1939 (Poidebard, 1927b, 55; Mouterde and Poidebard, 1945, xii) and in October or November in 1927, 1928, 1930, 1936 and 1937 (Poidebard, 1928b, 1930a, 1931a; Mouterde and Poidebard, 1945, xii). Stein followed suit, flying from March to May in 1938 and November 1938 to May 1939 (Gregory and Kennedy (Stein), 1985). Spring and autumn therefore appear to be the best times, avoiding the hot weather and poor visibility of summer. Upstanding features will presumably be the main targets, and it will be necessary to gain experience of finding and recording sites shown by rock and soil colour, by shadows, and by vegetation marks. Spring would be the time for crop marks, if they occur on parts of the cultivated land which has increased in area so much recently. On page 240, some suggestions are made about sites which seem particularly promising.

This chapter would not be complete without mention of the imagery from spacecraft which pass over the Middle East. Both unmanned satellites and the manned space shuttle supply information about the land surface over which they pass. Images compiled from signals transmitted by satellites are the main source of information. Photographs taken from the space shuttle may also be available to the public in the future. Many kinds of information are recorded, for which there are numerous applications in the study of the landscape. Archaeologists can learn much that has a bearing on the country through which the *limes* runs, and can make deductions about ancient conditions in the region. However, though the imagery gives the general picture, it has been recorded from so far above the ground and covers such great areas that its scale is extremely small, and it does not give the fine resolution needed if small archaeological features are to be recognized and studied. At the time of writing, therefore, its value for the study of ancient fortifications is restricted. Much more advanced imagery probably exists, but is not made public, though if the present rapid rate of progress continues, highly detailed imagery may be released in the future.

· PART C ·
The Sites

· CHAPTER FIVE ·

Water Supply

During the dry season between approximately May and September, nomads were dependent on access to springs, wells and shrinking pools. By controlling these sources, Rome could police large areas relatively economically.

Water was also vital along the trade arteries. There, the routes themselves could either link existing water sources, or be provided with a source. In practice, both at road stages and control points on transhumance routes, a great deal of work was put into collection and conservation of the water which was quite abundant during winter rains. On wadis this could be achieved by building dams to store water in the rainy season for use later (Figs. 165, 183); elsewhere, run-off from the surface could be channelled into cisterns (Figs. 89, 120, 130, 147) or reservoirs (Figs. 86, 89, 98, 111, 117, 124, 128, 130, 147, 153, 155, 157). Groundwater could be tapped and led some distance by constructing the underground channels known as foggaras or qanats (Figs. 22, 79, 87), and in other places wells could be dug (Figs. 36, 38, 98, 157).

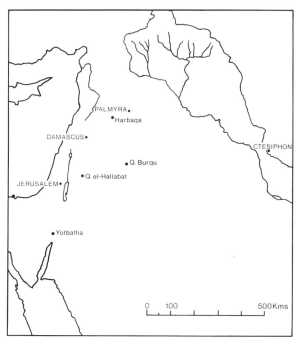

FIGURE 16 Location map.

HARBAQA, SYRIA (Fig. 17)

This low level oblique photograph of the Harbaqa reservoir must be one of the most striking archaeological air photographs ever taken. It is a pity, however, that there is nothing to bring out the great size of the dam (see below). The camera was aimed towards the sun so that shadows emphasize the dam wall and the deep gullies cut through the silt that has filled it (cf. Schlumberger, 1939, Pl. XXVII.2; 1986, pl. 49 a and b).

The barrage lies some 80 km (50 miles) west-south-west of Palmyra on a route to Damascus. It is located half way between the forts at Qasr el-Heir el-Gharbi (Fig. 171) and el-Basiri (Poidebard, 1934, 47; Pls. XXX, XXXI), in a pass linking them across the Jebel Rawaq. As Poidebard's other photographs and map show (Pls. XXXIII–XXXVII), the dam is one element in an impressive and extensive system of ancient water collection and distribution, agricultural remains, military installations and roads.

Recent excavations have provided information about the dating of some of the elements in the system. Nothing earlier than the Roman period has been traced, and the original construction of the dam at Harbaqa and the earliest settlement at el-Heir date from the first century AD. The region was dependent on the prosperity of Palmyra, and it declined with the latter's fall in the later third century. Later came a small garrison in the fourth and fifth centuries at Qasr el-Heir, supplied by wells and cisterns, and, in the sixth century, a fortified Ghassanid monastery, the tower of which survives. Finally, in the early Islamic (Ommayad) period, the entire system was restored and a fort – erroneously identified by Poidebard as a Roman *castellum* – was built at Qasr el-Heir abutting the Ghassanid tower (Schlumberger, 1986, 16ff; 24ff).

Although little enough can be said about the settlement associated with the barrage, the immense size and capacity of the latter suggest a major undertaking. The dam is 345 m. (1125 ft) long, 18 m. (59 ft) thick at the base and still

FIGURE 17 Harbaqa, Homs, Syria (34°15′N 37°37′E): oblique view looking south-south-east. *Photograph: de Boysson (January-March 1930). From Poidebard, 1934, Pl. XXXIII.*

20.5 m. (67 ft) high. The lake formed measured some 1550 × 800 m. (5000 × 2600 ft) at its greatest extent (Schlumberger, 1986, 2ff). At the very least this must have been a major road station on the Damascus-Palmyra route (cf. below, Figs. 151-60).

QASR BURQU, JORDAN
(Figs. 18 and 19)

At this desolate spot in the desert of north-eastern Jordan about 150 km (95 miles) east of the legionary fortress and city of Bostra, an ancient reservoir in the Wadi Minqat holds water from the winter rains. An arrow shows the position of the probable Late Roman tower of Qasr Burqu, which was surrounded by an enclosure wall and rooms of the Early Islamic period, though none of these buildings shows well on the photograph (cf. Figs. 172-3). The black areas visible in the foreground are bare basalt rock. The numerous enclosures or corrals of indeterminate date, their walls built of basalt boulders, were made to pen the animals of nomadic visitors who were

attracted by the water.

The importance of the location must have developed from the use made of the north–south route along the Wadi Minqat. Later, presumably exploiting an existing tendency for water to pond at that spot, the construction of a dam *c.*100 m. (320 ft) long, created a large artificial lake, a *ghadir*, *c.*460 x 90 m. (1500 x 300 ft), at the end of which Qasr Burqu is situated (Poidebard, 1934, 97-101, 121-4, Pl.XCII.2,3; Field, 1960, 94-9, 150-8; Gregory and Kennedy (Stein), 1985, 240-7; Gaube, 1974). The pond may be seen dried out on Figure 172.

FIGURE 18 Qasr Burqu, Irbid, Jordan (32°37′N 37°58′E): oblique view looking north-west from a height of 800 ft (250 m.). *Photograph: Royal Air Force (07.30; 28 May 1937). Stein Archive (Institute of Archaeology, London, RAF no. 00576).*

FIGURE 19 Qasr Burqu, Irbid, Jordan (32°37′N 37°58′E): plan of the qasr, dam and reservoir. *Traced with permission, with minor modifications, from an unpublished drawing in the British Museum prepared by Surveyor Iltifat Hussein for Sir Aurel Stein in 1939. Stein Archive (British Museum, Department of Western Asiatic Antiquities, Small Archive, Plan 31).*

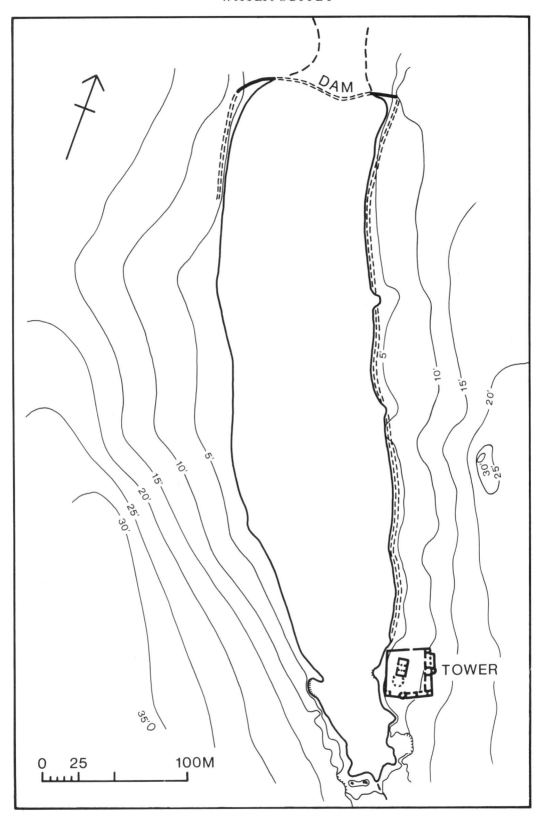

DAM

35·0

TOWER

0 25 100M

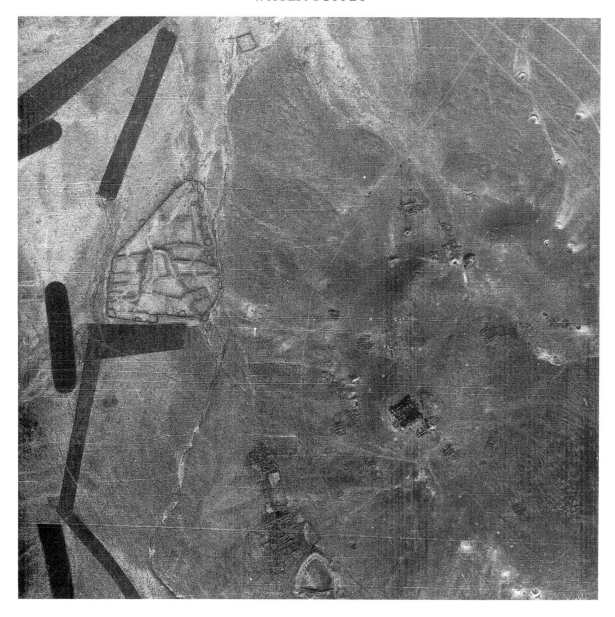

QASR EL-HALLABAT, JORDAN
(Figs. 20 and 21)

Shadows emphasize various structures around the hill, on which stands a small *castellum*. Apart from the fort itself (1), various groups of houses (4), a substantial agricultural feature west of the fort (3), two dry wadis (5) and a large silted up reservoir (2) may readily be identified. This last was supplied from channels which can still be traced on the hill slope, and its waters were supplemented by several open cisterns (6),

FIGURE 20 Qasr el-Hallabat, Al-Asimah, Jordan (32°06′N 36°20′E): vertical view from a height of 12,500 ft (4000 m.). *Photograph: Hunting (September, 1953). Copyright: Royal Jordanian Geographic Centre. Supplied from Aerial Photographic Archive for Archaeology in the Middle East, inv. no. HAS 58.008*

revealed by the dark openings of their collapsed roofs and the paler colour of the light soil cast up around them. There are two further cisterns beneath the courtyard of the fort.

The final phase of occupation before modern

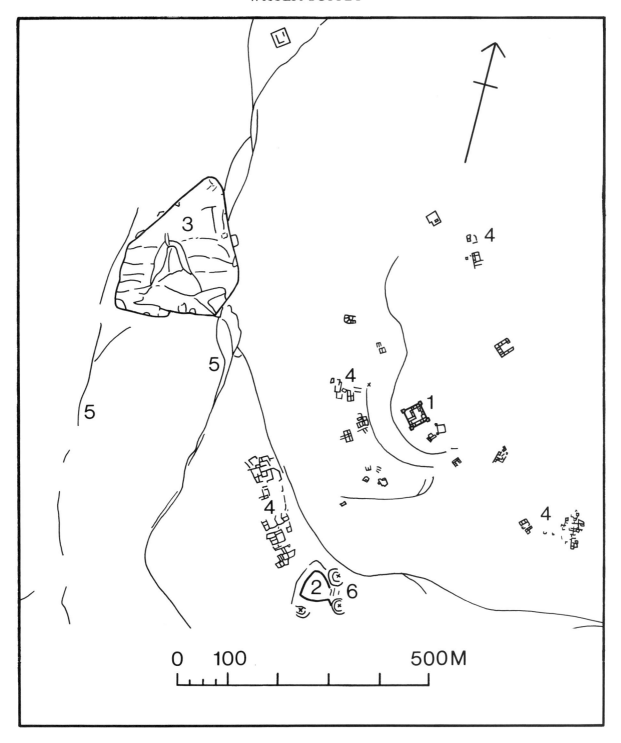

times was in the Ommayad period (cf. Fig. 147), but there is clear evidence for the Roman origin of the fort. The water collection system may belong to the Roman period.

FIGURE 21 Qasr el-Hallabat, Al-Asimah, Jordan (32°06′N 36°20′E): plan of the site drawn from the air photograph. *After Kennedy, 1982, 61, fig. 10.*

YOTBATHA, ISRAEL (Fig. 22)

Yotbatha, ancient *Ad Dianam* (preserved in the Arabic Ain Ghadian), was the site of a small Roman post in the Wadi Araba, lying some 40 km (25 miles) north of Aqaba. The remains of the fort are undistinguished, sand covered and looking rather similar to the site at Gharandal, further to the north (Fig. 159). Pottery and coins point to a date in the fourth century (Rothenberg, 1971, 218ff including low oblique air photograph), as now confirmed by a Tetrarchic inscription (Meshel and Roll, 1987).

The importance of the site for present purposes lies not in the fort, nor in the various other remains or structures of dates ranging from the Chalcolithic, through the Nabataean to Late Roman, but rather in the marvellous water-harvesting network that brought water into the settlement. The system consists of water channels and *foggaras* which brought water from underground sources along the edges of the Wadi Araba into the settlement, where it is thought to have been used to irrigate date palm groves. The latter – still identifiable on air photographs from the regular pattern of bunch grass – seem to have covered as much as 400 ha. (*c.*1000 acres).

The notable feature on the illustration is a line of large rings, a very recognizable pattern. Each ring has a pale-toned centre, where fine material, presumably wind-blown, reflects more light. The rings are dark because of the rocky material of which they are formed, and are emphasized by shadow. They are raised rings of stony debris with sunken centres, the upcast from the wells of a *foggara*. An alternative word is a *qanat*, or in English, a chain well. This was an underground channel, reached by a series of vertical shafts. Water was tapped from a distant underground source at higher level and ran down the tunnel, to emerge ultimately and run in an above-ground channel to its destination. Several such chains have been found around Yotbatha, some only a few hundred metres long, others as much as 3–4 km (2–2.5 miles).

Though probably pre-Roman in date, the system was apparently still in use in the Roman period. Such water collection systems are most common in Iran, where they were first developed. They are frequent in our region also, where they are found near several military sites, as here (Figs. 79, 87) (Evenari *et al.*, 1982, ch. XI).

FIGURE 22 Yotbatha, Hadarom Hanegev, Israel (29°44′N 35°03′E): oblique view of *foggara* running towards the fort at Yotbatha. *Photograph: Survey of Israel. After Evenari, Shanan and Tadmor, 1982, fig. 105a. Reprinted by permission.*

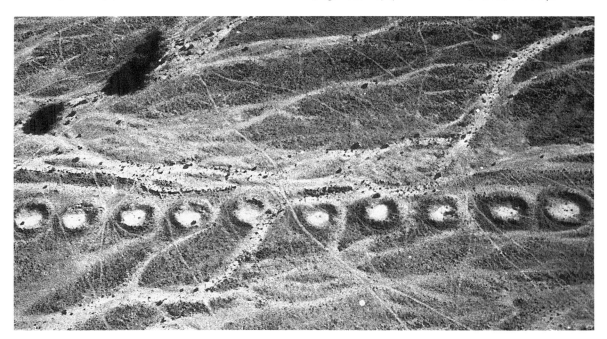

· CHAPTER SIX ·

Roads and Communications

Roads and routes, some of them very ancient, already existed in the region before the coming of Rome. The great Royal Road from Persia passed through the north; and along the coast of the Levant the ancient *Via Maris* ran south to Egypt. Trade routes followed particular lines of communication from the Red Sea and Persian Gulf, and from northern Iran. Thence, great routes ran across northern Mesopotamia (the 'Silk Road'), up the Euphrates, across the Syrian Desert and across the deserts of northern Arabia.

Road construction was begun by the Roman forces quite early in their occupation of the region, and roads can often be dated by the milestones that survive in many places. The first major undertaking was the reconstruction in AD 56 of a large part of the great coastal highway, the *Via Maris*, which was rebuilt and provided with milestones from Antioch to Ptolemais. Many other projects followed, of which the major roads of the *limes* were among the most important. In the reign of Vespasian, presumably in the aftermath of the annexation of Commagene in 72, a road seems to have been laid out running south from Samosata; in the same year, one was certainly constructed from Raphanaea towards Apamea, and another from Palmyra to Sura on the Euphrates in 75. Under Trajan, the new province of Arabia received the great *Via Nova Traiana*, some of the milestones proclaiming that it ran *a finibus Syriae usque ad Mare Rubrum* ('from the boundaries of Syria as far as the Red Sea'). This ran southwards from the provincial capital Bostra (Fig. 71) to Aila (modern Aqaba/Eilat) on the Red Sea, often utilizing the former King's Highway and passing on the way a number of forts such as Samra and Humeima

(Figs. 89, 144). Far to the north-east, a milestone in Trajan's name has been recovered beside a road across the Jebel Sinjar between Nisibis and Singara (Fig. 73). In the Severan period a road was built in western Osrhoene in 205, *ab Euphrate usque ad fines regni Sept Abgari* ('from the Euphrates as far as the boundaries of the kingdom of Septimius Abgar' [the client-king of Osrhoene]); in 208/10 a road was laid out across the basalt desert of northern Arabia to the Azraq Oasis (Fig. 28); in 232 another milestone attests a road from the Khabur to Singara. Finally, there was important road work in the late third to early fourth century reorganization of the *limes*; a number of Tetrarchic milestones have been found along the *Strata Diocletiana*, which linked the Euphrates with Damascus and served many forts (Dunand, 1931), e.g. Khan el-Hallabat (Fig. 151), Khan el-Qattar (Fig. 153), Khan Aneybeh (Fig. 155) and Khan el-Manqoura (Fig. 128).

Roads were of course repaired and maintained, often over long periods. The *Via Nova Traiana* is dated by its earliest milestones to 111 and was still being repaired at least as late as the reign of Julian (360-3). At some of the milestations on it, clusters of stones – as many as 14 are attested at one place – erected under successive emperors, demonstrate the enduring commitment of the Roman authorities to the upkeep of their road. Towns and villages studded the roads of the fertile area; in the desert, the roads were provided with guard posts (e.g. Fig. 24) and road-stations or caravanserai (e.g. Fig. 40). The best-known examples of the latter are to be found along the caravan routes in the desert east of Palmyra.

By the end of the fourth century, an impressive network of roads had been developed. Although it is unrealistic to attempt a rigid classification, the various roads may be grouped into three general types under headings proposed by Poidebard (1934, 165-7), which were as follows.

a FULLY PAVED ROADS (*voies pavées*), e.g. that across the Ledja, which gives a good impression of the construction of a metalled road surface (Fig. 24). Considerable lengths of similar metalled road survive on the *Via Nova Traiana* (Fig. 31) and certain other roads.

b UNSURFACED ROADS (*voies de terre aménagées*), the most common type, according to Poidebard. The surface of these roads was cleared and their course marked by the line of stones on each side that had been removed from their surface, and they were only paved in bad places, such as the crossings of wadis. This type of surface was adopted for some important roads, such as the *Strata Diocletiana*. Long straight lengths usually occur on reasonably level ground, e.g. Palmyra to Hit (Fig. 27; cf. fig. 15), but the line was adapted to the terrain in hilly country, e.g. the stretch of the *Via Nova Traiana* where it crosses the Wadi Mujib (Fig. 33).

FIGURE 23 Location map.

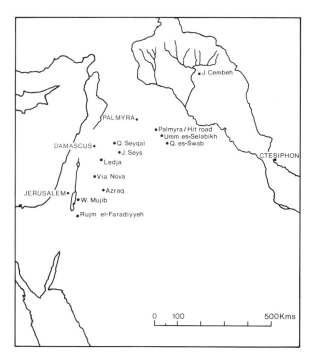

c CARAVAN TRACKS (*pistes caravanières*). These unmarked tracks across the desert are known because of the watch towers, guard posts and wells that are found along them.

The observer on a reconnaissance flight, if one were possible, should find it easy to follow the course of a reasonably well-preserved paved road. The improved roads may also show well because of their lateral lines of stones, e.g. Figure 33, and in some cases by the clearing of stones from their surface, e.g. those to Azraq (Fig. 28) and to the Jebel Seys (Fig. 26). On the prints of vertical air surveys, our present source of new aerial information, both types of roads should be identifiable, though the improved roads may be difficult to find when the scale of the photograph is below 1/10,000.

ROAD ACROSS THE LEDJA, SYRIA (Figs. 24 and 25)

On this impressive vertical photograph, the Roman road is seen crossing the contorted surface of the great lava flow, the Ledja. The construction of the road can be appreciated – the larger stones at the edge and at the median line, and the way it was built up to cross hollows in the rocky surface. At the point marked by an arrow, the site of a watch tower (Edj-Djamin) is marked by a heap of stones in which the shape of a square foundation can be seen (see Poidebard, 1928a, overlay to Pl. XLI).

This is part of the road linking Damascus to Bostra via Mismiyeh (*Phaena*) and Ahireh (*Aerita*), which lie on either side of the Ledja. Its date of construction is unknown but a milestone of 185/6 records: *vi[am] a Phaena Aeritta[m] restituit* ('the road from Phaena to Aerita restored'). Others point to the dates 175 or even 162 for construction or previous repairs. Along the road's course of some 30 km (19 miles) across the Ledja, Dunand recorded 18 watch towers, 6.5 m. (21 ft) or 13 m. (42 ft) square, and 18 complete or fragmentary milestones. The road itself is 6.5 m. (21 ft) wide (Dunand, 1933; Poidebard, 1934, 29-33; MacAdam, 1986, 68-71).

FIGURE 24 Roman road across the Ledja, Dera, Syria (33°07′N 36°30′E): vertical view from a height of 1600 ft (500 m). *Photograph: de Boysson (08.50; 29 July 1927). From Poidebard, 1934, Pl.XII.*

FIGURE 25 Roman road across the Ledja, Dera, Syria (33°07′N 36°30′E): map of the road, towers and milestones. *After Dunand, 1933, 523, fig. 1.*

JEBEL SEYS, SYRIA (Fig. 26)

The Roman road across the desert, which is here covered by basalt rocks, may be traced across the centre of the photograph by the light-toned strip from which the stones have been cleared and piled on each side to form a dark edge. Poidebard says that the road was invisible at ground level. Numerous other tracks cross the desert including, on the left margin of the photograph, one used by motor cars.

The grey areas in the middle distance are mud flats, two of which (showing white) have evidently been flooded by the autumn rains. Beyond is the crater of Jebel Seys, an extinct volcano. On its outer slopes, almost in line with the road, are the ruins of a settlement, wells and fort, which Poidebard took to be Roman (Poidebard, 1934, Pls. LIV–LVIII). However, while a Roman post of some sort there is not implausible, excavation has not so far revealed anything of that period. The largest building, the

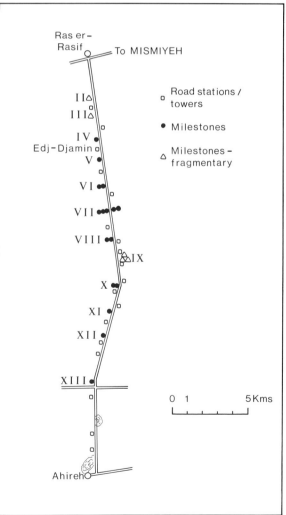

FIGURE 26 Jebel Seys, Suweida, Syria (33°20′N 37°22′E): oblique view looking west. *Photograph: de Boysson (08.30; 17 October 1930). From Poidebard, 1934, Pl. XCIII.*

so-called *castellum*, is now dated to the eighth century (Sauvaget, 1939c, 239–56, esp. 252–6; Creswell, 1969, 472–7).

It has been suggested that the volcano is the *Mons Jovis* of the *Notitia Dignitatum (Or. XXXII.33)*, which was the base, under the *Dux Foenicis* of the *Ala Prima Damascena* (Dussaud, 1927, 271), but that presents some difficulties.

Some 48 km (30 miles) further on, the road reached Habra Merfiyeh es-Smeyr, a road-station with reservoir; 16 km (10 miles) further east again Poidebard discovered a tower and circular signal platform (Pls. XCIV–V).

ROAD FROM PALMYRA TO HIT, SYRIA (Fig. 27)

The lonely desert road from Palmyra to the Euphrates valley at Hit is visible from the air from a little north-west of Giffa in Syria almost to Qasr Amij in Iraq, a distance of about 270 km (about 170 miles). According to Stein, its course is marked by a low ridge of stones on each side, removed from the road to improve its surface (Gregory and Kennedy (Stein), 1985, 220). The dark bands seen on Figure 15 no doubt indicate similar lines of stones.

Poidebard's description of the photograph shown on Figure 15 says that the aircraft (which can be identified as a Potez 25) was being used as a measure of the road width. The Potez 25 was 9.1 m. (30 ft) long and the road is therefore about

FIGURE 27 Roman road from Palmyra to Hit, Homs, Syria (approx. 34°10′N 39°15′E): oblique view taken looking north-west *c.* 100 km (62 miles) south-east of Palmyra. *Photograph: de Boysson (07.45; 3 March 1930). From Poidebard, 1934, Pl.C.*

15 m. (almost 50 ft) wide between the dark bands at this point. Elsewhere Stein reported a width of 8 m. (*c.* 25 ft) (idem, 1985, 220).

Poidebard identified stages on the route including: Umm el-Amad, where he found a second-century inscription honouring a benefactor of the caravans, Umm es-Selabikh, (Fig. 40) with the text of 225 naming a *strategos* at Ana and at Gamla, and Qasr es-Swab (see further under Fig. 36) (Poidebard, 1934, 105-14).

AZRAQ OASIS, JORDAN
(Figs. 28, 29, and 30)

Figure 28, a mosaic made in 1927 from at least 13 photographs, shows the northern edge of the Azraq Oasis (lower left corner) and the black desert that surrounds it on three sides. The desert surface is mainly covered by black basalt boulders (Fig. 29), though hollows are floored by mud flats, formed by silt washed there during the winter rains. The black boulders and pale-toned silt form a characteristic dark and light pattern on the photographs. Since they were taken, there have been great changes. Azraq, then a remote and almost deserted place, has become a busy little town, and the land shown at the bottom of the photograph is now covered with houses. The area illustrated is now crossed by an asphalt

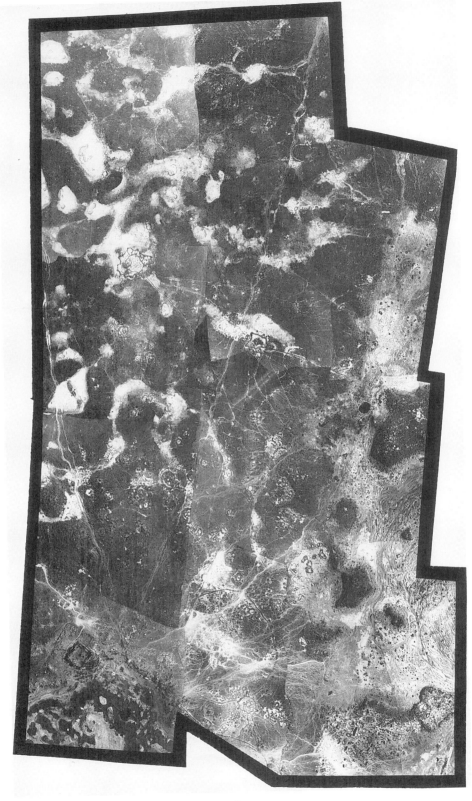

FIGURE 28 Azraq Oasis, Al-Asimah, Jordan (31°55′N 36°49′E): vertical views (mosaic) from a height of 9000 ft (2800 m.). *Photograph: Royal Air Force, Transjordan (06.00; 29 April 1927). Crawford Archive (Institute of Archaeology, London, inv. no. AP 1044). Cf. Rees, 1929b, Pl. VI.*

highway, part of the road linking Amman in Jordan with Baghdad in Iraq. Photographs such as this are very valuable records.

The Azraq Oasis lies almost 80 km (50 miles) south-east of Bostra (Fig. 71). Perennial springs supply copious amounts of water to two major pools: one in the north, beside which was constructed the well-preserved Roman fort, the Qasr el-Azraq (Figs. 56, 126; cf. Kennedy, 1982, 69ff, pl. XVIIIa); and a second at Azraq Shishan, 6 km (3.6 miles) to the south, where there is a great reservoir, possibly originally of Roman construction (Kennedy, 1982, 96-107).

A major Roman road runs north from the Azraq Oasis. After some 16 km (10 miles) it divides. One branch goes north-west via Umm

FIGURE 29 Azraq Oasis, Al-Asimah, Jordan (31°55′N 36°49′E): ground view of the Roman road looking north. *Photograph: D.N.Riley (June, 1985).*

el-Quttein (Fig. 86) to the provincial capital of Bostra (Fig. 71); the other runs north through Deir el-Kahf (Fig. 124) and Imtan into southern Syria. With the growth of the modern town at Azraq, traces of this road in the immediate vicinity of the fort are now lost, and even further afield its course is unclear. Three main tracks (A–B, A–C and A–D) and a large number of minor tracks are visible on the illustration. From the evidence of early travellers, it would seem that the Roman road is the track A–B, which runs off the photograph on the upper left edge. It is the wider and has more clearly defined edges, but is less straight than A–C and has numerous deviations. It is simply a track cleared through the rocks, which were heaped on either side forming the distinct border seen here (Fig. 28). Since its preparation, many short detours have been made – probably mainly in modern times – to one side or other, presumably to avoid obstacles which had not been cleared well in the first place. The line therefore has become irregular.

Part of a milestone has been found beside the Roman road several kilometres beyond the upper edge of the mosaic, where its line is better defined. Fragments of several others are to be found

collected inside the Roman fort and an almost complete example re-used in an oil press on the nearby Early Islamic site of Ain es-Sol (below). All are Severan, dated to 208/10 (Kennedy, 1982, 170-5; Kennedy and MacAdam, 1985, 105ff). In contrast, the milestones from Umm el-Quttein and the stretch of road beyond to Bostra are Tetrarchic (284-305) or later (Fig. 86). Consequently, the road constructed in the Severan period is most likely to be that running north through Imtan and Deir el-Kahf (Fig. 124) rather than that running through Umm el-Quttein.

An intriguing inscription from Qasr el-Azraq seems to be a terminal stone recording the

FIGURE 30 Azraq Oasis, Al-Asimah, Jordan (31°55′N 36°49′E): sketch plan of the area covered by Figure 29. *Drawn by D.N.Riley.*

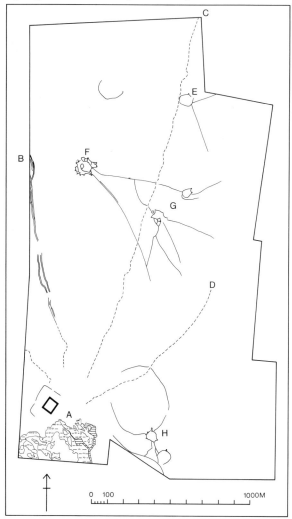

distances from Azraq to various places, and construction work by detachments of several legions, probably in the Tetrarchic period (Kennedy, 1982, 169-86; Gregory and Kennedy, 1985, 270, 416ff; Kennedy and MacAdam, 1985, 100-4; cf. Speidel, 1987). Interestingly, it names Dumat, modern Jauf in northern Saudi Arabia. This gives useful confirmation of Roman influence at one point at least on the great Wadi Sirhan route, which stretches off to the south-east from the Azraq Oasis and takes the traveller to Jauf, some 250 km (150 miles) away.

The line A-C is more difficult to date. It is apparently the road to Qasr Ain es-Sol, where a Severan milestone has been found used in an olive press (Kennedy and McAdam, 1985, 99ff.) The site lies beside a spring and was certainly in use by the Early Islamic period. The track may, therefore, have been cleared or at least already in use in the Roman period (Kennedy, 1982, 169-77).

Many other antiquities may be seen in addition to the Roman road and fort. There are several 'kites' (Fig. 30 E, F, G, H), ancient structures used in hunting herds of gazelle, which were driven into the space between the long converging walls and then into the enclosure at the end, where the hunters waited (Helms and Betts, 1987). Near Azraq fort is a large curvilinear walled enclosure (H), now covered by houses, and there are a large number of smaller enclosures and hut sites visible elsewhere on the photograph. The 'kites' and the other enclosures probably date from many periods between the early neolithic and the present. There is a large amount of interesting material here (cf. Riley, 1982).

VIA NOVA TRAIANA, JORDAN (Figs. 31 and 32)

The *Via Nova Traiana* is illustrated both by air and ground photographs, the latter taken looking south-west from point A on the air photograph. Recent agricultural activity has brought cultivation up to the road on either side and resulted in the ploughing up of some stretches. The ground view shows the foundations of the road — large field stones contained within a shape provided by parallel side kerbs and a central spine. Originally this foundation would have been

FIGURE 31 *Via Nova Traiana,* Adjlun, Jordan (32°20′N 36°20′E): vertical view of the Roman road west of Umm el-Jemal. *Photograph: Hunting (1953). Copyright: Royal Jordanian Geographic Centre. Supplied from Aerial Photographic Archive for Archaeology in the Middle East, no. HAS 58.028*

covered by beaten earth (Kennedy, 1982, 144ff).

The line of the Roman road runs diagonally (between the two arrows) across Fig. 31, which shows an area in northern Jordan just south of the modern Syrian frontier. At this point, north-

west of Umm el-Jemal (Fig. 130), which is linked to it by a spur road (not visible), two other important features are seen. First, at B is the outline of a small roadside tower set within the tumbled walls of a square enclosure. Such structures are found at various points along the road, most, as here, coinciding with a milestation. However, no tower is visible at the previous milestation – Mile 13 from Bostra. At C, 1 km ($c.\frac{1}{2}$ mile) east of the road, is the ruin of Qasr el-Baiq, which is partly submerged under the modern village. The *castellum* at this site is dated by an inscription to 411 (cf. Parker, 1986, 22ff).

FIGURE 32 *Via Nova Traiana*, Adjlun, Jordan (32°20′N 36°20′E): ground view looking south along the Roman road between milestations 13 and 14. *Photograph: D.L. Kennedy (1976).*

WADI MUJIB, JORDAN (Fig. 33)

The Wadi Mujib – some 35 km (22 miles) north of Kerak – is the largest of the lateral wadis leading down into the eastern side of the Dead Sea. In antiquity – as today – it presented a formidable obstacle to communications. In the early second century AD, Roman military road builders constructed a road – a section of the *Via Nova Traiana* – across the wadi, descending the precipitous north side in a series of short steep alignments to the water course 600 m. (2000 ft) below (Glueck, 1939, 112f). The photograph

(presumably taken from 200 ft above the northern edge of the gorge) shows the road on the lower slopes of the south side clearly marked by a ridge of stones on each side; on the upper slopes it disappears, but probably follows the crest of a ridge.

Milestones still survive recording construction in 111 and repairs/reconstruction in 162, 193/4, 213/9, 288, and 361-3 (Thomsen, 1917, 49ff, nos. 125-7).

RUJM EL-FARIDIYYEH, JORDAN (Figs. 34 and 35)

The collapsed stone walls of a road-station on the *Via Nova Traiana* are seen as a dark rectangle. At this point the road runs along the eastern rim of the Wadi Ja'is, a tributary of the Wadi Hesa (the northern rim of which is seen on the horizon),

FIGURE 33 Wadi Mujib, Al-Kerak, Jordan (31°27'N 35°47'E): an oblique view looking at the southern edge of the gorge from 200 ft (60 m.). *Photograph: Royal Air Force (07.10; 25 May 1937). Institute of Archaeology, London, RAF no. 12728. Cf. Glueck, 1939, 112, Fig. 43; Bowersock, 1971, pl. XV.* which in turn runs into the south-east corner of the Dead Sea. The well-built structure measures some 36 × 42 m. (118 × 137 ft), with a courtyard flanked by rooms on at least three sides. Pottery is predominantly Nabataean and Roman, which may suggest re-use from the Nabataean into the Roman period.

Other features of this site, not visible on the photograph, are worth noting. On the cliff edge 70 m. (220 ft) to the west is a tower commanding the local spring. A second tower lies 1 km (*c.* 1 mile) to the north, just west of the road. The road itself has a foundation of stones collected from the surrounding fields. It is set within raised kerbs and is 6 m. (19 ft) wide at this point (MacDonald *et al.*, 1988; cf. Gregory and Kennedy, 1985, 436f). A succession of milestones dating from Trajan to Constantine has been reported (Thomsen, 1917, 52-4, nos. 133-54).

FIGURE 34 Rujm el-Faridiyyeh, Al-Kerak, Jordan (30°57'N 32°42'E): oblique view looking north from a height of 200 ft (60 m.). *Photograph: Royal Air Force (08.30; 25 May 1937). Institute of Archaeology, London: RAF no. 12741. Cf. Glueck, 1939, 50, fig. 27.*

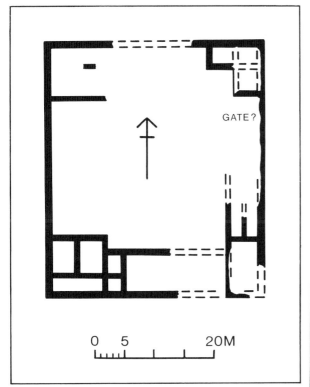

FIGURE 35 Rujm el-Faridiyyeh, Al-Kerak, Jordan (30°57′N 32°42′E): plan of the road-station beside the Wadi Ja'is. *Traced with permission from MacDonald et al., 1988, fig. 59.*

QASR ES-SWAB, IRAQ
(Figs. 36 and 37)

The ruins of buildings far in the desert some 170 km (106 miles) south-east of Palmyra, just inside the frontiers of Iraq, mark one of a number of stopping places on the great caravan route through the al-Qa'ara depression (Gregory and Kennedy (Stein), 1985, 203; *contra* Poidebard, 1934, map), linking Palmyra to Hit on the Euphrates, and thence to the ports of the Persian Gulf. The choice of site was determined by water supply, which was always obtainable in the Wadi es-Swab, either from pools or from shallow wells.

On this photograph the January sun lights the remains of two major structures (B and C on Fig. 37) on the south-east bank of the wadi. The large enclosure B (53.6 m./176 ft square) was perhaps a caravanserai. It is well constructed with

FIGURE 36 Qasr es-Swab, Al-Anbar, Iraq (33°49′N 39°45′E): oblique view looking west from a height of 400 ft. (c.125 m). *Photograph: Royal Air Force (10.33; 17 January 1939). Stein Archive (British Museum, Department of Western Asiatic Antiquities, Small Archive, Air Photographs – Iraq-Stein, RAF no. 14508).*

a central courtyard and rooms facing onto it, and there is an annexe on the north-west side. Building C (c.21 m./70 ft square) might have been the residence of the senior officer. Both B and C are said to be of the same build as the structure at Umm es-Selabikh (Fig. 40). As there, however, the military may have been not regular Roman forces but a detachment of irregular Palmyrene caravan police (Poidebard, 1934, 112–14; Gregory and Kennedy (Stein), 1985, 211–20).

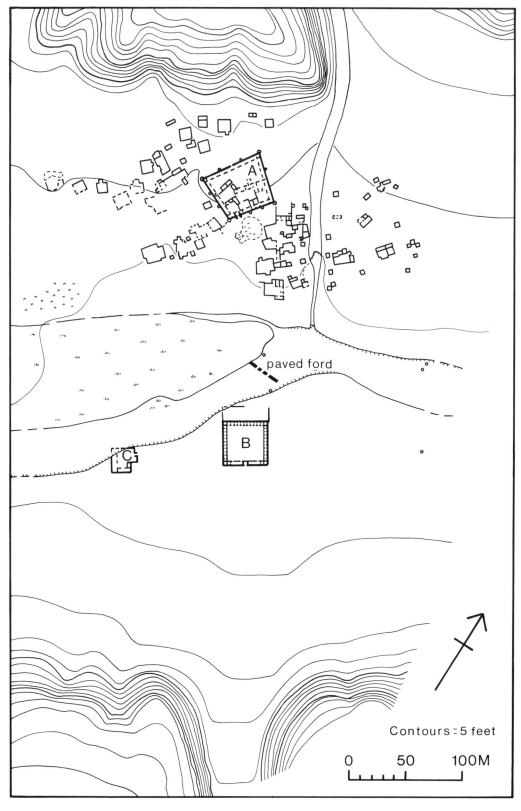

paved ford

A

B

C

Contours=5 feet

0   50   100M

FIGURE 37 Qasr es-Swab, Al-Anbar, Iraq (33°49′N 39°45′E): plan of the road station. Prepared by plane table survey over six days, it is broadly the same as Poidebard's (1934, Pl. CVII), but differs in having a number of minor structures not on the latter's plan and in the alignment of the major buildings. The main omission is the paved ford. *From an unpublished drawing in the British Museum, prepared by Surveyor Iltifat Hussein for Stein in 1939. Stein Archive (British Museum, Department of Western Asiatic Antiquities, Small Archive, Plan 28).*

The buildings on the more defensible north-west bank are not shown on the photograph, being beyond its right-hand edge. Building A (see Fig. 37), is a large trapezoidal enclosure (*c.* 68.6 × 57.9 m./225 × 190 ft), crudely built and with no sign of any regular internal layout. It is surrounded by a scatter of smaller structures

which Poidebard thought were the *canabae* of Roman soldiers outside what he took as their fort. Stein, however, saw no Roman influence in the large enclosure, which he could not date, and took the external structures as simply the buildings of traders which grow up around a stage post such as this.

QASR SEYQAL, SYRIA
(Figs. 38 and 39)

The low ruins of the stone buildings of this roadside station stand on high ground 90 km (56 miles) east–north–east of Damascus, beside a caravan track from that city to the Euphrates at

FIGURE 38 Qasr Seyqal, Damascus, Syria (33°42′N 37°13′E): vertical view of the road-station. *Photograph: de Boysson (n.d.). From Poidebard, 1934, Pl. XVII (cf. XVIII).*

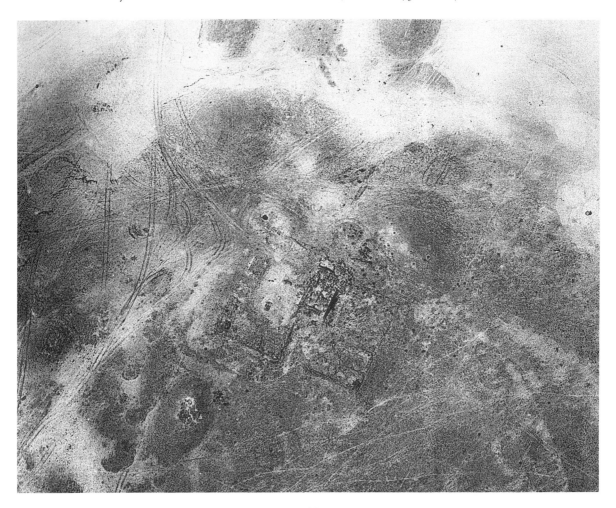

Hit. This desert route joined the Palmyra to Hit route some distance east of Qasr es-Swab (Fig. 36). Many motor car tracks and numerous animal tracks are seen on the surface of the steppe, which has a stable gravelly surface typical of the *hamada* desert.

Poidebard identified several sites of this type, which he described as *'postes d'étape'*. They usually consisted of a wall circuit (54.2 × 36.5m./178 × 120 ft), sometimes with an internal tower, as at this site. There are no towers on the wall itself or at corners. Internal perennial wells are a feature of such sites (1934, 45), which are often found by roads or at road junctions. Although Poidebard categorized them as Pre- and Post-Diocletianic (1934, 53), none has in fact been dated (cf. Fig. 40).

FIGURE 39 Qasr Seyqal, Damascus, Syria (33°42′N 37°13′E): plan of the road-station. *After Poidebard, 1934, Pl.XVIII:*

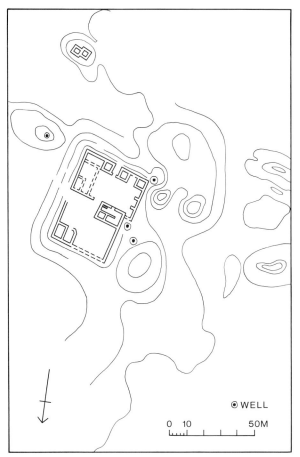

WELL

0   10   50M

UMM ES-SELABIKH, SYRIA
(Figs. 40 and 41)

Although their image is not sharp, the low walls of the road-side station are easily seen on the photograph. Poidebard observed that the layout, clear from the air, was very difficult to interpret at ground level (Poidebard, 1934, 109).

The site lies beside the Wadi el-Miyah some 120 km (75 miles) south-east of Palmyra on the route to Hit, but before it reached Qasr es-Swab (Fig. 37). Poidebard identified two elements: a building beside the road for a small cavalry detachment and a square enclosure (18 x 20 m./ 59 x 65 ft) which he interpreted as the residence of a Roman officer incorporating a cult-place. He saw this guard-post as part of a series of military installations extending over some 24 km (15 miles) along the Wadi el-Miyah. Sixteen kilometres (10 miles) to the west, along the route from Palmyra, were located two circular signal platforms (Poidebard, 1934, Pl.CIV).

Unknown to Poidebard, shortly before his aerial reconnaissance, Cantineau (1933, 178ff) had recorded on this site a mutilated inscription in Palmyrene. The date is clear – June, 225. It refers to '[....] who is general [*strategos*] at Ana and at Gamla, and his lieutenant [?] Kaphathuth, son of Salom'. Ana is Anatha on the Lower Euphrates (Fig. 62); Gamla is thought to be Gmeyla, a suburb of Ana 4 km (2½ miles) downstream (Kennedy and Northedge, 1988). Cantineau thought that the text, re-used in an Arab cemetery, may have come from a small shrine.

JEBEL CEMBEH, SYRIA (Fig. 42)

It is difficult fully to understand this photograph, which shows an interesting feature – the barrier, consisting of either a wall or a ditch, that starts about 4 km (2½ miles) south-east of the fort of Khirbet Hassan Aga (Fig. 94) and continues for about 20 km (12½ miles) eastwards to the fort at Qseybeh. The wall runs from A to B on the photograph and near it is a road, probably Roman (C to D). This road appears to be metalled, but no details were given by Poidebard. A desert 'kite' (cf. Fig. 30) is seen on the right of the photograph.

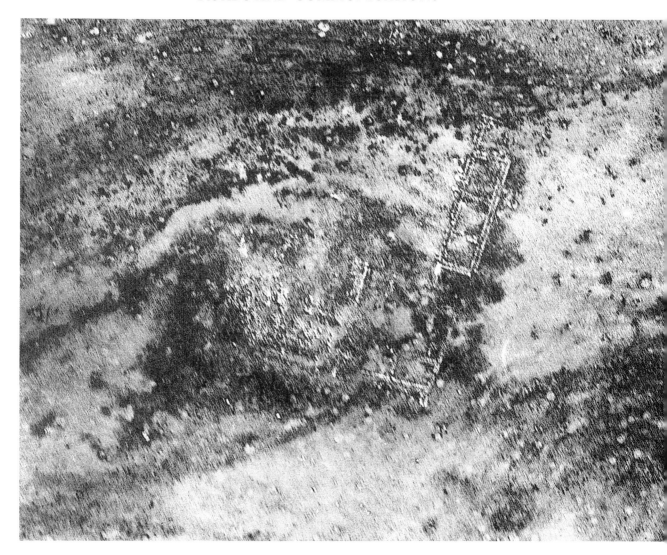

FIGURE 40 Umm es–Selabikh, Homs, Syria (34°1'N 39°25'E): vertical view. *Photograph: de Boysson (07.45; 3 March, 1930). From Poidebard, 1934, Pl.CIII.2.*

FIGURE 41 Umm es–Selabikh, Homs, Syria (34°1'N 39°25'E): plan of the road-station. *After Poidebard, 1934, Pl.CIV.*

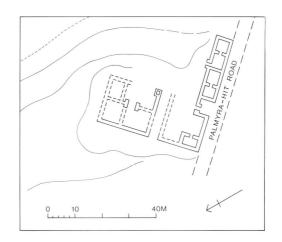

These features seem never to have been studied by anyone else; today they are of difficult access in a sensitive border area in north-east Syria. Poidebard saw the wall and associated forts, towers and road as designed to cover a possible invasion route over the low Jebel Cembeh towards Amida, passing between the River

Khabur and the difficult barriers of first the Jebel Jeribeh and then the more daunting Jebel Sinjar (Poidebard, 1934, 152ff). The principle is plausible; how it was intended to work is much less obvious: the wall is modest – 1.7-2.0 m.($5\frac{1}{2}$-$6\frac{1}{2}$ ft) wide and only 1 m. (3 ft) or so high; elsewhere the barrier is a ditch varying from 1.7 to 4 m. ($5\frac{1}{2}$-13 ft) in width, which is seen as a vegetation mark on Figure 14. Two forts at el-Khan and a number of features believed to be Roman,

including another road, lie in front (i.e. to the south) of it. If indeed Roman, this was a barrier closer in nature to the low wall of the *Fossatum Africae* in Algeria (Baradez, 1949) than to the walls in Britain or Germany.

FIGURE 42 Jebel Cembeh, Hasakeh, Syria (36°21′N 41°0′E): vertical view. *Photograph: Jullian (1928–9). From Poidebard, 1934, Pl. CXLVII.*

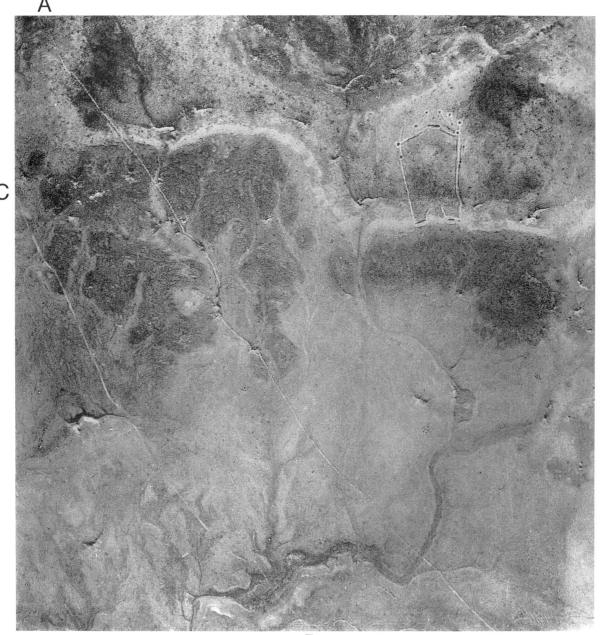

· CHAPTER SEVEN ·

Temporary Camps And Siege Works

It was traditional Roman military practice in hostile areas to fortify encampments during their stay, even if for just a single night. In the course of sieges, such camps were also prepared, and circumvallation walls or earthworks and siege ramps might be erected (Caesar, *Bell Gall, passim*; Josephus, *Bell. Iud.* III.76-93; Vegetius, *Epitoma rei militaris*, I.21; cf. Gichon, 1986, 295ff). Even when they are not mentioned, much less described, in the literary evidence for the military in the East, they can plausibly be inferred: thus, it would be astonishing if Aelius Gallus had not fortified his encampments in the course of his campaign down the west side of the Arabian peninsula (26/5 BC), and, given the nature of the terrain, some may one day be identified – especially if aerial photographs are made available (Isserlin, 1979, 3; cf. Crawford, 1929, 502).

Temporary camps, whether occupied by troops on the march, for days or months on campaign or some other duty, or in the course of a siege, are in fact well-attested in the Middle East in general from literary sources. Thus, in Armenia Lucullus placed a wall of circumvallation around Tigranocerta (Appian, *Bell. Mith.* 84), and later, in Cassius Dio, is the account (XXXVI.5.3ff) of the three winter encampments of the Roman army along the Cyrus/ Kera River on the Armenia-Albania border in 66/5 BC. During an attack on one of these, the Roman general, faced with too long a circuit to defend, threw up another circuit inside. Strabo makes no specific mention of siege works in connection with Aelius Gallus' campaign, but camps might be expected at least at Marsiaba, which he besieged for six days (Isserlin, 1979, 3).

For a later period, Tacitus' accounts of eastern campaigns, especially those of Corbulo and Paetus in the time of Nero, offer several references to temporary camps. Thus, in AD 58, Corbulo toughened his troops, especially the Syrian garrisons which had grown used to peace and a largely sedentary existence, by putting them into camps in northern Armenia and punishing some by obliging them to camp outside the ramparts (*Ann*. XIII.36). Later, *hiberna*, 'winter-quarters', were built on the Cappadocian Euphrates by Paetus in 62 (*Ann*. XV.7) with a 'ditch and moat' (*Ann*. XV.10). In the same year, Corbulo crossed the Syrian Euphrates and occupied the opposite bank, building first auxiliary forts, and then a legionary camp (*castra*) (*Ann*. XV.9.2). Soon after, Paetus' dispositions at Rhandeia in Armenia comprised a double legionary camp and a fort (*castellum*) for the non-combatants; the legions had previously camped separately. There were granaries inside the camp (*Ann*. XV.10-16).

Two pieces of literary evidence are especially useful. First, there is the testimony of Josephus, concerning Roman military organization and practices. This is presumably based largely on his own observations while a captive with the armies of Vespasian and Titus in the course of their campaigns against the Jewish rebels in 66–70. He described the choice and preparation of a site; the rapid raising in the shape of a square of a rampart pierced by four gates and, perhaps, the provision of a ditch; the erecting of towers and setting up of light artillery; and finally, the regular internal layout of streets, tents and headquarters. Departure, conversely, involved the burning of the encampment (*Bell. Iud.* III. 76-90).

Next, and also from Josephus, there is the account of the siege of Jerusalem in 70, and Titus' construction (in three days) of a circumvallation almost 8 km (5 miles) long together with 13 camps (*Bell. Iud.* V. 446 and 508). No vestiges have been identified.

Despite Poidebard's reference to marching camps (above, p. 53), relatively few sites with physical remains of temporary camps are known from the East, though we are better served for siege works. Apart from campaigns in Armenia, there are two regions in which one would expect to find either or both. First, in central Mesopotamia, along the Lower Euphrates and in northern Babylonia, where Rome laid siege on several occasions to Seleucia and Ctesiphon. At present, the only relevant traces known are at Hatra (Fig. 53) and, perhaps, Dura Europos (Fig. 58). Second, in Judaea and Arabia, where campaigns were directed against Jewish rebels or to punish the king of the Nabataeans. In this region there are only some hints of marching or temporary camps (Fig. 56; Strobel, 1974b, 175-81; cf. Fig. 178), but there are four sets of siege works, with many camps, which include the most famous and spectacular in the Empire. Masada (Fig. 44) is well known; Machaerus (Fig. 47), Battir (Fig. 49) and Nahal Hever (Fig.

51), less so. All are included here as probably representative of Roman practice in the East at other sites from which as yet we have no evidence.

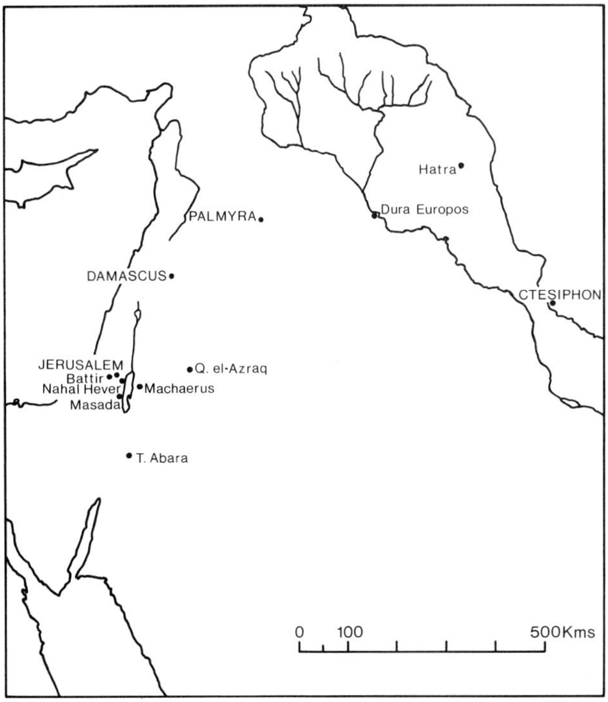

MASADA, ISRAEL
(Figs. 44, 45 and 46)

The great mass of the rock of Masada stands out from the bare ground between the Dead Sea and the barren hills to the west. The precipitous cliffs on all sides are well illustrated by Figure 44, as is the ramp, constructed by the Roman siege army, which ascends the cliff on the west side. The dark spots in the wadi bed on the left are bushes.

In Figure 45 the dry-stone walls of the camps and a short part of the wall of circumvallation show very distinctly as dark lines. The entrances of the largest camp (B on Fig. 46) have internal *claviculae*. Inside the camps, the ruins of low walls outline the remains of semi-permanent buildings, the roofs of which were probably formed by the leather tents used by Roman troops. The traces outside Camp C of a larger camp of about twice the size (*c.* 105 × 95 m./ 345 × 310 ft.; 1 ha. / 2.47 acres), and of another smaller enclosure to its east (Richmond, 1962, 146) are noteworthy. The former is evidently earlier, perhaps even from a different campaign, and may be compared with the probable camp at Tell Abara (Fig. 55). Its size would be adequate for about 750 men (using the calculation of *c.*300 men to the acre: Collingwood and Richmond, 1969, 11; cf. Hanson and Campbell, 1986, 87 n.78).

Other photographs show several more camps around the rock, and a range of other structures. One camp (F) has a wall cutting off a small part, thus reducing it in size. Outside the camps are

FIGURE 43 Location map.

FIGURE 44 Masada, Hadarom Hanegev, Israel (31°19′N 35°21′E): oblique view looking north from a height of 1500ft (500 m). *Photograph: Royal Air Force (10.24; 10 February 1936). Institute of Archaeology, London, RAF no. 11897.*

FIGURE 45 Masada, Hadarom Hanegev, Israel (31°19′N 35°21′E): vertical view of Camps A, B and C. *Photograph: Royal Air Force (8 November 1928). Institute of Archaeology, London. Cf. Richmond, 1962, Pl. XIX.*

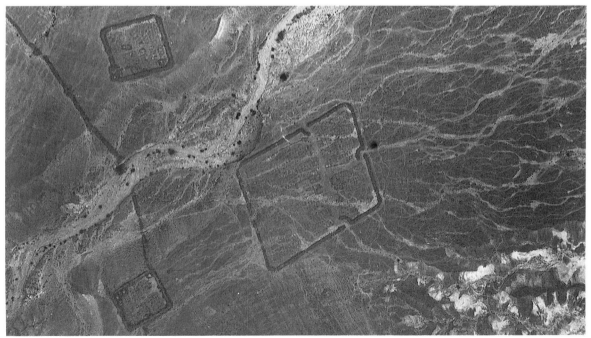

97

FIGURE 46 Masada, Hadarom Hanegev, Israel (31°19'N 35°21'E): sketch plan of the fortress and Roman siege-works. *After Richmond, 1962, fig. 5.* [A-H = Roman camps; J = engineers yard; W = Herod's palace; X = wall of circumvallation; Y = siege ramp; Z = aqueducts.]

the ruins of small buildings, the *canabae* of camp-followers, while further along the circumvallation is an enclosure described by Richmond as an engineers yard (J). On the wall of circumvallation itself, are the remains of small towers at intervals. The great assault ramp 'as big as a railway embankment' (Richmond, 1962, 154) is particularly striking. It shows as a pale feature on the right side of the rock in Figure 44.

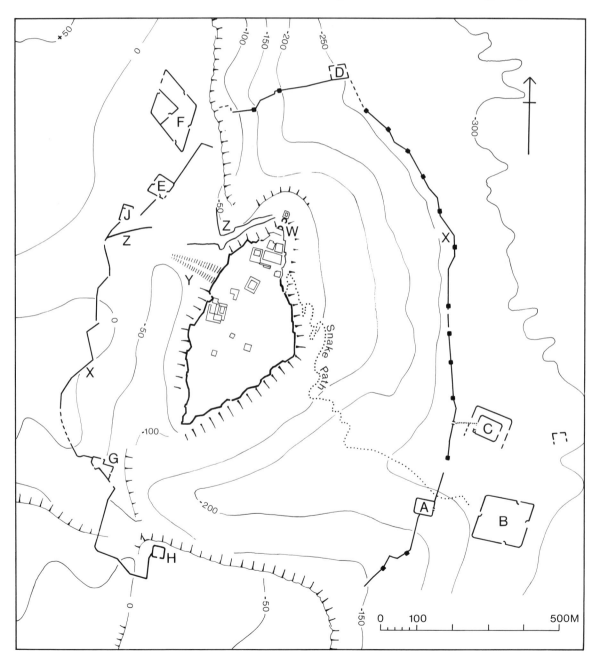

Masada lies on the western shore of the Dead Sea south-east of Jerusalem. The attractions of the site as a fortress go back to the mid second century BC at least, but it was only with its fortification by Herod the Great and his construction of a palace there that it took on great significance. Under Roman rule the fortress was probably garrisoned; there was certainly a Roman force there – as at Machaerus – at the outbreak of the Jewish Revolt in AD 66 (Josephus, *Bell. Iud.* II. 408). After the defeat of the rebel forces and the capture and destruction of Jerusalem, the new governor of Judaea, Flavius Silva, conducted a siege of the Zealot defenders who had seized it from its Roman garrison. A graphic account of the site, its siege and the final suicide of the defenders in the spring of, probably, 74 (Eck, 1970, 98-100; Campbell, 1988), is given by Josephus. Silva subsequently installed a new garrison (*Bell. Iud.* VII. 275-407).

Most of the physical remains are astonishingly well preserved, the camps and the wall of circumvallation with towers all being very clear. In recent years, however, some regrettable damage has been caused by the facilities installed for the large number of tourists who now visit the fortress on the rock. On the basis of a detailed examination of the individual camps, the traces of barracks and their likely garrison, Richmond calculated that Silva's forces consisted of a legion (divided between camps B and F), a *cohors milliaria*, two *cohortes quingenariae peditatae*, and one *cohors quingenaria equitata*; a total force of some 7500 men, almost entirely infantry (Richmond, 1962; cf. Hawkes, 1929; Schulten, 1933; Yadin, 1966, 206-23).

Excavation in the camps has turned up a few stratified coins, none later than 73. Excavations in Camp F have shown two floor levels in some structures, the upper presumably being due to a detachment of troops that was left behind – some below in this camp for a short time, others above in the fortress itself, perhaps for a rather longer period (Yadin, 1967).

MACHAERUS, JORDAN
(Figs. 47 and 48)

The Roman siege of Machaerus is overshadowed in the account of Josephus (*Bell. Iud.* VII. 163-216) by that of Masada, which was more protracted and ended in a dramatic fashion. Also, the remains at Masada are very striking and readily accessible, while those at Machaerus are less remarkable and more difficult to reach.

On this vertical photograph, shadows demonstrate the rugged nature of the landscape better than any map. In the centre, the excavated ruins of the Herodian fortress palace of Machaerus are easily seen, standing on the summit of a steep hill which forms part of a long ridge between two deep valleys. Near it is the assault ramp, which clearly was never completed. Two siege camps, D and H, are shown well by the darker tone of their walls, but the other camps are much harder to find on the photograph. The map summarizes the results of field work on the ground, and with its aid B, C, I and L can just be seen. E, F, G, K and P are not visible. They would presumably only show on air photographs of larger scale taken when the sun was in position to throw the necessary shadows at each site. However, the greater part of the wall of circumvallation can be followed with the aid of the map, and at one place slight shadows appear to mark a new length that was not recorded by the ground survey.

Machaerus – the palace fortress where John the Baptist is believed to have been executed by Herod Antipas – was located on the southern border of the Peraea, where it met the territory of the king of Nabataea. Like Masada it had a garrison of Roman troops in AD 66 and passed into the hands of Jewish rebels during the revolt. After the capture of Jerusalem it was assaulted by Lucilius Bassus at the head of a force which included the *Legio X Fretensis*. Josephus describes the fortress on its peak, the lower town on the slopes immediately below, and the natural defensibility of the site surrounded by steep-sided ravines. Bassus is said to have decided to fill in the ravine to the east and elsewhere Josephus speaks of 'platforms'. As may be seen from the photograph and plan, the Roman forces in fact constructed a line of circumvallation some 3 km (2 miles) long, with 10 or 11 camps and an assault camp. There is another camp well beyond the circuit on the slopes to the west (beyond the right edge of the photograph near the top). The camps are all much smaller than at Masada,

FIGURE 47 Machaerus, Al-Asimah, Jordan (31°34′N 35°38′E): vertical view of the palace and siege works. *Photograph: IGN (1978). Courtesy of Royal Jordanian Geographic Centre and Michel Piccirillo.*

raising the possibility that the main force was based in an as yet unidentified camp or camps, presumably at a place which could more easily be supplied; an obvious location would be where the current village stands on flatter ground east of the fortress. Although a new stretch of the circumvallation can be added from the air photograph, the latter has not been traced for its entire circuit and it may in fact have been incomplete

at the moment of the capitulation of the defenders (Vardaman, 1968; Strobel, 1974a and b; Corbo, 1978).

BATTIR, WEST BANK
(Figs. 49 and 50)

The third series of siege works illustrated is near the modern village of Battir, which lies 8 km (5 miles) south-west of Jerusalem in the hilly country familiar to visitors approaching the city by road from Tel Aviv. The importance of this place has long been known (Carroll, 1923/4 [for earlier references]; Alt, 1927; Schulten, 1933), but it has not yet been thoroughly explored.

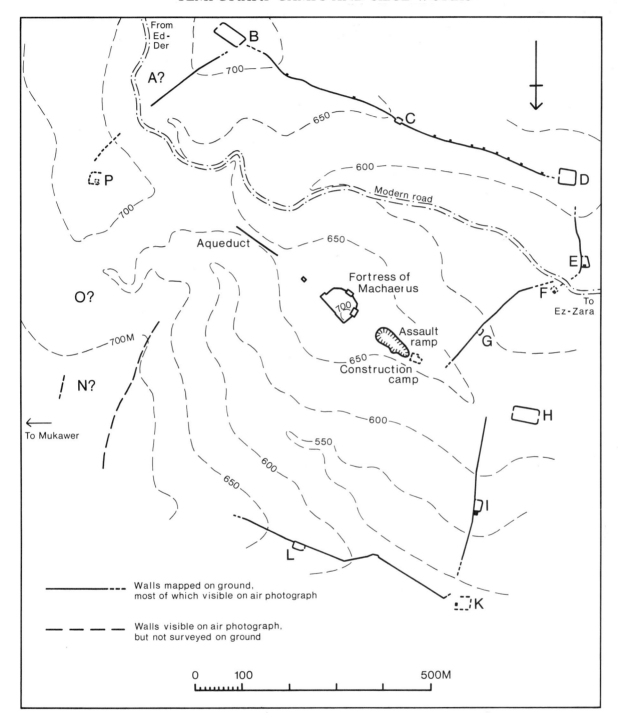

FIGURE 48 Machaerus, Al-Asimah, Jordan (31°34′N 35°38′E): plan of the fortress palace and the surrounding siege works and camps. *Drawn by D.N.Riley from the air photograph and after Strobel, 1974b and Corbo, 1978.*

Battir is well known as the site of Bar-Kochva's headquarters, *Bettar/Bethar*, the last great centre of resistance during the Second Jewish Revolt against Rome in the years 132-5 (Smallwood, 1976, 455f), but literature has little to tell us:

the war reached its climax in the 18th year (134-5) of Hadrian's reign at Bethar, a very strong citadel not far from Jerusalem. It was a long siege and the rebels were finally destroyed by starvation and thirst. (Eusebius *HE* IV.6.3)

On the photograph there are no shadows to indicate the relief of the land, but the height contours are suggested very well by the narrow cultivation terraces that cover the hillsides from top to bottom. On Figure 50 a black spot marks the site of the Jewish stronghold which is known to the Arabs as Khirbet el-Yahud ('Jewish Ruins'). It is located on the flattish top of a steep sided and isolated hill, which is connected with a higher hill to the south by a saddle (X) between the heads of two minor valleys. It has been suggested that there was a siege ramp on this saddle, built against the defences of Bethar, but the place has now been covered by houses. Certainly, in the 1920s the hill opposite bore a broken monument known to the native Arabs as 'The Stone of the Catapult' (Carroll, 1923/4, 88). Excavation was commenced in 1984, but has concentrated on the Jewish fortress (Ussishkin, 1986-7, 49ff).

The adjacent higher hill was known in local legend last century as 'the place from which the King bombarded the Jews' (Carroll, 1923/4, 88). It has more level ground on its summit, and there is little doubt that much of the shapes of two camps may be traced in the modern field walls, though various slight deviations indicate that the original lines of their defences have not been exactly followed (Reifenberg, 1950, 41 and Fig. 3). The larger camp (A), which covers some 8.3 ha./20.5 acres (*c.*218 × 380 m./710 × 1240 ft), is the better preserved. The smaller (B), perhaps 2.63 ha. / 6.5 acres (198 × 133 m. / 645 × 435 ft) in size, is traceable by field walls on two of the sides, but on the other two no more than slight differences in the appearance of the surface suggest the line on Figure 49.

At distances varying from *c.* 1.5 to 4 km (1 to 2½ miles) south and east of camps A and B, four other hill top camps (C, D, E and F) were

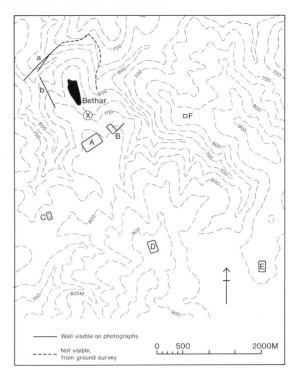

FIGURE 50 Battir, Al-Quds, West Bank (31°42′N; 35°11′E): plan of the site showing the Jewish fortress and the Roman siege works. *Drawn by D.N.Riley based on Kochavi, 1972.*

identified during the archaeological survey of the newly occupied territories carried out after the 1967 Six Day War (Kochavi, 1972, 24). The site of camp F is seen on the lower right corner of Figure 49, but its walls cannot be identified. Camp D, *c.* 3.3 ha. (8.2 acres) in size, is traceable by present-day field walls on air photographs, but is outside the area covered by Figure 49. The site of E appears to be being built over.

Survey in the area has also located part of a wall of circumvallation, known since the 1920s (Alt, 1927; Schulten, 1933). The only parts that show well on air photographs are lengths a and b, running down hillsides north-west and west of Khirbet el-Yahud, but the survey map gives a considerable extra length north and east of the site. Much of the wall has probably been destroyed in the building or repair of cultivation terraces, so its line may be lost in many parts.

The size of the two largest camps (A and B,) would suggest accommodation for some 6000 and 1800 men respectively. If they are contempor-

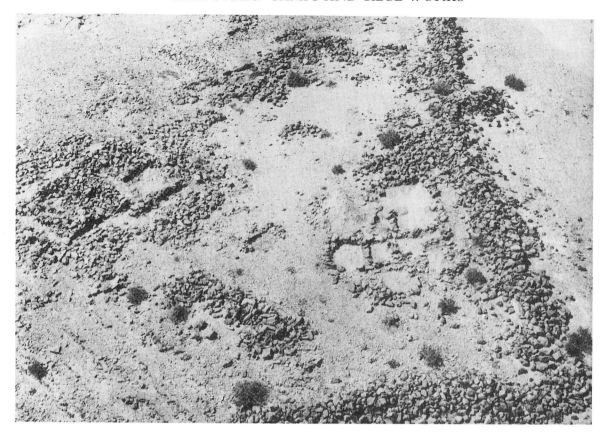

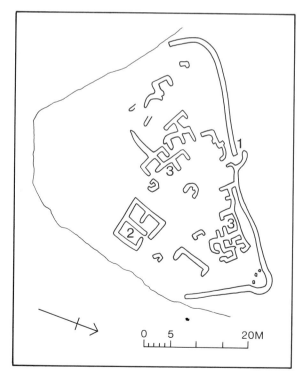

FIGURE 51 Nahal Hever, Hadarom Hanegev, Israel (31°22′N 35°20′E): oblique view looking west. *Photograph courtesy the executors of Y.Yadin. Cf. Yadin, 1971, 47 plate.*

FIGURE 52 Nahal Hever, Hadarom Hanegev, Israel (31°22′N 35°20′E): plan of the camp. *After Yadin, 1971, 48.*

ary, with the addition of further troops in Camps C, D, E and F, the total siege force may have been some 10-12,000 troops. That many were legionaries is likely, and the units may be those on a rock-cut inscription naming detachments of legions *V Macedonica* and *XI Claudia*, whose parent units, normally permanently stationed in Moesia Inferior, had evidently all contributed men to the Roman forces putting down the revolt (Applebaum, 1976, 45). So large a force accords with the status of the place and its role in the final phase of a bitter and bloody war.

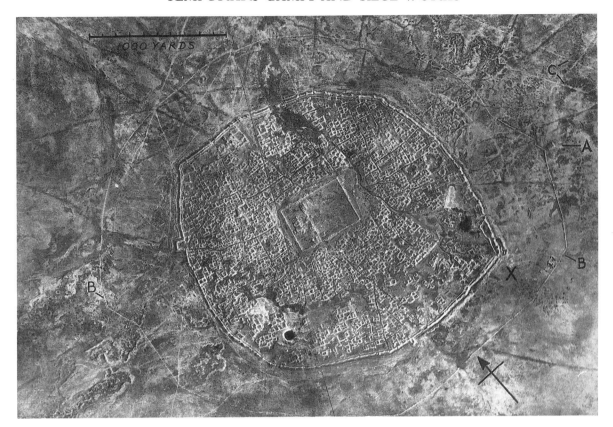

NAHAL HEVER, ISRAEL
(Figs. 51 and 52)

This is one of two camps (Yadin, 1971, 46-9) which lie above steep cliffs facing one another on each side of the Nahal Hever, a gorge running towards the Dead Sea between En-Gedi and Masada. Their location in that remote spot is to be associated with the fugitives known to have taken refuge in caves in the cliff face. Below each camp is a cave, known respectively as the 'Cave of the Letters' and the 'Cave of Horrors'. It is the camp above the former which is here illustrated. The low-level oblique view of the camp during excavation seems to show every stone of its wall and of the ruins inside it.

With a steep cliff edge on one side, only half the perimeter of the camp had a wall (right of photograph), in the middle of which is an entrance defended by a *clavicula* (1) (cf. Fig. 45). The area enclosed is *c.* 1250 m. (13,366 ft) square (Yadin, 1971, 49). Apart from a quite substantial structure identified as a possible headquarters (2),

FIGURE 53 Hatra (Al-Hadr), Neineva, Iraq (35°36'N 42°44'E): vertical view of the ruins of Hatra. *Bradford Archive (Pitt Rivers Museum, Oxford University).*

most of the ruins are probably to be seen as the traces of the low stone walls of the otherwise largely timber and leather quarters of the troops (3). It has been estimated that some 80-100 soldiers may have been accommodated. From the cave below, the excavators recovered an extraordinarily interesting series of documents, preserved by the dry climate. They make clear that the siege was part of the mopping-up operations at the close of the Second Jewish Revolt, the so-called Bar-Kochva War. That being the case, it may be that the soldiers belonged to the *Cohors I Milliaria Thracum*, attested in the region in the early second century (Speidel, 1979).

HATRA, IRAQ
(Figs. 53 and 54)

Figure 53, a remarkable photograph of the whole of the ruins of Hatra and the surrounding country, is made up of two prints from a vertical survey made in the 1950s. It was first published by J. Bradford (1957, pl. 24) and has his writing on it. He suggested that the mound A had perhaps been made for siege engines. BB is a wall of circumvallation, showing partly by shadow, partly as a soil mark. CC are long white soil marks which perhaps indicate old routes.

Next (Fig. 54) comes a very low level view taken for Sir Aurel Stein from above point X on Figure 53, looking west along the ruins of the immense mud brick walls towards the south gate. To the left of the wall, a vegetation mark is formed by the better growth of plants in the

FIGURE 54 Hatra (Al-Hadr), Neineva, Iraq (35°36′N 42°44′E): oblique view looking west from a height of 300 ft (100 m.). *Photograph: Royal Air Force (10.58; 23 April 1938). Stein Archive (Institute of Archaeology, London, inv. no. A.P.1583).*

deep defensive ditch. Just inside the wall is what looks like a second wall. To the right of the centre of the photograph is one of the standing pools of water found inside Hatra, several of which appear as black patches on the vertical view.

Hatra lies at perennial springs in the north Mesopotamian desert 50 km (31 miles) west of the Tigris and 115 km (72 miles) south-east of Singara. It developed in the first century AD into a major caravan city and, by the end of the second century was renowned for its splendid sanctuary of the Sun God and for its wealth (Cassius Dio LXXVI.12.2). The walls enclosed some 400 ha. (1000 acres). A large area at its centre was occupied by the great Temple of the Sun, around which are the densely packed houses of an oriental city. Streets weave their way from gates to temple, but there is no trace of systematic planning. The defences are impressive. A tall curtain wall with numerous towers may be seen on the vertical view (Fig. 53). The apparent inner, and more modest, circuit, seen best on the oblique view (Fig. 54), may explain Cassius Dio's reference (LXXVI.12.1) to the troops of the

Emperor Septimius Severus breaking down part of the *outer* circuit.

Hatra first appears in Roman history in 117 at the time of Trajan's vain assault on it. In 199/200, Septimius Severus twice failed to capture it in the course of his Second Parthian War, his sieges being those for which we have the only detailed accounts (Cassius Dio and Herodian (III.9.3-7)). It seems, finally to have been captured – by the Sasanian Persians – in 239/40, after a previous failed attempt in 227.

To which siege, or sieges the line of circumvallation is to be assigned, is unknown. It lies 400 m. (1300ft) from the city walls, a safe distance from the skilful Hatrene archers of whom Dio wrote. Dio also referred to the artillery used by both sides. The remains of a catapult were discovered in recent excavations behind one of the towers, where it must have fallen during a siege, probably the final siege by a Sasanian army (Baatz, 1978, 3-9). There are no traces in these photographs of the siege camps to be expected if the works were Roman, although Trajan's and/or Severus' troops must surely have constructed camps. Andrae (1908-12) claims to have seen one and Crawford reports seeing two more probable camps from the air during his 1928 trip (1955, 194; cf. 1929, 502), but these were beyond the circumvallation and not, therefore, in the area covered by any of the photographs at present available. From the parallels at Masada and Machaerus, at least some of the camps should be on the circumvallation wall. However, we should bear in mind that at both those sites, the ground was very different from the open spaces around Hatra. Unless the expected traces of them have been covered over by wind-blown material and/or were dismantled by the Sasanian besiegers to repair the circumvallation, it seems probable that the army's camps were more distant from their opponents than at Masada and Machaerus. Equally, however, it may be best to treat the visible lines as belonging to the final, successful, Persian siege, even if they were a re-use of Roman work (Gregory and Kennedy (Stein), 1985, 57-63; 396f; cf. Bradford 1957, 74).

Ironically, despite the repeated success of the city in resisting Roman armies, at the end a regiment of Roman troops seems to have been admitted. Latin inscriptions attest the presence in

FIGURE 55 Tell Abara, Ma'an, Jordan (30°19′N 35°35′E): vertical view. *Photograph: IGN (14.14, 1981). Royal Jordanian Geographic Centre. Supplied by A.C.Killick.*

the time of Gordian III (238-44) of the *Cohors IX Maurorum*, and it is arguable that the rapprochement with Rome should go back at least to the rise of the Sasanians (Kennedy, 1988). Whether Roman troops were still in the city at the time of its final capture by the Sasanians is unknown.

TELL ABARA, JORDAN
(Fig. 55)

The large enclosure – c.150 x 120 m. (c.500 × 400 ft), 1.8 ha. (4.5 acres) – has recently been noticed by A. Killick on a print of this photograph, which comes from a vertical survey of the region. It is on a quite steep but rounded hill 2 km. (1.25 miles) south-south-west of the fortress at Udruh (Fig. 79) (Killick, 1986, 436ff; 1987, 28ff). No signs of any internal structures are visible. There are openings on the east and west walls of the enclosure, the former being masked by an external clavicular barrier. The structure looks very much like those known in the western provinces as temporary camps. If so, it would represent the first such structure known anywhere in the East apart from siege-camps and the probable site at the Azraq Oasis (Fig. 56). In appearance it is very similar to the large camp outside Camp C at Masada (Fig. 45). Its proximity to a sizeable Nabataean and Roman settlement at Udruh is intriguing.

FIGURE 56 Qasr el-Azraq, Al-Asimah, Jordan
(31°53′N 36°50′E): vertical view. *Photograph: Royal
Air Force, (c.1927). Crawford Collection (Institute of
Archaeology, Oxford).*

No date is yet available, but the distinctive
entrance, if indeed it is the *clavicula* seen more
clearly on the photographs of Masada and Nahal
Hever (Figs. 45 and 57), suggests construction at
a similar period to the camps at those places. On
the analogy of such camps in Britain, its size
would suggest a force of some 1350 men (Collingwood and Richmond, 1969, 11); a legionary
vexillation (*c.* 3 cohorts) perhaps, a force of
auxiliaries or some combination of the two.

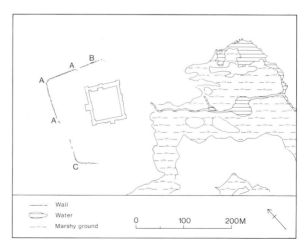

Wall
Water
Marshy ground

0   100   200M

QASR EL-AZRAQ, JORDAN
(Figs. 56 and 57)

The Azraq Oasis lies some 80 km (50 miles) east of Amman, a little less south-east of Bostra. As described above (Fig. 28), it is the most important perennial source of water in the Syrian Desert after that at Palmyra. The walls of the fort, which still stand to a good height, are emphasized on Figure 56 by shadows of the morning sun (about 08.00, to judge from its direction). An outer enclosure wall (A on Fig. 57), perhaps the remains of a Roman temporary camp, is also clear, and there are many bedouin enclosures. Pools of water (black), grass covered marshy ground (dark) and mud flats (pale) cover a large area near it (upper right).

The fort and suggested temporary camp are located on higher ground just west of the north spring and pools. The overall size of the possible camp cannot be calculated with any confidence. The section AAA is certain, B fairly certain, but C is more doubtful. The sides AA and AAB give dimensions of *c.* 100 and 125 m. (300 and 180 ft), implying a minimum internal size of *c.* 1.25 ha. (3 acres), though the further hints at C suggest it could have been at least twice that size. As previously mentioned (p. 84), the fort (discussed below, Fig. 126) is now surrounded by houses, which have covered the site of the enclosure.

The Severan milestones on the road into Azraq (Fig. 28) and the Severan building inscriptions from the dependent fort at Uweinid (Fig. 105) give the earliest certain date for Roman occupation at the oasis. The date of this suggested camp may belong to this period also.

DURA EUROPOS (SALIHIYEH), SYRIA (Fig. 58)

The history of Dura Europos is discussed more fully and appropriately in the next chapter. This photographic mosaic is included here because it records a little-noted feature. Uncommonly amongst the many air views of Dura Europos, it covers a considerable area outside the land wall of the city. Along the upper right edge of the photograph, just beyond the necropolis, can be seen the remains of a wall. This is mentioned only once in the literature on Dura, where it is described as 'a low earthen wall' (Toll, 1946, 1). A note to that text observes that there are other walls further out in the desert. The author suggested that the wall was the work of the Persian army to protect itself both against the garrison and the 'impurity' represented by the necropolis.

Later French maps show this wall to be part of one of three enclosures along the river on the north side of the city. Preliminary investigation by P. Leriche has noted that the bank is of earth with a mixture of stones, but there is no indication of date and he suspects these enclosures might even be modern (pers. comm., 20 June 1988).

The striking feature of this bank is the entrance (*c.* 4 m (13 ft) wide according to Leriche), which is not just a gap, but a gap fronted by a parallel bank protecting it against direct approach. We know a great deal about Roman castrametation and can identify this bank as a *titulum*, characteristic of the gate design of many Roman temporary camps in the West (Collingwood and Richmond, 1969, 9–12). *Titula* may also have been used to protect entrances through Roman siege works, the best example at present known being at an opening through Caesar's circumvallation of the Gallic fortress of Alesia (Goguey, forth., fig. 9). If the bank with *titulum* at Dura *is* Roman, the obvious period for its construction would have been in the second century at the time of the campaigns of either Trajan or the armies of Marcus Aurelius and Lucius Verus (cf. Fig. 53). On the other hand, too little is known of Sasanian siege practices to be confident of rejecting them as the builders.

Also visible on the photograph, showing as a dark line, is the trace of the ancient road running up towards the major gateway, the Palmyra Gate. The road coming in on the centre right is modern.

FIGURE 57 Qasr el-Azraq, Al-Asimah, Jordan (31°53′N 36°50′E): plan of the fort and vicinity. *Drawn by D.N.Riley from the photograph.*

FIGURE 58 Dura Europos (Salihiyeh), Deir es-Zor, Syria (34° 38′N, 40° 43′E): vertical view of the city from a mosaic of prints. *Photograph: L'Armée de l'Air[?] (1935). Dura Europos Collection, Yale University Art Gallery, inv. no. Y2.*

· CHAPTER EIGHT ·

Fortress Cities

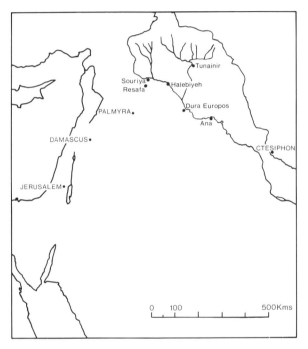

FIGURE 59 Location map.

From the early days of the Roman military occupation of the region, garrisons were established inside existing cities. The usual purpose in these early days was not to defend the urban population, whatever their origin, but to acquire easy billeting and supplies, and to police the populace. In contrast are those urban centres which later became military strong-points against hostile forces, e.g. Sura, Halebiyeh and Resafa (Figs. 63–7), most of which initially lay along the Euphrates, the great invasion route into Syria; later they developed elsewhere, in Mesopotamia in particular, as existing cities were fortified or re-fortified and garrisoned.

In the literature there are references to fortress cities being defended by Roman garrisons in the very early years of the province. Thus, Antioch and Laodicea were defended against civil war opponents, while Apamea and Tyre were held against Parthian forces. After this there is a long gap in the evidence in the Early Empire and it is not until the later second century that there are again references to cities becoming strongpoints. After that, however, there are many references as the long-standing but seldom fulfilled possibility of Parthian invasion was replaced by the reality of several Persian ones. The course of wars from the third century onwards was often centred on a struggle to seize crucial fortress cities, some with powerful garrisons. The pages of Ammianus Marcellinus and, later, Procopius, are full of the accounts of Persian assaults on such cities as Bezabde, Nisibis and Amida on the one hand, and the fortress cities of the Euphrates valley on the other. Procopius' account of the building work of Justinian in the sixth century, the *Buildings*, is of course our major source of evidence for military construction in any part of the Roman period.

DURA EUROPOS (SALIHIYEH), SYRIA
(Figs. 60 and 61)

Low sunlight draws attention to the walls of the city, the grid pattern of streets, the wadis in the foreground and the distance. A very similar oblique photograph of the site is reproduced on Pl. LXXXVIII of *La trace de Rome*. The walls of ruined buildings show very clearly in the large areas excavated by the Franco-American expedition then in progress, which may be compared

FIGURE 60 Dura Europos (Salihiyeh), Deir es-Zor, Syria (34°38′N, 40°43′E): oblique photograph of the ruins looking south-east. *Photograph: L'Armèe de l'Air[?] Supplied by Dura Europos Collection, Yale University Art Gallery, negative no. 2184.*

FIGURE 61 Dura Europos (Salihiyeh), Deir es-Zor, Syria (34°38′N, 40°43′E): plan of the fortress city. *Adapted from the map by A.H.Detweiler of 1935 in the Dura Europos Collection, Yale University Art Gallery, by kind permission.*
A = main gate ('Palmyra Gate'); B = citadel, enclosure wall and palace; C = military chapel; D = palace of the Dux Ripae; E = baths; F = shrine of Dolichenus; G = barracks; H = amphitheatre; I = principia; J = house of a senior officer; K = Temple of Azzanathkona (also used to store the archives of the Cohors XX Palmyrenorum); L = Mithraeum; M = brick wall of the military quarter.

with those in Figure 58 above. Elsewhere, most of the site of the ancient city is surprisingly level because of the complete collapse of the upper parts of the mud brick buildings, which had buried the ancient surface by a layer 0.6 to 2 m. (2 to 6 ft) deep (Hopkins, 1979, 50). The high stone walls of the citadel may be noted, partly eroded by the Euphrates, which flows past the city and winds into the distance, the route followed by Roman, Parthian and Sasanian armies.

Dura Europos was a strongly defended fortress city built on the site of an earlier native defended settlement (*Duru* fort), but taking its shape from its re-foundation by the Seleucid general Nicanor, *c*.300 BC, at which time it also acquired the latter, Greek, part of its name. Natural

defences of the river on the east and deep wadis running into it on the north and south were strengthened by walls, while on the west, the circuit was completed by a strong wall still standing to several metres.

In AD 114, Dura, then still a Parthian city,

was the site of a Roman victory, commemorated by the construction of a triumphal arch just outside the city (off the photograph on the bottom right) (Hopkins, 1979). It was not until *c.*164, however, that it was seized to become part of the now extended Roman frontier defences. Dura provides an excellent though rare example (cf. Kurnub, Fig. 183) of the accomodation for an implanted urban garrison within the circuit of an existing stronghold. In the early third century the regional commander, the *Dux Ripae*, was resident in a palace (D) in the northern part of the city, while nearby, some 9 ha. (22 acres) of the western (upper left) corner of the city was taken over and walled off by the army (M). Within this area, have been excavated a *principia* (I), barrack blocks (G), baths (E) and even an amphitheatre (H) (uncommon, military or civil, anywhere in the East), albeit laid out in a less orderly fashion than within a purpose-built fort. Inscriptions give us a great deal of evidence for the large garrison of legionaries and auxiliaries, but it is from the huge cache of papyri discovered in the Temple of Azzanathkona (K), the archives of one of the units, the *Cohors XX Palmyrenorum*, that most has been learned (Welles *et al.*, 1959). The capture and sack of Dura by Shapur I in, probably, 252 (Balty, 1987, 229-39; cf. MacDonald, 1986) ended not only the century of Roman occupation, but – probably after a very brief Persian occupation (MacDonald, 1986, 64-8) – the life of the city: in 363, the Emperor Julian passed the ruined and desolate city in the course of his expedition into Parthia (Amm. Marc. XXIV.1.5).

ANA, IRAQ (Fig. 62)

Ana Island and a strip of flat land below the steep banks bordering the Euphrates, some 350 km (220 miles) due east of Palmyra, were occupied for millenia by the buildings of a succession of important settlements, as were other river islands in the region. It has remained occupied down to the present and nothing of the Roman period is visible on the surface.

For most of the Roman and Byzantine period, it was a Parthian or Sasanian city. Its location on the Middle Euphrates, however, exposed it to attack in time of war and it changed hands several

times. The earliest attestations from the Roman period are of the first and second centuries AD and reveal first the popularity of its deity, Aphlad, amongst Palmyrene merchants, then that Palmyra apparently maintained troops there. They were presumably caravan guards at what would have been a stop along the trade route from the Persian Gulf.

The city was probably seized in 115 by Trajan's armies on their march to Ctesiphon, and again in 164/5 when those of Lucius Verus passed by. These would have been brief occupations, but in the early Severan period, certainly by 219, it was firmly in Roman hands and seems to have remained so for half a century until captured by the forces of Shapur I in, probably, 252 (cf. Fig. 60). Significantly, the Palmyrenians seem to have retained their forces there still.

Whether it again changed hands in the course of the expeditions down the Euphrates of the Palmyrene prince Odenathus, and the Emperors Carus and Galerius, is unknown. When Julian arrived there in 363 it was certainly a Persian fortress although its garrison surrendered and were transferred to Roman service in Syria (Amm. Marc. XXIV.1.6-10). It may have been held for a few years – it is recorded, anachronistically perhaps, as a Roman fortress in the *Notitia Dignitatum (Or.* XXXIII.20; cf. 11). By the end of the fourth century it had become and was apparently to remain a part of the Persian frontier defences against both Rome and the nomads. Its final mention in our period comes from the account of a short-lived Roman seizure of the fortress in 591. (For all of the above see Kennedy and Northedge, 1988.)

The island, densely settled until its desertion before flooding by dam water in the last few years, is some 950 × 200 m. (3100 × 654 ft), rising in the centre to *c.* 13 m. (42½ ft) above the river level. Recent excavation has suggested that the stone embankments around the perimeter date to the Partho-Sasanian period, though perhaps overlaying a neo-Assyrian circuit in places. The oldest visible remains – including the bridge piers running across the channel to the left (southwest) of the island – are of the Middle Islamic centuries. The street pattern, based on a longitudinal central pathway, may preserve a very ancient layout. Excavation beneath the mosque found remains of the Hellenistic and Roman period, including almost 1000 Seleucid coins in graves and three hoards of the same period including rich jewellery deposits (Northedge *et al.*, ch. 2; cf. Gregory and Kennedy (Stein), 1985, 146–51, 403f).

SOURIYA, SYRIA (Fig. 63)

The ruins of ancient Sura were recorded well by Poidebard's two photographs (Fig. 63 and

FIGURE 62 Ana, Al-Anbar, Iraq (34°28′N 42°01′E): *vertical view from 5000 ft (1600 m). Photograph: Royal Air Force (10.28; 19 January 1939). Stein Archive (British Museum, Department of Western Asiatic Antiquities, Small Archive, Air Photographs – Iraq-Stein, RAF no. 05810).*

Poidebard, 1934, LXXX), taken when the site was completely deserted. The photograph published here is an oblique view, showing the defences of the city, outlined by shadows, and its situation beside the Euphrates.

The visible remains consist of five major elements. First, there are the traces of many buildings within the outer circuit; second, a square fort (A), 220 x 200 paces (Sarre and Herzfeld, 1911, 153ff, and fig. 66), with projecting angle towers and, apparently, four intermediate towers along each side; third, a major circuit wall (B) with broad outer ditch, enclosing an area some 1150 x 400 paces; fourth, the western end of this area is enclosed within its own, more substantial, walls (C). This part at least of the circuit appears to be the combination of towered

FIGURE 63 Souriya, Raqqa, Syria (35°53′N 38°48′E): oblique view of the site looking west. *Photograph: Aéro Levant (n.d.). From Poidebard, 1934, LXXIX.*

wall and outer works, described by Procopius. Finally, there are many buildings outside the walls, some of which may be seen on the left of this view, though they show better on Poidebard's other photograph.

The Elder Pliny mentions *Sura* simply as the place where the Euphrates turns east (*HN* V.87). However, a milestone of AD 75 from Erek on the Palmyra to Sura road strengthens the possibility that the site may have been garrisoned by the Flavian period as the point where two major highways joined; one was from Palmyra, and the other the ancient route down the Euphrates. For the third century, the so-called *Res Gestae Divi Saporis* records Sura as the fourth place seized by Sasanian forces on their march up the Euphrates in 252. Later still, according to the *Notitia Dignitatum*, it was the seat of the *Praefectus Legionis Sextaedecimae Flaviae Firmae* (*Or.* XXXIII. 28; cf 6). In the time of Justinian the city was captured and sacked by Khusrau I (Procopius *Wars* II.v.8–33) then massively re-built by that emperor (Procopius *Buildings* II.ix.1f).

Although it had a legionary garrison in about AD 395 when the *Notitia Dignitatum* was compiled, it is not certain that any of the fortifications now visible belong to that period. Indeed, the movement of *Legio XVI Flavia Firma* from Samosata to Sura may have occurred as early as the Severan period (Kennedy, 1988). A legionary fortress of that period would have required some 16-20 ha. (40-50 acres), approximately half the total walled area at Sura. The small square fort (A), some 4 ha. (10 acres) in the centre, lying where the old course of the river once washed the walls, is probably best interpreted as the citadel for a rather later garrison. It may be that in the aftermath of the sack and the loss of a large part of the population, Justinian's architects designed a circuit to encompass a rather smaller area (C) including this fort (A) on the eastern end overlooking the river.

RESAFA, SYRIA (Fig. 64)

The massive walls of the city and the ruins of the cathedral of St Sergius are emphasized in a striking manner by shadows on this morning photograph, taken with the camera facing towards the sun. Shadows also show the sites of many buildings outside the walls. The area inside

FIGURE 64 Resafa, Raqqa, Syria (35°37′N 38°45′E): oblique view from the north-west. *Photograph: Petit (n.d.). From Poidebard, 1934, LXXV (cf. LXXVI.1).*

the walls and patches of land outside are pockmarked by pits dug by treasure hunters.

The fortress city of *Rosapha/Risapa/Resapha*, later *Sergiopolis*, lies on the road between Sura and Palmyra, 28.5 km (18 miles) from the former, 155 km (97 miles) from the latter (Poidebard, 1934, 82). It is known from ancient sources, beginning with Ptolemy in the Hadrianic period, but only comes to prominence rather later. The *Notitia Dignitatum (Or.* XXXIII, 27, cf. 5) gives it as the base of *Equites Promoti Indigenae.* Later, Procopius (*Buildings* II.ix.3-7) describes how an attack by the Saracens seeking plunder from the site had caused the authorities to construct a modest wall. Subsequently, in the early sixth century, Justinian provided a grander wall commensurate with its status and wealth, and installed a garrison. The Persian king Khusrau I is credited with making an unsuccessful attack.

Later still, it seems to have become the residence of the pro-Roman Arab *phylarch* Al-Mundhir (Alamundaros), son of Jabala, the Ghassanid (Musil, 1928, 260-72; Sauvaget, 1939a).

The most striking features of the site are the great church and huge underground (and not visible) cisterns inside the walled town, and the massive walls with covered internal colonnaded walkway, 29 towers of various shapes and 21 solid rectangular bastions. The circuit encloses an irregular rectangle, 356 × 543 × 422 × 558 m. 1164 × 1776 × 1380 × 1825 ft (21 ha./ 52 acres) (Musil, 1928, 299-322; Karnapp, 1976).

HALEBIYEH, SYRIA
(Figs. 65, 66 and 67)

The position of the great fortress town on the banks of the Euphrates is well illustrated by Poidebard's vertical photograph (Fig. 65), on which its walls and the larger ruined buildings are outlined by shadows. Little can be seen of the other buildings. The distant oblique (Fig. 66) emphasizes the extraordinary nature of the terrain around the river and the superb location of the town.

The ruins of Halebiyeh have survived much better than those of Zelebiyeh, the adjacent town on the opposite bank a little downstream (marked by an arrow on Fig. 66), much of which has been eroded into the river. Seen from the north-west, the massive walls of Halebiyeh are emphasized by deep shadows in the oblique photograph (Fig. 66). The situation of the town is demonstrated well – the Euphrates winding past, the flat land on which the town stands, and the cliffs behind it, on a spur of which is the citadel. When visited on the ground, the flatter land nearer the river is found to be covered with low ruins of buildings, which include much of the friable local gypsum rock, and it is surprising that more does not show on the photograph. The explanation is probably due to the way the site slopes towards the river, i.e. towards the sun at the time when these photographs were taken, so that few shadows are visible, and also to the accumulation of surface debris that has probably been carried

FIGURE 65 Halebiyeh, Deir es-Zor, Syria (35°40'N 39°49'E): vertical view. *Photograph: Aéro Levant (n.d.). From Poidebard, 1934, Pl. LXXXIV.*

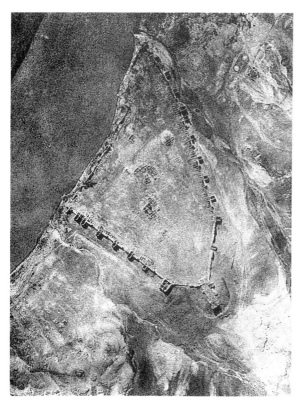

down from the steep slopes near the citadel.

The sites lie on the Middle Euphrates some 190 km (120 miles) north-east of Palmyra, at a point now known as el-Khanouqa, 'the Strangler', where the river valley narrows, passing through steep cliffs on either side. The two towns could maintain tight control of movement up either bank of the river in what was otherwise a very barren area (Musil, 1927, 332ff; Poidebard, 1934, 86ff; Lauffray, 1983, Ch. IV).

The physical remains of the walls and citadel at Halebiyeh are considerable, as may be gauged from the relative size of the Landrover (marked by arrow) seen in the ground view (Fig. 67). The curtain survives on the land side to a height of several metres with stretches of walkway intact; huge towers can still be climbed via the internal staircases. The citadel has lost its roofing and internal floors, but is otherwise in an excellent state of preservation. Even today, the fortress presents a formidable appearance. The walls run for *c*.385 m. (1200 ft) along the river front, *c*.350 m. (1100 ft) on the north side and *c*.550 m (1700 ft) on the south, encompassing an area of some 12 ha. (30 acres), some of which, on the steep ascent to the citadel, is dead ground (Lauffray, 1983).

According to ancient tradition, the fortress city was built by and named for the Palmyrene queen, Zenobia. It is best known to us, however, from the writings of Procopius. Khusrau I in 540 made a brief effort to force the surrender of what is said to be an unimportant fortress (*Hist.* II. v.4-7). Later, Justinian is credited with massively re-building the site as a great fortress city, with immense walls, a citadel, baths, colonnades and a powerful garrison (*Buildings* II.viii.8-25). In 610, it was captured by the Persians (Musil, 1927, 331ff).

TUNAINIR, SYRIA
(Figs. 68 and 69)

This photograph, taken from a considerable height, records vegetation marks and shadows, which give the positions of many ancient features on this important site. Poidebard produced a detailed plan from air photographs, although earlier visitors had judged the site impossible to plan without clearances and excavation (1934, 141). The large mound in the centre left, an

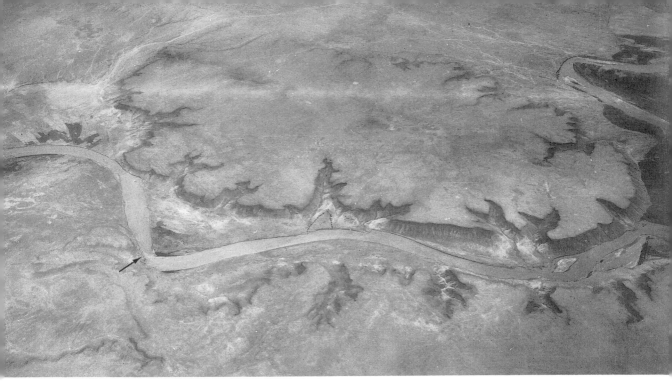

ancient tell, is covered by remains of buildings, which also extend to the upper left of the area covered by the photograph. Near the right margin there are very distinct pale toned vegetation marks on the walls of a large building identified by Poidebard as the tower of Procopius (below). On the small island in the river, between this tower and the large mound, are the ruins of part of a bridge. On both sides of the River Khabur are modern irrigated fields.

The region had passed permanently into Roman hands in the time of Marcus Aurelius but, although a garrison is not unlikely at what appears to have been a major settlement, none is known then or in the third century. The earliest indication of any military involvement at *Thannuris* is provided by the *Notitia Dignitatum*, which records *Equites Sagittarii Indigenae, Thannuri* (*Or.* XXXVI. 28; cf. 17). Thereafter, one has to leap ahead more than a century to the account by Procopius of Justinian's refortification work in Mesopotamia: Thannourios (one of two sites of that name he said) was converted into a 'truly formidable' fortress, and nearby, at a spot where the Saracens were in the habit of crossing the River Khabur and attacking the settled Roman population, Justinian 'built a very large tower of hard stone... in which he established a very considerable garrison' (*Buildings* II. vi. 13-16).

FIGURE 66 Halebiyeh – Zelebiyeh Pass, Deir es-Zor, Syria (35°40′N 39°48′E): oblique view looking south west. *Photograph: Aerial Photographic Archive for Archaeology in the Middle East (n.d.).*

FIGURE 67 Halebiyeh, Deir es-Zor, Syria (35°40′N 39°48′E): ground view from the citadel looking east across the south-east walls towards Zelebiyeh in the distance. *Photograph: D.L. Kennedy (August, 1976).*

FIGURE 68 Tunainir, Hasakeh, Syria (36°24′N
40°53′E): vertical view. *Photograph: G. David (n.d.).*
*From Poidebard, 1934, Pl. CXVI (cf. Pl.
CXV).*

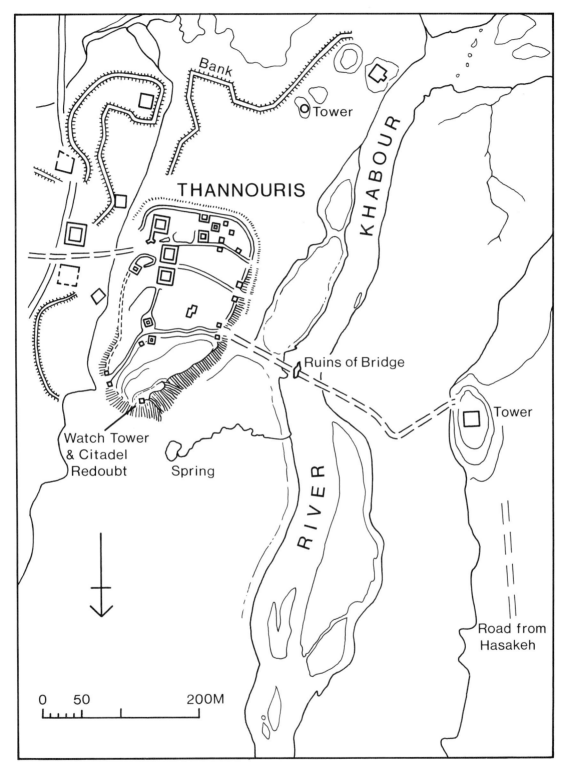

FIGURE 69 Tunainir, Hasakeh, Syria (36°24′N 40°53′E): plan of the tell and Roman remains.

Traced from the relevant portion of Poidebard, 1934, Pl. CXVII.

CHAPTER NINE

Legionary Fortresses

The term 'fortress' is here employed to define the bases of legions, the largest discrete units in the Roman army, both in the Early Empire, when they consisted of some 5000 men, and in the Late Empire, by which time they had shrunk to perhaps as little as one-fifth of that. Normally fortresses were garrisoned by a single legion, but occasionally there were more than one, or, conversely, only a part unit. In the Syrian provinces only a few fortresses for single whole legions have been identified. There are other sites known to have been occupied by legions, but the evidence about them is much less certain, depending on mentions by ancient authors and on inscriptions, which are as yet unsupported by excavation or survey on the ground.

In order to set the scene, this account of fortresses in the Middle East will begin by summarizing what is known about the history of the legions in the region from literary and epigraphic evidence, which gives the actual places at which some legions were stationed at certain dates. Because our information is limited there are considerable problems in the identification of fortress sites.

· History ·

Although a legionary garrison of, probably, two legions was established in Syria by Pompey (Caes. *Bell. Civ.* III.4), little is known of where they were located and nothing of any actual fortress; still less is known of where the great concentrations of the civil war period were placed: in 44 BC Cassius seems to have had 13 legions there, and for several years many of Antony's 22 or 23

legions must have been in the Syrian part of his half of the empire. In practice we read of one or more legions in garrison at Apamaea (Dio XLVIII.25ff), perhaps another at Antioch (Cic. *ad fam.* XII.15.7), and what were probably parts of legions on temporary detachment at Tyre (Jos. *Ant. Iud.* XIV) and perhaps Damascus (Jos. *Bell. Iud.* I.236; *Ant. Iud.* 14.295; cf. 288).

With Augustus, the normal legionary garrison of Syria was increased from two to four legions, but at no time in his long reign is there any hint of their permanent locations; the only information of this kind concerns one which was placed in Jerusalem temporarily in 4 BC (*Jos Bell. Iud.* II.40). With the Julio-Claudian period more is known: Cyrrhus was specifically reported as the fortress (*hiberna*, literally 'winter-quarters') of *VI Ferrata* in AD 18 (Tac. *Ann.* II.57); by 67 *XII Fulminata* was at Raphanaea in southern Syria (*Jos Bell. Iud.* VII.18) and *X Fretensis* was apparently on the Euphrates, perhaps at Zeugma. In the Early Empire, as in the Late Republic, the legionary soldiers were probably billeted in the towns, but no evidence has yet been recovered.

For the Flavian and Antonine period, legions can be placed with confidence: at Jerusalem after 70 (*X Fretensis*); at Caparcotna in the Jezreel Valley from, probably, the reign of Trajan (*VI Ferrata*); at Bostra after 106 (*III Cyrenaica*) (Fig. 71). Raphanaea (*III Gallica*) and probably Zeugma (*IV Scythica*) continued as legionary bases, while Samosata became one from probably 72 (initially *VI Ferrata* and/or *III Gallica*, then finally *XVI Flavia Firma*). Under the Severi, the new Mesopotamian legions can be added: at Singara (*I Parthica*) (Fig. 73) and perhaps at Nisibis (*III Parthica*). By the end of the fourth century the list can be amended, according to the *Notitia Dignitatum*, to include the following: Apatna (*III Parthica*) and Circesium (*IV Parthica*) in Osrhoene; Sura (*XVI Flavia Firma*) (Fig. 63) and Orisa (*IV Scythica*) (cf. Fig. 84) in Syria Coele; Danaba (*III Gallica*) and Palmyra (*I Illyricorum*) (Fig. 82) in Syria Phoenice; Betthorus (*IV Martia*) (Figs. 76–7) in Arabia and Aila (*X Fretensis*) in Palaestina (below, p. 125). Physical remains are known at few sites (see in general: Keppie, 1986; Kennedy, 1987). Conversely, at Udruh (Figs. 79, 80) there are the remains of an apparent fortress that is not recorded in the sources.

Finally, the short-lived legionary fortress base at Apamaea may be mentioned. This city, the former Seleucid military capital of Syria, had Roman troops in garrison in the Late Republic (above, p. 122). Recent Belgian excavations on the site have produced epigraphic evidence for the presence there almost three centuries later, in the Severan period, of a considerable force, including the *Legio II Parthica*. The latter was normally based at Albanum south of Rome but seems to have been stationed at Apamaea during the Parthian War of Caracalla and Macrinus (216-18) and at the time of the Persian War of Severus Alexander (231-3). Partly from traces on very small scale air photographs, the excavator has proposed the location of a large camp just east of the city (Balty, 1987, 239-41).

· *Classification* ·

Six places are illustrated, of which three, or probably four, seem to be clearly identifiable as legionary fortresses. The remainder – because of their modest size – would probably have been included in one of the subsequent sections dealing with forts, but for the fact that legions are known or suspected to have been there. They may be divided into three categories:

• Larger fortresses: Bostra (Fig. 71) is the only known eastern fortress comparable to the sites familiar in the Western Empire. It is a large rectangle enclosing 16.8 ha. (41.5 acres), an area appropriate for the *c*.5000 men of the *legio III Cyrenaica*, which was stationed there from the early second century onwards.

Singara (Fig. 73), which was first garrisoned permanently in the early third century, had an area of c. 17 ha. (42 acres). Its plan was irregular, perhaps because of the hilly site on which it stood.

Nothing is known of the interior buildings at either place.

• Smaller fortresses: Lejjun and Udruh (Figs. 76-7, 79-80) are strongly defended sites, 4.6 ha. (11.4 acres) and 4.7ha. (11.6 acres) respectively in area. The former began its life in the late third/ early fourth century and would have been suitable for a legion of that period. Udruh may have had an earlier origin, but the visible fortifications are strikingly similar to those at Lejjun. The interior buildings of both survive in ruins.

• Possible smaller fortresses: Palmyra (Tadmor) (Fig. 82) and Souriya (above, Fig. 63) were cities (the former by far the more important of the two) that are known to have had legions stationed in them at a fairly late period. As noted above (p. 115 and Fig. 63), the visible remains at Souriya are largely those of the fortress city, and there are problems in accepting the *c*.4 ha. (10 acres) fort as the base of *Legio XVI Flavia Firma*. Tayibeh (Fig. 84) may have been the location for a Late Empire legion. The possible site of a

FIGURE 70 Location map.

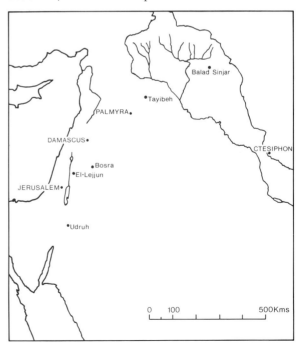

modest fort there (area perhaps 2 ha./5 acres) could have accommodated a very small fourth century legion.

FIGURE 71 Bosra eski-Sham, Dera'a, Syria (32°31′N 36°28′E): vertical view. *Photograph: Royal Air Force (c. 1930). From Israel Department of Antiquities. Supplied by A. Segal. Cf. Segal, 1981, III, fig. 7*

· Comments ·

At first sight it is disappointing to find that the long list of literary references to places where legions were stationed is only followed by such a short list of sites with actual remains of fortresses.

However, several sites shown on the air photographs are clearly of great archaeological importance, being almost free of later building. Their state is changing: at Udruh, for example, a modern village has grown near the spring and there has been much robbing of stone from the fortress, but to the archaeologist it is still a splendidly preserved site. It is very satisfactory to know that excavations have taken place at both Udruh and Lejjun in the last few years, so that a beginning has now been made on the task of unravelling the history of two fortresses at least.

At Aqaba, a place which has been inhabited continuously, because of its situation at the head of one arm of the Red Sea, there have recently been important discoveries, which perhaps suggest the later development of sites that were not deserted after they were lost by Rome. Here a newly discovered fortification seems to have a plan almost exactly like that of a half-size version of Lejjun – but it is dated to the Early Islamic period (Whitcomb, 1988, 28; cf. Fig. 76). During excavations a fragmentary Latin inscription of the Tetrarchy or the house of Constantine was discovered (MacAdam, 1989, forth.). As mentioned above, Aqaba, the ancient *Aila*, was the base of *Legio X Fretensis* from the early fourth

century at least, and it is therefore tempting to associate the inscription with the construction of its fortress. The Islamic fortification now being investigated may have been influenced by the design of Lejjun (and/or Udruh) or even by the as yet unidentified fortress of *X Fretensis* at Aqaba.

BOSRA ESKI-SHAM, SYRIA
(Figs. 71 and 72)

This vertical view shows the plan of the modern city of Bosra, the ancient *Bostra*, very clearly. Although Poidebard must have flown near the town, or over it, he published no photograph in *La Trace de Rome* or elsewhere. The site of the legionary fortress has now been identified with confidence in the north of the town. The large rectangular enclosure of *c.* 463 × 363 m./1520 × 1190 ft (16.8 ha./41.5 acres) covers approximately the space required by the *Legio III Cyrenaica*, which is known to have been stationed there from soon after the creation of Arabia in 106. None of the internal buildings has been identified, but stretches of wall, parts of the south gate and stamped legionary tiles have all been recorded. Just outside the south-west angle is a major perennial spring (Sartre, 1985: 96; Brulet, 1984).

Also clearly visible in the photograph are the circus and the theatre (re-used as a fortress in the Middle Ages), and two large reservoirs. Within the town itself, it is easy to pick out the line of the major colonnaded street running from the West Gate and one or two of the others which intersect. The white line to the right of the theatre is a scratch on the negative, not a road.

Bostra was the point of commencement for the great *Via Nova Traiana*, which was constructed between 106 and 11 to link Syria to the Red Sea (Figs. 31–4).

BALAD SINJAR, IRAQ
(Figs. 73, 74 and 75)

Figure 73 is still the only known vertical photograph showing the whole area of the Roman town of Singara. Much of the circuit of walls and towers is outlined by shadow. The rest of the circuit can be followed by the streets of the modern town. To the east of the town (the left), the defences enclose an outlying hill, on which

FIGURE 72 Bosra eski-Sham, Dera'a, Syria (32°31′N 36°28′E): sketch plan of the city and fortress. *Drawn by D.N.Riley after Sartre, 1985, Ill. 1, and from the air photograph.*

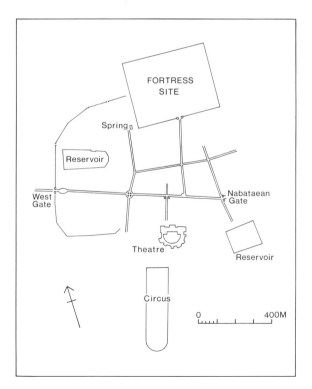

was the citadel. Much of the land shown is on the foothills of the Jebel Sinjar and the only flat ground is the cultivated area seen at the top of the photograph. The stream bed which runs through the defences from north to south is an important element in the plan. It carries water for only part of the year (Gregory and Kennedy (Stein), 1985, 9). Today the stream simply passes through wide breaks in the defences. In antiquity

FIGURE 73 Balad Sinjar, Neineva, Iraq (36°40′N 41°51′E): vertical view from a height of 13,500 ft (4,100 m.). *Photograph: C.I.D.F. (n.d., 1925/32). From Poidebard, 1934, Pl. CLIV*

there were probably conduits under 'water gates', and the stream may have been embanked within the city and would have required bridges (cf. Dara: Whitby, 1986, 742–9).

The steeply sloping ground at the eastern end of the fortress is shown by an oblique view from a perilously low flying height (Fig. 74), one of two dozen photographs taken from Stein's aircraft. In the foreground is part of the north wall, emphasized by shadow, and in the distance the modern town.

The site was occupied briefly by the forces of Trajan (Dio LXVIII. 22.2) and, presumably Lucius Verus, in the course of their respective

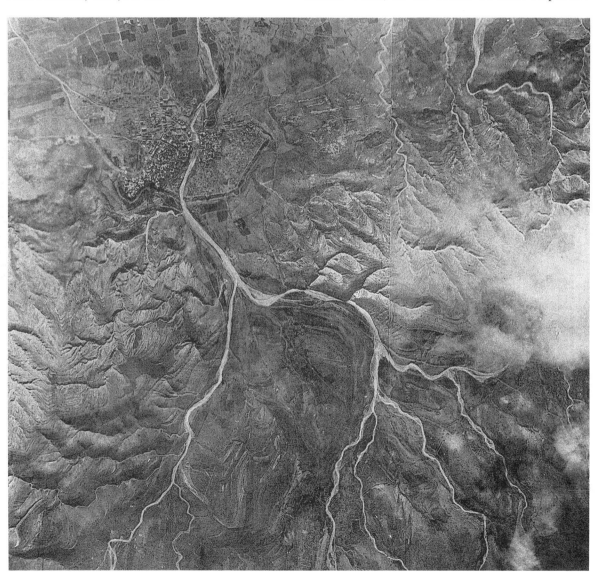

Parthian Wars. Only under Septimius Severus was a permanent garrison, consisting of two legions, placed in Mesopotamia (Dio LV.24.4). The recently discovered lower part of a long-known inscription from Aphrodisias in the province of Asia, dated to the reigns of Severus and Caracalla, reads: '*I Parthica Severiana Antoniniana* which legion is at Singara in Mesopotamia by

the River Tigris' (Speidel and Reynolds, 1985). We cannot trace the history of the fortress over the next century and half, but Cassius Dio, writing in the years after Severus' death in 211, made it clear that even in his own time the salient of north-eastern Mesopotamia, intended to be a 'bulwark for Syria', was proving indefensible (LXXV.3.3). It is probable that in the mid-third century the region was held for a time by the Persians (Oates, 1968, 99). Later, Ammianus Marcellinus (XX.6.9; cf. XIX.9.9) reports that during numerous sieges, Singara had always been too distant to reinforce and several times had been taken together with its garrison. It appears

FIGURE 74   Balad Sinjar, Neineva, Iraq (36°40′N 41°51′E): oblique view looking east-south-east from a height of 100 ft (30 m.). *Photograph: Royal Air Force (10.50; 24 March 1938). Stein Archive (Institute of Archaeology, London. Inv. no. AP.1769).*

in Roman history for the penultimate time in 359-60 when, despite the resistance of two legions in garrison, *I Flavia* and *I Parthica* (Amm. Marc. XX.6.8), the forces of Shapur II broke in; three years later, the Emperor Jovian officially ceded it to the Persians (Amm. Marc. XXV.7.9).

The surviving defences consist of the citadel on an outlying hill, together with an irregular wall circuit with massive U-shaped towers at intervals. The walls enclose an area of high ground split by the southwards flowing seasonal stream. The lower ground in the western half of

FIGURE 75 Balad Sinjar, Neineva, Iraq (36°40′N 41°51′E): plan of the fortress. *After Oates 1968, fig.8 and Stein, unpublished drawing in the British Museum, Department of Western Asiatic Antiquities, Small Archive, Plan 29, with additions.*

the site contains a large permanent pool, a source of water which was vital in this arid region. Allowing for dead space inside, the circuit encloses some 17 ha. (42 acres) of usable ground. Oates has dated the surviving defences to the early fourth century (1968, 106; cf. Lander, 1984, 226). Probably by that date, certainly by the time of its seizure by the Persians half a century later, the small legions of the Late Empire garrison would have required only a portion of the area available within the circuit. Thus, for the last generation or two of its existence it would be more accurate to describe Singara as a 'Fortress City' (cf. above, Ch. 9).

The shape of the circuit is so unlike that of a traditional Early Empire legionary fortress (cf. Bostra, above Fig. 71), as to raise doubts about the Severan origin of it. The legion stationed

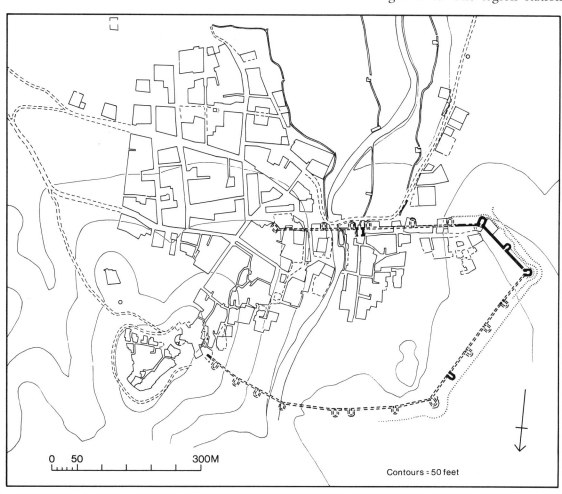

0 50   300M

Contours = 50 feet

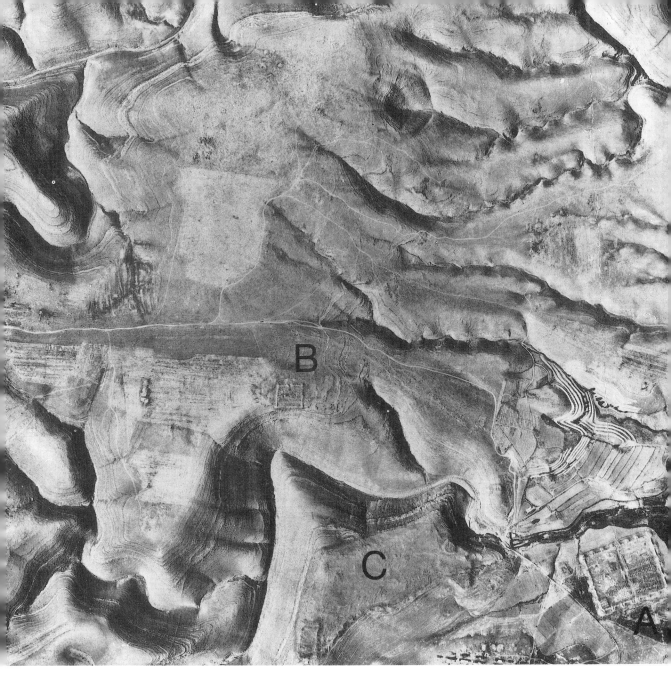

FIGURE 76 El-Lejjun, Al-Kerak, Jordan (31°13′N
35°48′E): vertical view of the fortress (lower right
corner) and Khirbet el-Fityan (centre). *Photograph:
Institut Géographique National. Royal Jordanian
Geographic Centre (15.27; 1982). Supplied by
S.T.Parker. Cf. Parker, 1987, 189, pl.20.*

there by Severus was one of three newly formed
by him. The sister fortress of one of the other
two – *II Parthica* – was at Albanum south of
Rome, where there is a fortification of traditional
'playing card' plan without external towers, more
elongated than usual, but otherwise perfectly
acceptable as part of the Early Empire military
architecture (plan most conveniently found in
Hassall, 1983, 123, fig. 13). Although the unortho-
dox plan of Singara is reminiscent in the Roman
West of such sites as Abrittus in Lower Moesia
(Lander, 1984, 219, fig. 225) and Pevensey in
Britain (S. Johnson, 1983, fig. 79), it may nevertheless closely preserve the shape of the earlier
Severan fortress. Certainly the configuration of

FIGURE 77 El-Lejjun, Al-Kerak, Jordan (31°13′N 35°48′E): oblique view looking north across the fortress from a height of 200 ft (65 m.). *Photograph: Royal Air Force (08.35; 25 May 1937). Aerial Photographic Archive, Institute of Archaeology, London, RAF no. 12743.*

FIGURE 78 El-Lejjun, Al-Kerak, Jordan (31°13′N 35°48′E): plan of the fortress. *After Parker, 1986, fig.25.*

the ground around the spring would have given little scope for a traditional 'playing card' shape, and none of the surviving air photographs gives any hint of an earlier and different circuit there, or in the immediate vicinity. The alternative explanation is that the circuit was already in place around the high ground in the late second century and that it was simply taken over by the Roman forces and later rebuilt with projecting towers.

The drawing of the fortress and its vicinity (Fig. 75) was made by superimposing the plan by Oates on part of a beautifully contoured survey of the area prepared by Stein's assistant, Iltifat

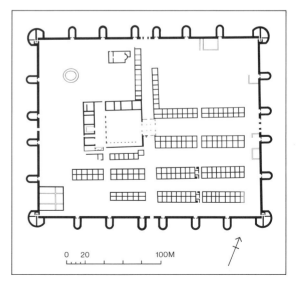

Hussein. This survey also shows the defences, but while the shape of the walled area is the same as that on Oates' plan, there are several discrepancies in the positions of the towers. Because of the heaps of debris covering parts of the circuit (Fig. 74), it has not proved possible to reconcile the problem areas by reference to the air photographs taken for Stein.

EL-LEJJUN, JORDAN
(Figs. 76, 77 and 78)

Two photographs, one oblique, the other vertical, show the site of the fortress at el-Lejjun (A on vertical). The vertical also shows the sites of the fort at Khirbet el-Fityan (B), which is described below (Fig. 120), and of a large Early Bronze Age town (C). Near the fortress, at the lower edge of the photograph, are the two lines of buildings of the early-twentieth-century Ottoman barracks.

Located in central Jordan, 16 km (10 miles) north-east of Kerak, the fortress, though much smaller than those at Singara or Bostra, is one of the largest known Roman fortifications in the East: 242 × 190 m./790 × 620 ft (4.6 ha./11.4 acres). It is of a large and impressive build: walls of mortared cut masonry 2.4 m. (8 ft) thick, with massive fan-shaped corner towers, 19 m. (62 ft) in diameter, and 20 U-shaped interval towers, which each project 11 m. (36 ft). They have been extensively robbed for stone, as can be seen on the larger-scale oblique photograph. The interior is filled by the ruins of a substantial *principia* (headquarters building) and several rows of barrack blocks. Various structures have also been identified in the *vicus* outside to the east and south of the fortress, though they do not show up well on the photographs. Water supply was assured by the important spring nearby. Two Roman roads pass by to the east; one of them, which goes to Qasr Bshir (Fig. 122), is marked by an undated milestone (Thomsen, 1917, 57, no. 176).

Excavation in recent years has shown that the original construction took place about AD 300. There was, however, extended occupation taking the fortress through to the sixth century, though with significant internal modifications.

Although proof is yet to emerge, it has long been common to identify this site by the entry in the *Notitia Dignitatum (Or. XXXVII.22)* which places under the command of the *Dux Arabiae*, the *Praefectus Legionis Quartae Martiae, Betthoro*. As already mentioned (p. 19), such legions, probably raised in the late third or early fourth century, are believed to have been rather smaller than their Early Principate counterparts. Certainly this fortress is only about one fifth the expected size for a legion, the excavator believing the garrison to have been 1000-1500 (Parker, 1986, 58-74; cf. now Groot *apud* Parker, 1987, 261-310).

UDRUH, JORDAN
(Figs. 79, 80 and 81)

The second of the late fortresses in Jordan is also illustrated by both vertical and oblique photographs, which are rather similar to those of Lejjun. Inside the walls of the fortress, shadows emphasize the traces of collapsed buildings, some of which are in straight lines. Outside its southeast corner, uneven ground shows the site of the *vicus* (at the right on the oblique, at the upper centre of the vertical). When the photographs were taken, the only recent buildings were a handful of small houses along the east side of the fortress (nearest the fields) and a large rectangular Ottoman fort on the north wall. Since then a village has grown, covering much of the *vicus* and part of the eastern side of the fortress.

Udruh lies 12 km (7.5 miles) east of Petra, located amidst a network of watch towers and roads. To the west is the great *Via Nova Traiana*. A perennial spring attracted settlement in antiquity as today, and a striking feature of the site is the agriculture stretching out from the northeast angle of the fortress near where the present spring lies. Additional water was supplied by foggaras, extensive traces of which have been identified to the south-east (beyond the area of the photograph).

The fortress is a polygon, or it might be called a slightly irregular quadrilateral, with a bend in one side. Walls of 246 × 207 × 248 × 177 m. (800 × 673 × 806 × 576 ft) enclose an area of *c.* 4.7 ha. (11.6 acres). Despite the less regular shape, its size and the appearance and dimensions of its defences are strikingly similar to el-Lejjun

(Fig. 76): four massive corner towers, again fan-shaped, with diameters of *c.* 20 m. (66 ft), and again 20 U-shaped interval towers, *c.* 8.5 m. (28 ft) wide, projecting *c.* 11.2 m. (37 ft). In the

interior, most of the buildings, like much of the wall circuit, have now been robbed away. A *principia* has been identified and investigated, but otherwise there are only faint indications of a regular layout (cf. Killick, 1987, 4).

The date is more of a problem. The current excavator has found no evidence yet which would lead him to see a foundation date for the circuit necessarily later than the Trajanic period. That there might well have been a military presence on so important a site in the early second

FIGURE 79 Udruh, Ma'an, Jordan (30°19′N 35°35′E): vertical view of the fortress. *Photograph: Hunting (September 1953). Copyright: Royal Jordanian Geographic Centre. Supplied from Aerial Photographic Archive for Archaeology in the Middle East, HAS 47.080.*

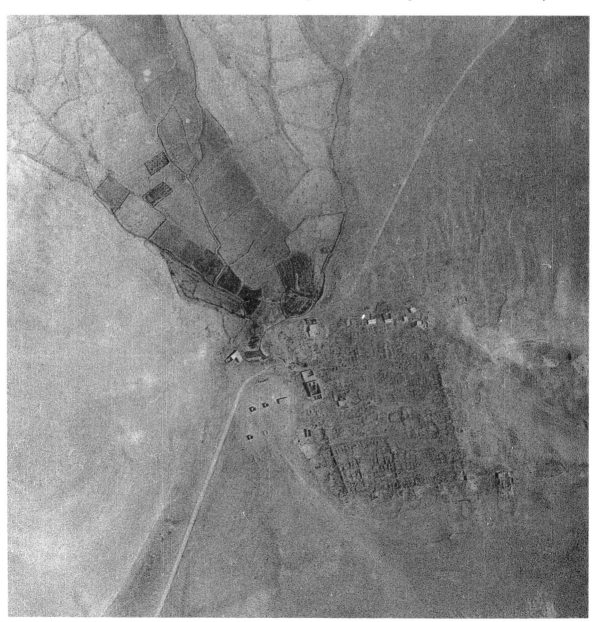

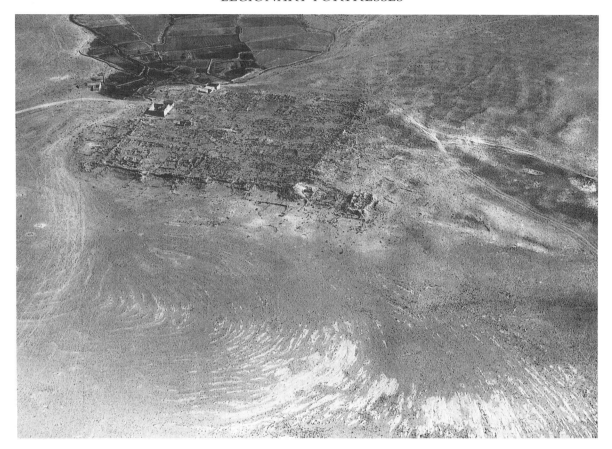

FIGURE 80 Udruh, Ma'an, Jordan (30°19′N 35°35′E): oblique view of the fortress looking east from a height of 400 ft. (c.125 m.). *Photograph: Royal Air Force (30 November, 1933). Stein Archive (Bodleian Library, Oxford, Stein Ms. 331, fol. 43).*

FIGURE 81 Udruh, Ma'an, Jordan (30°19′N 35°35′E): plan of the fortress. *After Killick, 1983, 113, fig. 2.*

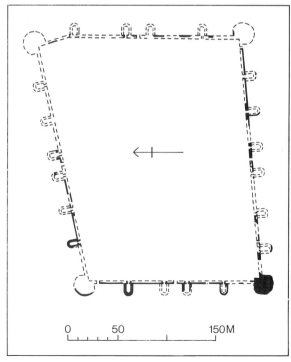

century is easily accommodated; that the circuit we see is of that date is more difficult to accept. At the other extreme, remodelling seems to have continued down into the sixth century (Killick, 1983; 1986; 1987; cf. Gregory and Kennedy (Stein), 1985, 425ff; Parker, 1986, 94–8).

As at Lejjun, the garrison could have been of the order of 1000 to 1500. For the early second century that is too large for any one auxiliary unit and too small for an entire legion; it would, however, accord with the size of a Late Roman legion.

FIGURE 82 Palmyra (Tadmor), Homs, Syria
(34°33′N 38°17′E): oblique view looking west.
Photograph: Petit (Autumn 1932?). From Poidebard,
1934, Pl.LXVII.

PALMYRA, SYRIA
(Figs. 82 and 83)

This striking photograph captures one of the
most impressive views of Palmyra, the Temple
of Bel from the south-east. In the clear desert air,
the houses of the modern village of Tadmor and,
beyond, stretching into the distance, the columns
and buildings of the ancient city are seen very
distinctly. In the background is the Valley of the
Tombs.

The location of Palmyra at the principal oasis
of the Syrian Desert, 160 km (100 miles) east of
Emesa and nearly 250 km (155 miles) north-east
of Damascus, made it an essential link on a major
route for caravan traffic from the Persian Gulf to
the cities of Syria and, beyond, to the ports
of the Levant, which shipped all round the
Mediterranean. Despite its relative isolation, it
could not hope to remain independent of Roman
power in the region. Roman political influence
can be detected through the interference of
governors of the Julio-Claudian period beginning

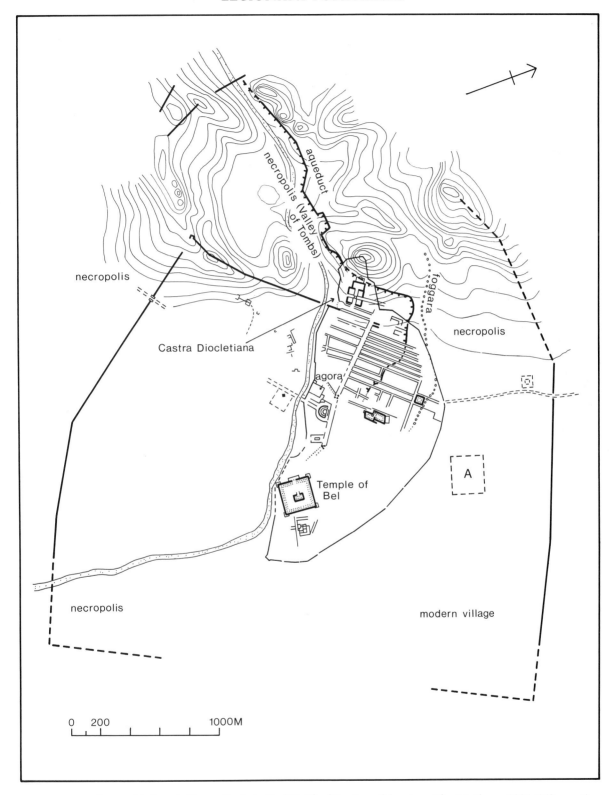

FIGURE 83 Palmyra (Tadmor), Homs, Syria (34°33'N 38°17'E): plan of the city. *After Matthews, 1984, 160, map 1.*

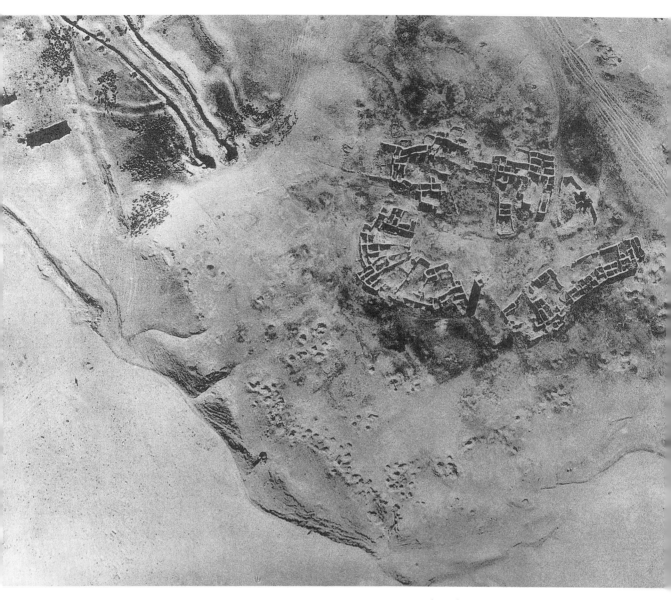

FIGURE 84 Tayibeh, Homs, Syria (35°5′N 38°55′E): vertical view from a height of 4400 ft (1350 m.). *Photograph: de Boysson (09.30; 23 October, 1930). From Poidebard, 1934, Pl. LXXI*

in AD 18 during the visit of Augustus' adopted son Germanicus. Likewise, the road built in 75 linking it to the Euphrates entailed a tightening of that control. Nevertheless, throughout the first two centuries of the Principate, Palmyra maintained its own forces to police the desert and provide protection for the lucrative caravans. There is no evidence of any permanent Roman

garrison and Palmyra appears as a client-state, ruled by an oligarchy rather than by a king or prince.

The earliest known Roman garrison, the first of a series attested by inscriptions, is the *Ala I Ulpia Singularium* in the 150s. Its successor is recorded as laying out an exercise area in 167 (Speidel, 1972). We do not, however, know the fort in which these regiments were based. There is a possible location for it in the rectangular enclosure (A on Fig. 83) north of the city (off Fig. 82 on the upper right) noted by French archaeologists in the 1920s, but soon lost beneath the modern village (Richmond, 1963, 49). That, however, was very large: c. 183 × 229 m. (600 × 750 ft), i.e. 4.2 ha. (10.33 acres), an area in excess of what would be required even by one of the rare *alae milliariae*. Although it may be best to treat this site with caution, it should be borne in mind that in the mid second century, Palmyra may have been the base for the *Ala I Ulpia (Palmyrenorum?) dromedariorum milliaria* (*AE* 1947, 171; cf. *CIL* XVI, 106). A fort to accomodate camels (if they were not simply coralled outside) would necessarily have been large.

The capture and then sack of the city by Aurelian in 274 led to its garrisoning by a legion, the *I Illyricorum*, which was still there at the time of the *Notitia Dignitatum* (Or. XXXII.30). The base associated with this force is the so-called Camp of Diocletian, an enclosed area of c. 8 ha. (20 acres) (which included some dead ground) on the hills at the western end of the great colonnaded street. It included a fine example of a military *principia* (Gawlikowski, 1984).

TAYIBEH, SYRIA (Fig. 84)

A deserted Arab village (now re-occupied) stands on a large square platform, which Poidebard identified as the site of a fort (1934, 79). The outline of the defences is not easy to see at first, but is made clearer by following the lines of pits dug to rob stone from the fort walls, seen on the lower part of the picture. At the upper left corner are trenches dug in modern times to channel water from a spring, near which can be seen numerous flocks of sheep and a bedouin tent. No sizes are given by Poidebard, but a rough estimate may be based on the size of the four-bay bedouin tent, from which it may be suggested that the length of the sides was about 150 m. (c.500 ft), and the area enclosed about 2.25ha. (5.5 acres).

The site has been identified with the ancient *Oresa*, a name given in various forms by Ptolemy (*Geog.* V. 14), the Peutinger Table and the *Notitia Dignitatum*. This last records: *Praefectus Legionis Quartae Scythicae, Oresa* (Or. XXXIII.27), under the *Dux Syriae*. The legions *XVI Flavia Firma* and *IV Scythica* had previously been based at, respectively, Samosata and Zeugma on the upper bend of the Euphrates. It is possible that both were brought round to the south-east at some stage after the creation of the province of Mesopotamia in the Severan period. In that case, with *XVI Flavia* certainly at Souriya/Sura (Fig. 63) and *I Illyricorum* at Palmyra, it is likely that *IV Scythica* would lie somewhere between the two. Tayibeh is almost exactly at the mid-point (Kennedy, 1988a).

As a prospective legionary fortress it is of course very small – less than one-seventh the size of Bostra and about half the size of even the small fourth-century fortresses at Lejjun (Fig. 77) and Udruh (Fig. 79). It would be necessary to assume a force of about 1000 men, though that is possible for one of the Late Empire small legions (above, p. 19). The only evidence from the site that points to occupation in the Roman period is a bilingual – Greek and Palmyrene – text of 134 (*IGRR* III: 1057).

· CHAPTER TEN ·

Forts

Scores of forts are known in the region. They range in size from the very large such as Ain Sinu I (Fig. 167), which at 10.6 ha. (26.2 acres) was bigger than the legionary fortresses of the Late Empire, to the very small like Upper Zohar (Fig. 149), which at 0.034 ha. (0.08 acres) was plainly no more than a modest garrison point. Most, however, are in the range 0.1–5 ha. (0.25–12.4 acres) Inscriptions provide evidence of date for a few, mostly in north Jordan, some are dated by association with a confirmed Roman road, and a few have been excavated, but many are treated as Roman only on the basis of location and character, i.e. they are in what is demonstrably a Roman military zone and have the regular appearance commonly associated with Roman military architecture.

In so far as they can be categorized by date, most of the forts are attributable to the Late Roman period, the fourth century or later. There is no known fort of the first century BC, only one, Tell el-Hajj, on the Euphrates (for which no aerial view is known), dates from the first century AD, a handful are or may belong to the second century, and rather more for the third century. Only after that do dated military installations become common. In part at least, the explanation is to be found in the first century AD practice of placing garrisons in the towns of the province and in the fact that large tracts of the desert region, where sites are well-preserved and aerial photography is useful, were at first policed by not Rome but the troops of a native ruler or the caravan guards of Palmyra. Town garrisons, a feature of the early province of Syria, re-appear in the Late Roman period, e.g. at Umm el-Jemal (Fig. 130), counterparts in the desert areas of the

great fortress cities like Amida, Dara and Nisibis (cf. Singara, Fig. 73) in the north. Dura-Europos (Fig. 60), heavily garrisoned in the late second and first half of the third centuries, may be seen as a link between the two periods.

The scarcity of well-established evidence of date makes it difficult to categorize forts. One cannot, of course, treat the military architecture of the desert frontier region in isolation from what was happening elsewhere in the East, or indeed within the Empire as a whole. To some extent this task has been tackled by the publication in 1984 of Lander's *Roman Stone Fortifications: Variation and Change from the First Century AD to the Fourth*. However, the present study not only includes a number of sites excluded by Lander, because they were outside his time frame or definition, but also others not then known to him or now better understood, as well as a few too uncertain as Roman to be useful for his purposes. It has seemed reasonable to include here a number of forts of uncertain date, both because they were identified as Roman by Poidebard or Stein and because, with the recent recognition that such previously uncertain sites as Bir Haidar (Fig. 91) and Ertaje (Fig. 180) were Roman, a similar date has become more likely for at least some of the problem sites (see further below, pp. 148, 224ff.

A systematic study of Roman military architecture in the East through to the Moslem conquests is required, and for that we can look forward to the doctoral research currently being undertaken at Sheffield University by Shelagh Gregory. For our purposes here, it has seemed best to keep the number of categories small. The division has been made crudely by design, i.e. by plan and architecture (if enough survives), and by size, though it has not always been clear where to draw the line between 'large' and 'small' forts. The term 'fort' has been used to define all military installations which fall in function between the bases for legions and the towers garrisoned by a handful of soldiers as a watch post (above, p. 19).

In the Early Empire, a typical fort, the evidence for which comes almost wholly from the West, was usually the 'playing-card' shape – rectangular with rounded corners. In practice there were many variations, but standard features were straight sides, rounded corners, and towers set *inside* the walls, except perhaps at the gates. The sizes of forts varied according to the accommodation required by the unit(s) in garrison, but normally even the smallest and commonest unit, a *Cohors quingenaria peditata*, needed about 1.5 ha. (3.7 acres). About one-fifth to one-quarter of the auxiliary regiments in the provinces under discussion were cavalry. Mostly about 500 strong, these would have required more than twice as much space, 3.5 ha. (8.6 acres). Moreover, we know that on occasion, two or more regiments (in one instance, Apsaros on the Black Sea, it is reported (Arrian, *Periplus*, VI.1) to have reached five) could be stationed together in a permanent fort which was naturally much larger than the average for a single unit (for sizes, see Hassall, 1983; cf. A. Johnson, 1983, 292ff).

Internally, the arrangement of buildings varied in Early Empire forts, though conforming to a broad scheme. Normally an *intervallum* road ran around the interior of the defences, and within it a headquarters building and a commander's house were located centrally, with much of the remaining space occupied by rows of regular barrack blocks; granaries, stores and workshops were also fitted in (A. Johnson, 1983).

In the Later Empire, the character of forts changed considerably, and here the evidence from the East can be drawn on more extensively. An important group of sites is that along the 'Voie des Hans', a section of the *Strata Diocletiana*. This road is marked by milestones giving distances and naming places which may be equated confidently with forts and regiments listed in the *Notitia Dignitatum*. In conformity with the reduction in size of all units (above, p. 19), forts are much smaller: thus, the *Cohors V Pacata Alamannorum* was located at Khan Aneybeh (Fig. 155) which covers only 0.19 ha. (0.47 acres), and the *Ala I Francorum* had only 0.17 ha. (0.42 acres) at Khan el-Qattar (Fig. 153).

Even allowing for the reduced size of units, forts are considerably smaller than might have been expected. At a number of forts this may be explained by the two-storey accommodation which reduced the ground area taken up by buildings (Figs. 124, 126, 147). In these forts the corners are angular, the plans are generally square or sub-square and the external walls may reach 4–5 m. (13–16.5 ft). The most striking new features, however, are the great towers which now appear, normally projecting partially or in entirety, and often massive both in build and height. On the smaller forts they normally appear at the angles and in some cases flank the gateways (e.g. Figs. 141, 146); on the larger there were also interval towers on the curtain walls (e.g. Figs. 116, 119). In plan, the towers were usually square or rectangular, but diamond-shaped (Fig. 132), fan-shaped (Figs. 129, 154), and semi-circular designs (Fig. 129) also appeared.

Internally, much was different from earlier forts. The *intervallum* road was commonly replaced by rooms built against the external wall, leaving an open central courtyard (e.g. Figs. 123, 125, 127), under which a cistern was often located. With rooms against the walls, the flat tops of roofs could offer a broad elevated platform between the towers for the use of the garrison, instead of the more modest rampart walkway of Early Empire forts. The towers provided extra space for stores and accommodation. The rooms in forts must have served the same range of functions as before, but it is unusual to recognize any distinctive types of accommodation, though, interestingly, the evidence for stabling is clear in a few of these later forts, mangers being a distinctive element in some rooms (e.g. Fig. 123).

The new appearance reflects a change in function. From the third century onwards, forts are no longer the fortified bases of an aggressive confident army, but the garrison places of an army thinly spread over more stations in smaller units, and increasingly on the defensive (see above, p. 45f). Forts had to anticipate attack, perimeters be shortened, and the defenders given every advantage of strength, height and angle of fire Roman military architecture could provide.

Finally, a point which is true of most sites discussed in this book (above, p. 19), and must be stressed – the later use of many Roman forts. Some were robbed of stone and perhaps largely obliterated, even in Roman times, but many others were reconstructed and remodelled both in the Roman period and in later centuries. This re-use was especially frequent in the Early Islamic period. It is a commonplace that Ommayad rulers and notables occupied Roman forts along the desert's edge. Qasr el-Hallabat (Fig. 147) and Qasr el-Azraq (Fig. 126) are examples. In discussing the sites of forts it is imperative to keep in mind that the remains we see may be more than the decayed structures of the Roman period. Nevertheless, it is clear from recent work at Qasr el-Hallabat and at Qasr el-Azraq that, while their re-use involved refurbishment and decoration, it did not involve the destruction of the characteristic structure of the Roman fort. Many forts along the *Strata Diocletiana ('Voie des Hans')* were probably re-used. No adequate fieldwork has been carried out yet along this route, so detailed information is not available, but the shapes we see on the photographs are likely to be essentially those of the forts of the Roman period.

In the four sub-sections which follow, sites have been grouped typologically where possible, and the individual sites or groups ordered in a sequence from the best attested to the least.

·Large Forts Without·
External Towers

The forts in this category may be compared with those built to house auxiliary units in the Western Empire between the first and earlier third centuries, but it will not be certain that like is being compared with like until there is much more information about the dates of the Eastern forts. Of the twelve illustrated, nine are in Syria or Iraq, of which only one (Fig. 91) has been investigated on the ground, however briefly, since the days of Poidebard and Stein, who have left little more than good photographs and ground plans. In contrast, two of the three sites in Jordan have been the subject of recent investigation.

The photographs supply information about the shape and size of the defences of the forts, and in two cases a little about the buildings within. In shape, the forts are about evenly divided between square and oblong, but details of the outline are seldom entirely clear and it is

FIGURE 85 Location map.

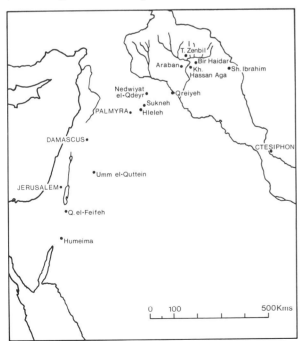

difficult to be certain that any had the rounded corners standard in the Early Empire in the West. Those illustrated here range in size from Qreiyeh at 4.85 ha. (12 acres) (Fig. 96) down to Sheikh Ibrahim at 0.78 ha. (1.93 acres) (Fig. 103) and Qasr el-Feifeh at 0.7 ha. (1.7 acres) (Fig. 88). When considering the size of the largest examples – Qreiyeh, Hleleh, Khirbet Hassan Aga and Humeima (Figs. 89, 94, 96, 98) – the areas of the small Late Empire legionary fortresses of Lejjun and Udruh may come to mind, but there are differences. Rather it is necessary to consider their capacity as Early Empire forts, in which case they could have accommodated several auxiliary units or even a combination of auxiliaries and legionaries. By the same standard Quttein, Bir Haidar and Nedwiyat al-Qdeyr (Figs. 86, 91-2) would be sufficient for the c. 500 men of an Early Empire regiment, but Sukneh, Feifeh, Tell Zenbil and Sheikh Ibrahim (Figs. 87-8, 100, 103) would have been rather small.

UMM EL-QUTTEIN, JORDAN
(Fig. 86)

This photograph of Umm el-Quttein shows the site as it was 25 years ago, when re-occupation of the deserted buildings of the small ancient town had not gone very far. Since then there has been much building and many changes. The print is unfortunately not sharp, having been greatly enlarged from the only available air photograph of the site, but this aerial view is most important because it shows what is probably the rectilinear shape of an otherwise unknown fort (arrowed) in the detached group of buildings in the northern part of the village (upper right). It also shows numerous other ancient features.

Quttein lies 26 km (16 miles) south-east of Bostra, just on the southern edge of the fertile Hauran. The remains recorded at the turn of the century included, notably, several early Christian structures and various tall towered houses (Butler,

FIGURE 86 Umm el-Quttein, Adjlun, Jordan
(32°20′N 36°37′E): vertical view. *Photograph:
Hunting (September 1953). Copyright: Royal Jordanian
Geographic Centre. Supplied from Aerial Photographic
Archive for Archaeology in the Middle East, no. HAS
61.129.*

1919, 137, ill. 116; cf. MacAdam, 1986, 367,
pl.13a). Most have now gone as a result of the
reoccupation of the site by a large modern village.
They are datable from the Nabataean to Early
Islamic period by dozens of inscriptions and from
coins found across the site. As with Umm el-

Jemal (Fig. 130), it would appear that a small native settlement had a Roman garrison imposed upon it. In the course of time, the settlement expanded northwards to adjoin the probable fort and, subsequently, when the army had moved out, civilians occupied the fort itself.

Most of the circuit of the fort defences is visible here except on the south-western corner. The overall dimensions are some 156 × 120 m./510 × 390 ft (1.87ha./4.6 acres), which would make this one of the largest forts in Arabia. An undated inscription from the site of a probable watch tower a few kilometres to the south-west records construction work by a detachment of the *legio III Cyrenaica*, but it is likely that the garrison of the apparent fort itself is that named on a large altar re-used in a building within the north-eastern corner of the circuit: *Cohors I[II?] Augusta Thracum Equitata*. There is some reason to believe that this unit must have been in this area in the early Principate; if so, the fort, about the right size for this regiment (500-strong and part-mounted), would have been built for it at that time (Kennedy and MacAdam, 1986; Kennedy, MacAdam and Riley, 1986.).

Just beyond the north-east angle is a large reservoir (A), similar to those at other sites (e.g. Fig. 128). A smaller ancient reservoir (B), lies just south of the fort. Both will have been fed by ground level aqueducts, one of which can be traced approaching the north side of the larger tank (C).

Just coming in on the left edge of the photograph is the surfaced Roman road from Bostra (D). Dated by milestones to the late third to early fourth centuries, its alignment, interestingly, is pointing not to the fort, but to the lower part of the town where the major towered buildings were once located. Beyond Quttein the road has been traced in places as far as the Azraq Oasis (Fig. 28).

Finally, we may note the large sub-rectangular enclosure (E), which is not visible on the ground. The texture of the ground in the interior is different from that outside. Its date and purpose are unknown; possibly a garden area.

SUKNEH, SYRIA (Fig. 87)

The rectangular earthwork shown partly by differences of surface texture and partly by shadow, covers the rubble walls (*murs de blocage*), of the fort. Poidebard's identification of round towers at the corners is possible but should be treated with some caution. Beyond and to the left of the fort, lines of pits give the courses of several underground channels or foggaras, dug to carry water from springs. From the appearance of the banks and mounds of soil near them, the foggaras had recently been cleared out.

The fort, which stands near a spring and a large village (*c.* 1500 people even in 1943), is about 65 km (40 miles) north-east of Palmyra, at the point where routes diverge, the one north to Sura, the other eastwards to Circesium. Between Sukneh and Palmyra is Erek, where a Flavian milestone was found (above, p. 77). During recent times it has been a strategically important point in the desert. In 1867 it was one of four posts (together with Deir es-Zor, Palmyra and Qaryateyn) given a force of Ottoman cavalry to control the bedouin (Lewis, 1987, 29ff). It remained a military station under the French Mandate, the location of a fort at the large village covering the northern approaches to Palmyra (Lunt, 1984, 109).

A statue base with a dedication to Jupiter was found at Sukneh, erected by Sex. Rasius Proculus, prefect of the *Cohors II Thracum* (*AE* 1911: 124). The text is dated to the second half of the second century (Devijver, 1976-80, R5). The site is not identified in the *Notitia Dignitatum*.

The rectangular enclosure visible in the photograph, was reported by Poidebard to measure 110 × 80m./360 × 260 ft (0.88 ha./2.17 acres). This would make it rather small for any Early Empire auxiliary unit: Quttein, for example (Fig. 86), is about twice this size for, apparently, a *cohors equitata*. (Cf. however small sites in Britain packed with barrack blocks: Pen Llystyn in Wales, 1.8 ha. (4.5 acres) is thought to have accommodated two infantry cohorts (Hassall, 1983, 118f) and Elginhaugh, 1.61 ha. (3.98 acres), with 14 barrack blocks (Hanson, 1988).)

FIGURE 87 Sukneh, Homs, Syria (34°54′N
38°52′E): vertical view. *Photograph: de Boysson (n.d.).*
From Poidebard, 1934, Pl. LXX.

QASR EL-FEIFEH, JORDAN
(Fig. 88)

The walls of a square enclosure with central
entrances in two opposing sides are shown very
clearly by the photograph. There are no visible
remains of structures inside. This is one of two
adjoining and very similar sites, 500 m. (*c.*1600
ft) apart, on the edge of the fertile Ghor el-Feifeh,
a region of marshland just below the southern
tip of the Dead Sea. Both were visited and
described by Frank (1934: 210ff, Pl.27 and Plans
11 and 12), before being photographed by Nelson
Glueck in the course of one of his flights with

Sq. Ldr. Traill in 1937 (Glueck, 1937, 20ff; cf.
above, p. 52). Glueck tentatively suggested a
Nabataean-Roman date; there is, however, no
dating evidence for this.

The easternmost site seen here is 84 × 84 m./
275 × 275 ft (0.7 ha/1.7 acres). As may be seen
from the photograph, a long aqueduct channel
runs from the hills to the enclosure, and then on
towards the second site (Glueck, 1939, 147,
150ff). Feifeh is conventionally identified with
Praesidium, which is just south of the Dead Sea
on the Madaba Mosaic Map (Avi-Yonah, 1954,
21). This place name should not be confused with
the *Praesidium* of the Peutinger Table, which is
identified with Khirbet el-Khalde, just north-east
of Aila on the Gulf of Aqaba. In the *Notitia*
Dignitatum are references to *Ala Secunda Felix*
Valentiana, apud Praesidium and *Cohors Quarta*

Frygum, Praesidio (Or. XXXIV.35 and 41). From the context in which they appear, it would seem that the first is certainly in the region immediately south of the Dead Sea, and probably the second too.

FIGURE 88 Qasr el-Feifeh (East), Al-Kerak, Jordan (30°27′N 35°27′E): oblique view looking south from a height of 200 ft (60 m.). *Photograph: Royal Air Force (07.30; 25 May 1937). Crawford Archive (Institute of Archaeology, London, RAF no. 12730)*

HUMEIMA, JORDAN
(Figs. 89 and 90)

Despite its inhospitable situation at a height of about 1000 m (*c.*3000 ft) in the desert of southern Jordan, the site shown by this photograph was clearly of some importance, consisting of at least one large military installation, numerous civil buildings, mainly houses, reservoirs, cisterns and an aqueduct system.

A grey-toned rectangle indicates the much ruined walls of a large fort (B), 204 × 147 m./ 660 × 475 ft (3 ha./7.4 acres), in the north-west corner of which the dark rectangle is an ancient reservoir. Inside its east gate (not clearly visible on the photograph but indicated on the map),

FIGURE 89 Humeima, Ma'an, Jordan (29°56'N 35°24'E): vertical view from a height of 12,500 ft (4000 m.). *Photograph: Hunting (September, 1953). Copyright: Royal Jordanian Geographic Centre. Supplied from Aerial Photographic Archive for Archaeology in the Middle East, inv. no. HAS 37.111.*

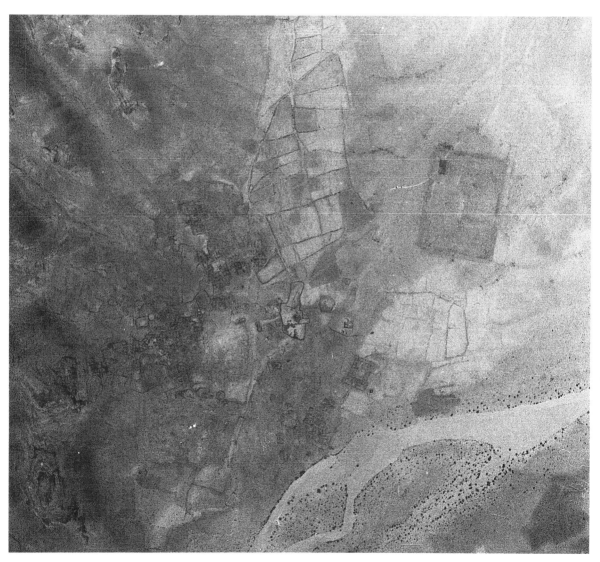

there may be traces of a line of buildings. There has been no excavation anywhere on the fort and we may only surmise an early date for it from its substantial size and the apparent absence of external towers (except those flanking the east gate, which have been seen on the ground: Eadie, 1984). It could have accommodated some 2000 infantry or a large cavalry force.

FIGURE 90 Humeima, Ma'an, Jordan (29°56'N 35°24'E): plan of the site. *Drawn by D.N.Riley from the air photograph.*

A survey team has recently planned a structure (D) south of the fort, which they identified as a *castellum*. Despite considerable enlargement from a copy negative, the details of this building appear to be clearer from the air than was evident to those working on the ground (cf. Eadie, 1984, Fig. 5a). As may be seen from the photograph, it is a very substantial structure, some 45 × 65 m. (147 × 212 ft). It consists in large part of ranges of rooms around four sides of a courtyard together with an apparent long room at the rear. It is very reminiscent of a military *principia* with

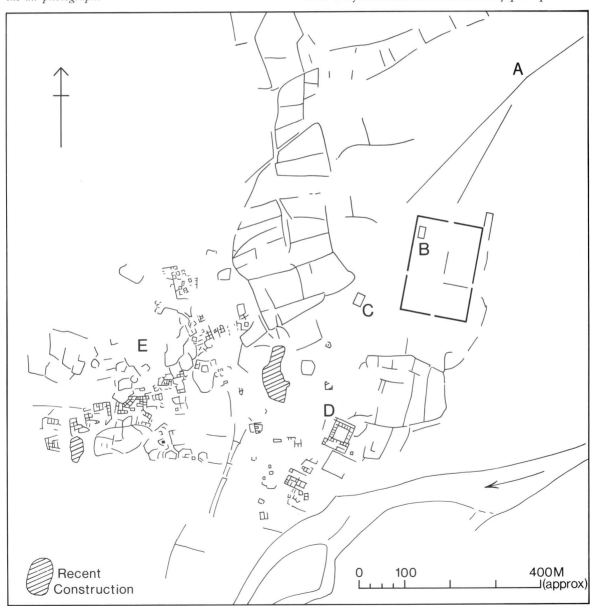

Recent Construction

0   100   400M
                                   (approx)

forehall (cf. A. Johnson, 1983, 104-32).

South-west of the fort, a network of dark lines shows the ruins of an extensive settlement. The buildings may be divided into two groups, of which that nearer the fort and including the large building (D), was more regularly planned than the other. This latter group (E), consists apparently of irregularly planned and located houses. Several churches have been identified by the ground survey.

Since the annual mean rainfall now is only 90 mm (3.5 in.), the elaborate water collection and storage arrangements must have been essential. There were cisterns, open reservoirs and a ground-level aqueduct bringing water from a spring 15 km (9 miles) away (Oleson, 1987). Its terminus may be seen just north of the large fort (A), with channels heading for the open reservoirs (B and C).

Something of the occupation history of the site may be traced from surface pottery sherds and literature. Pottery collected across the site gives a spread of dates from Nabataean to Early Islamic. This accords neatly with the literary evidence. Humeima has been identified with *Auara*, a town said to have been founded by the Nabataean king Aretas III (87-52 BC). The place name appeared again in Ptolemy's list (compiled in the early second century AD) of towns in the region, in the Peutinger Table road map and in the *Notitia Dignitatum (Or. XXXIV.25)*. It was mentioned in the fifth century Beer-Sheva Edict and finally in 687 sold to an Islamic notable, said to have constructed there a fortified dwelling.

The *Notitia* reference is of importance here. It attributes to the site the *Equites Sagittarii Indigenae*, a locally recruited regiment of mounted cavalry. Where this unit was based is not known – the fort is far too large for a small Late Empire unit of perhaps only 100–200 men. The '*castellum*' (D) would be a more appropriate size but its plan might make it a more likely candidate for the fortified Islamic dwelling.

Not visible on the photograph, but passing through or nearby is the *Via Nova Traiana*, the foundations of which and several milestones have been found both to the north and south. In this generally barren and very hot terrain, the presence of water at Humeima would have made the site a vitally important one for travellers.

Although this enlargement of part of a high-level vertical, the only photograph available, is unfortunately too small in scale to show many details of the ancient structures, we can take advantage of the large area covered to examine a little of the surrounding landscape. On the left of the photograph the darker toned area slopes up to the Jebel Qalkha, while on the right the paler toned part indicates the more reflective surface of flatter land near the Wadi Qalkha, a seasonal stream which crosses the lower right corner. There is little vegetation visible, except the bushes near the watercourse, seen as dark spots, but the fields in the middle of the photograph would have been used for crops similar to those still grown in the region with the aid of sparse winter rains. (Eadie, 1984; Oleson, 1987.)

BIR HAIDAR, SYRIA (Fig. 91)

In the foreground of this oblique photograph is the platform of what appears to be a decayed fort, c.120 × 100 m./390 × 325 ft (1.2 ha./3 acres), superimposed on which is a small square fort. Mounds along the wall line suggest towers, but none was detectable at ground level (information from Prof. D. Oates, 5 October 1987). Beyond the fort are the remains of many more buildings in an undefended area. A considerable amount of land is covered by modern cultivated fields, which have no doubt been extended much more widely in recent years.

The site is referred to as 'Camp au nord d'al-Hol' by Poidebard, and lies almost half way between Tell Brak and Lake Khatuniyeh, 12 km (7.5 miles) north of the latter. Although Poidebard was in no doubt that he was dealing with a Roman fort, his only evidence was its location and character (Poidebard, 1934, 158). Recently, however, pottery paralleled at Ain Sinu and dated to the first half of the third century has been identified, thus confirming that the site was occupied in the Roman period at least. It has been suggested that the superimposed structure was a 'small fort or *mansio*' (Oates, 1982, 198). Professor Oates now believes (pers. comm. 24 July 1987) that the site is that named on a modern map as Bi[r?] Haidar rather than the 'Tell Abu Jerade' he originally suggested (D. Oates, 1982, 198).

FIGURE 91 Bir Haidar, Al-Hasakeh, Syria (36°33′N 41°14′E): oblique view looking south. *Photograph: G. David (1930?). From Poidebard, 1934, Pl. CLI.*

NEDWIYAT EL-QDEYR, SYRIA
(Figs. 92 and 93)

On the smooth surface of the Hamada Desert may be seen the walls of the fort, which are shown on the south, east and west sides by quite distinct vegetation marks and on the north side by faint soil marks. It is not clear whether the corners of the fort are round or square. Inside the fort, traces of buildings appear as vegetation marks. Outside the walls, slight shadows give the position of a wide ditch, and to the left is part of a large structure, which is shown faintly by pale-toned vegetation marks and a line of what appear to be stone-robbing pits. In the foreground are wells, near which is a flock of sheep. The importance of this source of water is indicated by many bedouin tents, regularly disposed (cf. Poidebard, 1934, 81).

The site lies just east of the road from Palmyra to Sura, 100 km (62 miles) north-north-east of the former. Although the shape of the fort is not certain, the 'playing card' outline cannot be dismissed. The gates are placed in the middle of the short sides and two-thirds of the way along the long sides. This information all points to a Roman fort, the style of which would best suit the first or second centuries. The size, *c.*120 × 80 m./390 × 260 ft (*c.*1 ha./2.47 acres), would suit a standard infantry cohort of some 500 men.

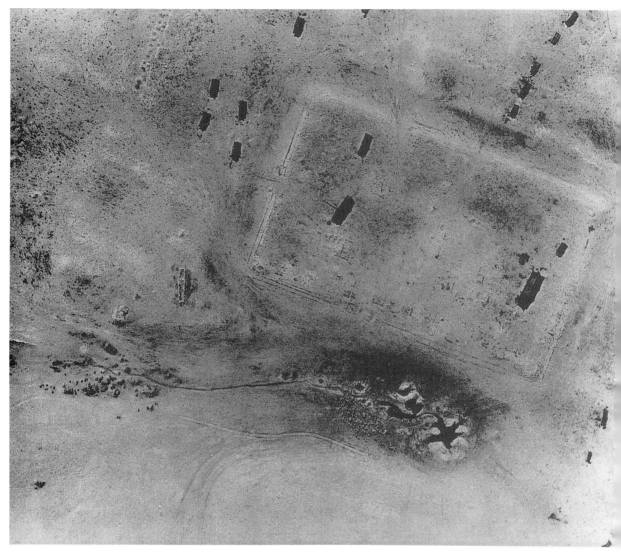

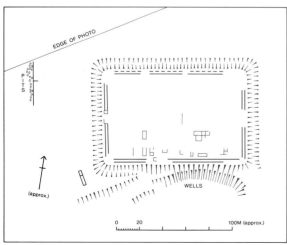

FIGURE 92 Nedwiyat el-Qdeyr, Homs, Syria

4600 ft (1425 m.). *Photograph: de Boysson (09.50; 23 October 1930). From Poidebard, 1934, Pl. LXXIII.* (35°16′N 38°50′E): sketch plan of the fort. *Drawn by* FIGURE 93 Nedwiyat el-Qdeyr, Homs, Syria (35°16′N 38°50′E): sketch plan of the fort. *Drawn by D.N.Riley from Poidebard's air photograph.*

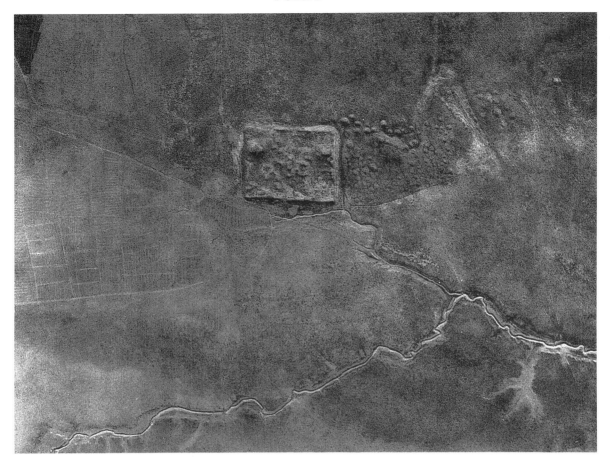

FIGURE 94 Khirbet Hassan Aga, Al-Hasakeh, Syria (41°04′E 36°20′N): vertical view. *Photograph: Jullian (n.d.). From Poidebard, 1934, Pl. CXLII.*

FIGURE 95 Khirbet Hassan Aga, Al-Hasakeh, Syria (41°04′E 36°20′N): plan of the forts. *From Poidebard, 1934, Pl. CXLIII.*

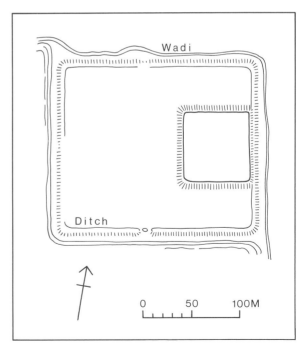

KHIRBET HASSAN AGA, SYRIA
(Figs. 94 and 95)

Rather faint shadows and highlights from the light of the sun in the south reveal a rectangular fort with a mound in one corner and a scattering of small mounds which continue towards the right of the picture. Poidebard's drawing has a smaller fort superimposed at one end of the larger, but it is difficult to see on this photograph.

The site lies 12 km (7.5 miles) south-east of Tunainir/Thannouris on the road to Singara. According to Poidebard's drawing, the larger enclosure is substantial, measuring 180 × 220 m. (590 × 720 ft), which gives an area of 3.96 ha. (9.8 acres). However, something appears to be amiss with this drawing, because the fort site seems too square, assuming that the photograph is a vertical, as it appears to be. The ratio of the long side to the short on the photograph is 1.36:1, from which it may be suggested that a better approximation to the dimensions is about 170 ×

230 m. (555 x 750 ft), or 3.9 ha. (9.65 acres). Whichever figures are correct, the area of the fort is comparable to some of the largest forts and small fortresses in the East (cf. Udruh, Lejjun, Qreiyeh, Figs. 76, 79, 96).

The smaller enclosure is said by Poidebard to be 75 × 75 m./245 × 245 ft (0.56 ha./1.39 acres). The most reasonable explanation may be that it was a smaller Roman fort overlaying an earlier and larger one.

FIGURE 96 Qreiyeh, Deir es-Zor, Syria (35°24'N 40°5'E): vertical view. *Photograph: Aéro Levant (1929?). From Poidebard, 1934, Pl. LXXXVI.*

QREIYEH, SYRIA
(Figs. 96 and 97)

Qreiyeh lies on a rocky plateau on the right bank of the Euphrates 44 km (27.5 miles) below Halebiyeh, and 40 km (25 miles) above Circesium, at a point where the river leaves the Halebiyeh-Tarbous defile and the routes from Tayibeh and Resafa reach it. There is a small fort

FIGURE 97 Qreiyeh, Deir es-Zor, Syria (35°24′N 40°5′E): plan of the fort. *From Poidebard, 1934, Pl. LXXXVII.*

on the facing bank on the other side of the river (Poidebard, 1934, Pl. LXXXVII).

The walls of the fort, apparently buried by a covering of silt, and the two surrounding ditches are shown by shadows and highlights in this excellent vertical view, which was taken with the sun in the east. Inside the walls, low mounds cover the remains of buildings. On the left (north) side of the fort is a rocky cliff. Outside the gate on this side, rock-cut steps descend to the lower ground of an old bed of the Euphrates, now cultivated fields.

At 220 × 220 m./715 × 715 ft (4.85 ha./12

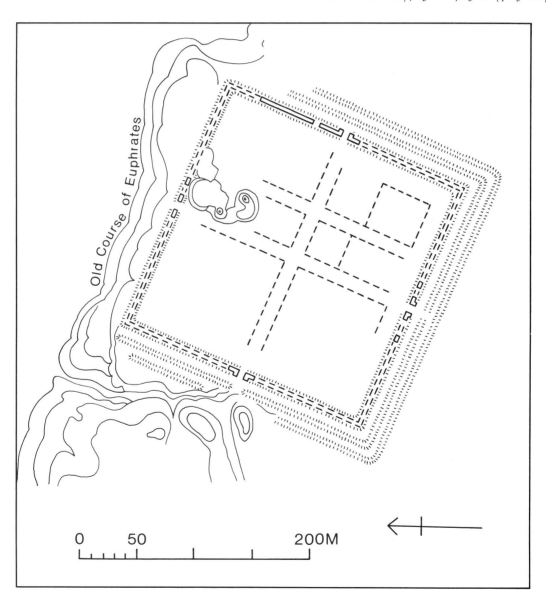

Old Course of Euphrates

0   50   200M

FIGURE 98 Hlehleh, Homs, Syria (34°45′N 38°44′E): vertical view. *Photograph: de Boysson (n.d.). From Poidebard, 1934, Pl.IV.1.*

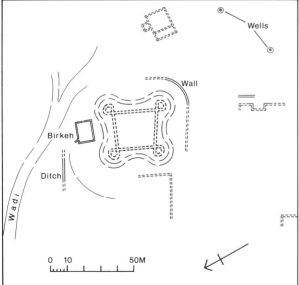

FIGURE 99 Hlehleh, Homs, Syria (34°45′N 38°44′E): plan of the fort. *From Poidebard, 1934, Pl.V, which had been prepared from the air photographs.*

acres), the fort is large, sufficient for some 1500 men. Walls are of stone set in mortar and 3-3.3m. (9.8−10.8 ft) thick, and there is a gate flanked by square bastions, 6.7 m. (22 ft) wide, in the middle of each side. Rather like Sa'neh (Fig. 135) the interior is bisected by a road, the halves then subdivided by lesser streets. Poidebard's excavations (not actually mentioned but inferred from features of his plan) produced no recorded dating evidence (Poidebard, 1934, 87f).

It has been suggested that the site should be identified with the *Birtha Arupan* named in the *Res Gestae Divi Saporis* (III.2) as one of the forts seized by the Persian king on his march up the Euphrates *c.*253 (Maricq, 1958, 338).

FIGURE 100 Fort at Tell Zenbil, Al-Hasakeh, Syria (36°39'N 41°00'E): vertical view. *Photograph: G. David (n.d.). From Poidebard, 1934, Pl. CXXI.*

HLEHLEH, SYRIA
(Figs. 98 and 99)

At ground level Poidebard reported that only the reservoir (*birkeh*) and a few indistinct wall traces could be seen. From the air, distinct pale toned negative vegetation marks gave the plan of the walls and towers of a small fort or *tetrapyrgium* and certain other walls. The small fort stood within a large outer enclosure which Poidebard reported as clearly visible when seen from the air '*avec contre jour*'. More water was supplied by two wells, the upcast around which shows as pale circles south-east of the fort (top right).

The site lies 48 km (30 miles) north-east of Palmyra beside the Roman road to Sukneh and Sura, and just at the entrance of the Pass of Rujm Saboun. The *tetrapyrgium* is small, *c*.28 × 30 m. (92 × 98 ft); the enclosure, on the other hand, is some 200 × 200 m./650 × 650 ft (4 ha./9.8 acres) (Poidebard, 1934, 76ff). It is usually identified as the *Helela* of the *Notitia Dignitatum* (Or. XXXIII.32), base of the *Cohors Prima Gotthorum*.

TELL ZENBIL, SYRIA (Fig. 100)

A text book photograph of a 'shadow site' which was taken with the sun in the south-west. The ruins seem to be those of a fort covered by wind blown silt. In his caption Poidebard said that it was a platform 96 × 96 m./315 × 315 ft (0.92 ha./ 2.3 acres) and 3 m. (10 ft) high. The outline of the wall of the fort and its external ditch and traces of interior buildings can be seen on the photograph, at the top of which is also what Poidebard termed an observation post on a hillock (12 m./40 ft high). He made a trial excavation here in 1927 to confirm that the site was Roman, but no results are recorded. He mentioned observation posts, '*tells observatoires*', at several places (e.g. Pl. CXXII), and in this flat country they would have been needed, so this interpretation is not impossible.

The fort is quite substantial: twice the size of Qasr el-Azraq (Fig. 126) and almost three times that at Deir el-Kahf (Fig. 124); there is, however, no suggestion here of buildings that have an upper storey.

ARABAN, SYRIA
(Figs. 101 and 102)

In this photograph, the plan of a fort is shown by vegetation marks, dark in most places, presumably on the lines of robbed-out walls, but light

FIGURE 101 Araban, Al-Hasakeh, Syria (36°15′N 40°38′E): vertical view from a height of 4000 ft (1200 m.). *Photograph: Aéro Levant (3 April 1931). From Poidebard, 1934, Pl. VII.2.*

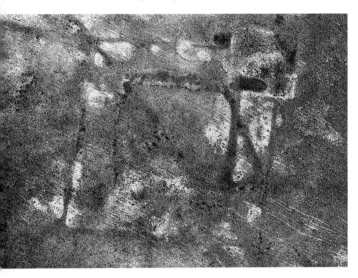

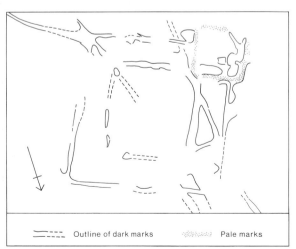

Outline of dark marks   Pale marks

toned in the upper corner, where it is probable that the foundations of a tower remain. The two dark lines which cross the site may be taken to be vegetation marks on the depressions formed by well-used tracks.

The site lies north of Tell Araban, west of the upper River Khabur. It has more recently been identified by van Lière and Lauffray (1954-55, 114) as Marazza, but their observation that the site covers 16 ha. (39.5 acres) shows that the building in the photograph here can only be part of the canal-fed site to which they allude. The size of the fort – shown on Figure 101 – is not given (Poidebard, 1934, 137), but it appears to have been fairly large. It seems to consist of a double square enclosure with a square tower in the south-west corner. The most likely explanation for the wall arrangement is that rooms were constructed between them. Since the tower foundations appear not to have been robbed-out, it may have been a later structure utilizing building material from the larger enclosure.

The town site of Araban to the south has been identified with the *Arabana* of the Peutinger Table and the *Oroba/Oraba/Horoba* of the *Notitia Dignitatum* (Or. XXXV.8; 20; 31), the base of the *Equites Sagittarii Indigenae* in Osrhoene. Occupation may well go back earlier, however; it has been suggested that the *Castell[um] Arab[um]* of a Dura papyrus (*P.Dura* 100 and 101) should be equated with this site and with the *Castellum Arabionis* of a fourth-century Christian source (Pennacchietti, 1986, 88 and n.15). Further north, in the province of Mesopotamia, the *Notitia* locates at *Mefana – Cartha*, a regiment perhaps once associated with the site: *Equites Sagittarii Indigenae Arabanenses* (Or. XXXVI. 25) (Poidebard, 1934, 136ff).

SHEIKH IBRAHIM, IRAQ
(Fig. 103)

The fort, which is shown by very distinct vegetation marks on the photograph, lies 75 km (47 miles) east of Singara, on the route from Tell Afar to Hatra. It is relatively large: 91.5 × 85 m./

FIGURE 102 Araban, Al-Hasakeh, Syria (36°15′N 40°38′E): sketch plan of the fort. *Drawn by D.N. Riley, from the air photograph.*

FIGURE 103 Sheikh Ibrahim, Neineva, Iraq (36°16′N 42°40′E): oblique view looking north-east from a height of 500 ft (150 m.). *Photograph: Royal Air Force (11.36; 23 April 1938). Stein Archive (Institute of Archaeology, London, inv. no. AP. 1690).*

300 × 280ft (0.78 ha./1.93 acres). Internal rooms ranged around a courtyard can be seen from the photograph. The importance of the site lies in its location on what was an important route. Stein believed that it should be identified with one of the 'Unnamed' points on the Peutinger Table on the road to Hatra (Gregory and Kennedy (Stein), 1985, 57; 81ff). However, there is no other evidence to suggest what the date might be.

·Small Forts Without·
External Towers

All the forts in this category are modest in size; indeed in Britain they would be described as fortlets. They may be divided into two geographical groups: the two forts in Israel and Jordan and the three in Iraq. The first group, both of which are certainly Roman, comprises Qasr el-Uweinid and Tell es-Seba (Figs. 105, 107). Unfortunately no dates have been established for any of the second group, El-Hamda, Dulalyah and Qasr el-Khidr (Figs. 109-11). They were visited on the ground by Stein, but he did not leave evidence to prove his supposition that they were Roman, and there is no record that they have been examined by an archaeologist since his time.

The forts in both groups were planned with a central court and rooms on the inside of the outer walls, so there is a measure of uniformity in their design. None of the buildings is reported to have stood more than one storey high, except for the tower inside the fort at Qasr el-Uweinid.

Looking at their sizes, in the first group Qasr el-Uweinid, 0.25 ha. (0.6 acres) in area, is the larger, but its area is barely one-sixth of what one would expect for a full Early Empire infantry auxiliary regiment (cf. Fig. 86 and above, p. 19). The smaller, Tell es-Seba, 0.01 ha. (0.025 acres) (Fig. 107), could have held only a handful of troops. The three Iraqi forts are fairly similar in size, ranging from the 0.12 ha. (0.3 acre) of Qasr el-Khidr to the 0.2 ha. (0.5 acre) of Dulalyah.

The building material is stone in all cases. The normal shape is square, but Qasr el-Uweinid and Tell es-Seba were given irregular plans to conform with their sites.

QASR EL-UWEINID, JORDAN
(Figs. 105 and 106)

Uweinid lies on the perimeter of the Azraq basin some 15 km (9 miles) to the south-west of the Azraq Oasis (Kennedy, 1982, 113-28; Gregory and Kennedy (Stein), 1985, 281-5; 421ff; Parker,

1986, 17ff). A variety of interesting features are seen on this old Royal Air Force vertical, including, at the lower right corner, the relatively well-preserved remains of the Roman fort, standing on a lava outcrop, around which bends the Wadi Butm. Unfortunately the scale of the photograph is small, so few details of the interior of the fort itself are visible, but it shows its position very well. Scattered clumps of vegetation are seen in the wadi, and elsewhere there are groups of 'hut circles' arranged in rings. The map shows a larger area of ground than the photograph, which is only part of the original Royal Air Force vertical.

The Uweinid fort is a small irregular quadrilateral: c.65 × 44 m./210 × 145 ft (c.0.25 ha./0.6 acres). Rooms are distributed around a central courtyard except in the south-west, where a large projection in the wall encloses a substantial free-

FIGURE 104 Location map.

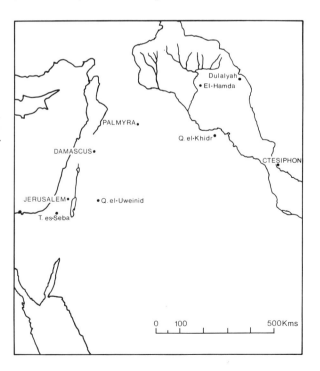

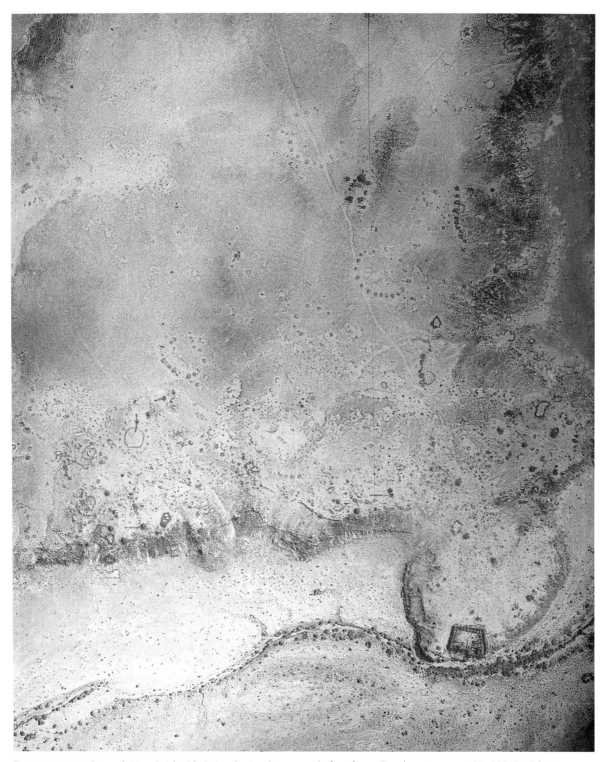

FIGURE 105 Qasr el-Uweinid, Al-Asimah, Jordan (31°47′N 36°43′E): vertical view. *Photograph: Royal Air Force, (1927?). Crawford Collection (Institute of Archaeology, London. inv. no. AP 1038). Cf. Rees, 1929, pl. II.*

standing tower, 9.5 × 9.5 m. (31 × 31 ft). To the south-west, across the Wadi Butm, but not on the photograph, are the remains of a second large tower, *c.* 12 × 12 m.(40 × 40 ft).

Like the other small fort at Aseikhin on the north-east side of the basin (Kennedy, 1982, 107-13), Qasr el-Uweinid must have been dependent on the large fort, Qasr el-Azraq (Figs. 126), which stood a few miles away beside the northern pools at the heart of the Azraq oasis. It is inconceivable that the extremely remote site of Qasr el-Uweinid would have been occupied when the Qasr el-Azraq was not. Two Latin building inscriptions from the site have been published (Kennedy, 1982, 124-6): one dates from 200/2, the other has the consular date 201. The latter is important because it describes the site as *Castellum et[s] Praesidium Severianum* and records the construction of a *balneum*, the sole reference to a bath building on an inscription from the East. However, there is no obvious bath building on the site – in any event, it is a curious location for one. This raises the possibility that the stone had been carried in from a more likely location near one of the Azraq pools. Sherds collected on the site have been identified as entirely third and early fourth century (Parker, 1986, 17), which does not accord with the dates of the inscriptions. The wide range of information from the site has not made its history easier to understand.

FIGURE 106 Qasr el-Uweinid, Al-Asimah, Jordan (31°47′N 36°43′E): plan of the fort and locality. *From Kennedy, 1982, fig. 27.*

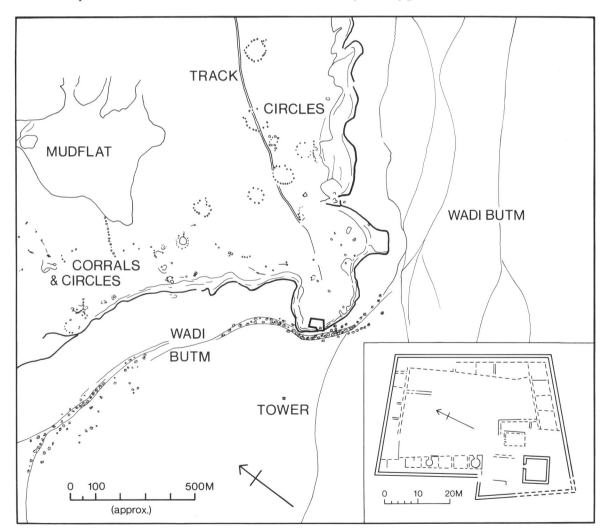

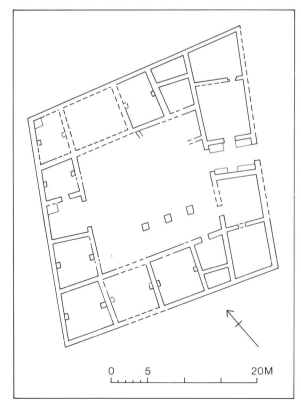

FIGURE 107 Tell es-Seba, Hadarom Hanegev, Israel (31°15′N 34°49′E): oblique view looking north-east. *Photograph: Avraham Hai (1970). Copyright: Institute of Archaeology, Tel Aviv University.*

FIGURE 108 Tell es-Seba, Hadarom Hanegev, Israel (31°15′N 34°49′E): plan of the fort. *After Aharoni, 1973, Pl.85.*

TELL ES-SEBA, ISRAEL
(Figs. 107 and 108)

The oblique photograph of Tell es-Seba was taken when excavation was in progress. The latest structure on the site was a small Roman fort which is here seen emphasized in the centre of the mound by the shadows of its low foundation walls.

The Biblical period Tell es-Seba lies 4.8 km (3 miles) east of *Berosaba*, on the northern edge of the Negev Desert. Although some early visitors to the tell saw no remains attributable to the Roman period, the low walls of the diamond-shaped fortlet of the photograph were in fact visible on the surface. They enclosed an area of broadly 31.5 × 31.5 m./*c*. 105 × 105 ft (0.01 ha./0.025 acres), with a central courtyard of *c*.16 × 16 m. (53 × 53 ft). Beyond the walls the surface was prepared as a court and the slopes of the tell itself strengthened by a glacis of stamped earth.

The fortlet could have accommodated up to 80-100 men, possibly a detachment from a parent unit in *Berosaba*. It is one of a chain of fortlets and forts to be found across the northern Negev between the Mediterranean on the west, and the Dead Sea and Wadi Araba on the east, part of a system commonly attributed to the fourth century.

Unfortunately there was no useful stratigraphy to give secure dating evidence at the site: a single coin (of 251-3) may point to construction in the third century, and some reconstruction has been dated to the Early Islamic period. When its first

phase was built and how long it remained occupied is unknown (Fritz, 1973).

In the early third century, *Berosaba*, the modern Beer-Sheva, was said by Eusebius (*Onom.* 50. 1-3) to have been a large village with a garrison, and at the end of the fourth century according to the *Notitia Dignitatum* (*Or.* XXXIV.18) this was the *Equites Dalmatae Illyriciani*. However, none of the Roman and Byzantine remains in modern Beer-Sheva can be identified as military.

EL-HAMDA, IRAQ (Fig. 109)

The site lies some 85 km (53 miles) south-west of Singara, on the road to Fadgami, a town beside the River Khabur. Both Poidebard and Stein refer to the clear line of a straight road which they took to be Roman, running for miles past the site. The fort, which measures 40 × 40 m./132 × 132 ft (0.16 ha./0.4 acres), stands between two branches of a wadi. It is emphasized on the photograph by vegetation marks, reminiscent of those at Tell el-Ghail (Fig. 139), which is in the same area of barren steppe. Stein reported

that the walls had decayed into ridges rising about 2 m. (7 ft) above the ground level and that the gate appeared to have been in the middle of the north face. He added that, 'On the gravel surface on the top of the western wall I picked up a Roman copper coin, apparently of the Emperor -----'. Unfortunately the name of the emperor is left blank in his account (Gregory and Kennedy (Stein), 1985, 48); in his *'Personal Narrative'* (n.d., 9) he describes it simply as

'late Roman'. The likelihood that the road was Roman makes it probable that the fort was a Roman post.

FIGURE 110 Dulalyah, Neineva, Iraq (36°15′N 42°50′E): oblique view looking south from a height of 300 ft (100 m.). *Photograph: Royal Air Force, (09.03; 7 May 1938). Stein Archive (Institute of Archaeology, London, inv. no. AP 1712).*

DULALYAH, IRAQ (Fig. 110)

Located 80 km (50 miles) east of Singara, close to the Tigris and on the road from Eski Mosul to Mosul, this is a small defended site, measuring 46 × 44 m./150 × 145 ft (0.2 ha./0.5 acres). Internal rooms are built against the walls and look out over a central courtyard. Stein noted Islamic features in the construction, but thought that it was Roman in origin, and was a station on a Roman road to the ancient crossing of the Tigris at Mosul.

FIGURE 111 Qasr el-Khidr, Al-Anbar, Iraq (34°06′N 41°42′E): oblique view looking north from a height of 500 ft (150 m.). *Photograph: Royal Air Force (10.54; 13 January 1939). Stein Archive (British Museum, Department of Western Asiatic Antiquities, Small Archive, Air Photographs–Iraq-Stein, RAF no. 14450).*

The ruins of buildings, surrounded by vegetation, evidently survived to a good height when this photograph was taken for Stein in May 1938. Unfortunately, when he passed the site again in November of the same year, the walls had been partly demolished to provide ballast for the railway then being built near them (Gregory and Kennedy (Stein), 1985, 114-17).

QASR EL-KHIDR, IRAQ
(Fig. 111)

The fort is some 40 km (25 miles) south-west of Ana, at a point where a desert route to Hit crosses the Wadi Khidr. The ruins of the stone walls have remained free from any later deposits and show well on the photograph. They enclose an area of 33.5 × 36.9 m./110 × 121ft (0.12 ha./0.3 acres), with rooms around three sides of a courtyard. Between the fort and the wadi, a large rectangular area, almost black on the photograph because of a better growth of vegetation, is a reservoir, 28 × 28 m. (92 × 92 ft) inside, with a 1.5 m. (5 ft) retaining wall. Stein called the fort a *castellum* but obtained no evidence of its date.

·Large Forts With·
External Towers

There are 13 forts described in this category, of which one is in Israel, seven are in Jordan, three in Syria and two in Iraq. Many of them are well preserved and they are often of imposing appearance. A ground view of one of the more striking has been included. A limited amount of information is available about the dates of the forts in Israel and Iraq and most of those in Jordan.

There is a very considerable variation in size between these forts. Ain Sinu II (3.7 ha./9.2 acres) (Fig. 113) is exceptionally large for the eastern frontier, and Umm er-Resas (2.2 ha./5.4 acres) (Fig. 137) is also unusually big. It may not be without significance that the former is one of the earliest-dated forts with towers, and that it is adjacent to much the largest fort discussed in this book (Fig. 167). The smallest, Deir el-Kahf (0.36 ha./0.89 acres) (Fig. 124) and Qasr Bshir (0.31 ha./0.78 acres) (Fig. 122) could have been classed as 'small forts' and placed in the next category (Small Forts with External Towers, see p. 194–212), but both are notable for their well-preserved remains of rooms on two storeys, which effectively doubled the accommodation for the garrison. Moreover, both are comparable in design with the large forts in this category.

The building material is stone in most cases, but two of the forts were made of mud brick. Both are in Iraq, where the technique was very commonly used, even for monumental buildings.

The wide variation in ground area implies great differences in the size of the units that could have been accommodated. Ain Sinu II (Fig. 113) would have had ample space for the largest auxiliary unit, or even two of the smaller. Umm er-Resas (Fig. 137) could easily have housed a major auxiliary unit of Early Empire size, as could Tell el-Ghail (1.35 ha./3.3 acres) (Fig. 139). The remainder could not have accommodated more than a part of a traditional *c.* 500-strong Early Empire unit, and it is probable that they held smaller Late Empire regiments.

The identification of the character and size of the garrison of a fort can be helped by looking at the internal structures. In a few cases (Figs. 128, 132 and 139) nothing is known of the internal arrangements, but the majority may be divided into three groups:
• forts with buildings set in the interior, leaving a space behind the walls (Figs. 113, 120, 135);
• forts with rooms both against the external walls and in the central area, with a roadway to separate the external from the central buildings (Figs. 115, 117, 130, 137);
• forts with rooms built only against the walls, leaving an internal courtyard (Figs. 122, 124, 127).

The third group is notable for buildings two storeys high, a feature not found in the others. These forts provided a considerable amount of accommodation, in spite of their relatively small

FIGURE 112 Location map.

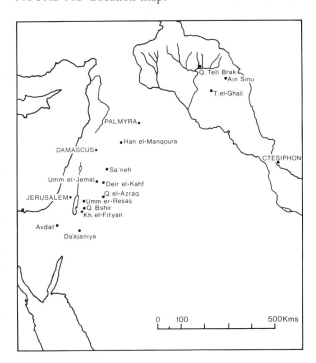

ground area. Deir el-Kahf, for example, had some 100 rooms on two floors (three in the towers). At all the forts in this group and at others such as Da'ajaniya, which is in the second group, allowance has to be made for the stabling which has been identified by the survival of mangers in many of the ground floor rooms. However, it is not possible to determine whether it was intended for horses, mules or donkeys, or even camels, much less what it was *actually* used for. Nevertheless, useful hypotheses can be constructed. Thus, at Deir el-Kahf, there would have been adequate accommodation for a 500-strong cohort at least. In contrast, the much larger ground area of the fort at Da'ajaniya probably provided quarters for fewer troops (perhaps half of a *cohors equitata*) in buildings which were seemingly single storeyed and included a great deal of stabling; the position was probably similar at Avdat I.

As noted above, in Early Empire forts – in the West at least – it is usually a simple matter to identify the functions of a structure by its distinctive character and location – barrack, stable, granary, storeroom, *praetorium* or *principia*. The change in design which introduced tall external towers and tall curtain walls, also involved changes in the internal layout. At one extreme there are Umm el-Jemal and Da'ajaniya with recognizable *principiae* in one half of the internal area and barrack blocks in the remainder. At the other extreme, there is Qasr el-Azraq with a *principia* protruding from an exterior wall, and the other rooms probably in two storeys built against the walls, providing accommodation in which it is only possible to distinguish between rooms intended for stabling and those for all other purposes. The new design may not have been adopted consistently. Umm el-Jemal, Da'ajaniya and Umm er-Resas, possibly transitional types, may be earlier than Azraq, which looks like the final stage of the process, but the building of the three forts was probably not widely separated in time. Avdat I is interesting as perhaps showing a transition from the Da'ajaniya design to that of Azraq; it is very similar to Da'ajaniya (including size) but has a probable *principia* projecting from of an external wall. Ain Sinu II is earlier and would help us to identify a pattern, but too little is known of the interior;

this is a key site for renewed excavation.

The towers of forts vary widely both in shape and size, from square and rectangular (the most common) to diamond, fan-shaped and semi-circular. Something is known about the tower shape at ten of the forts discussed below. In two instances, Ain Sinu II and Tell Brak I, square/diamond and semi-circular appear side by side.

Towers are in various positions. They are always on the angles, and on some forts are also at intervals along the walls and/or flanking the gates. Usually they project, but in a few instances, towers straddle the walls (Figs. 117, 122, 124, 126; cf. Figs. 130 and 137).

A hypothesis for the development of these forts, based on the current evidence, would be to see:

• the introduction of external towers in the Severan period, but no change in the internal layout;
• at the end of the third century, the design changed to give a mixture of accommodation, both centrally and against the external walls;
• finally, in the early fourth century, the curtain walls raised and rooms of one or two storeys built exclusively against this wall.

AIN SINU II, IRAQ
(Figs. 113 and 114)

In the foreground, vegetation marks show the site of the '*Castellum*', one of two adjacent forts, located near a spring at the eastern end of the Jebel Sinjar range, which is seen in the background. The forts – here termed Ain Sinu I and II after the designation of the excavator – were sufficiently well preserved to have been first reported and described by Herzfeld in 1887 (Sarre and Herzfeld, 1920, II, 305 and fig. 283), though his inaccurate description of their position caused Stein and his pilot to have to make 'repeated enquiries and air reconnaissances' before they found them (Gregory and Kennedy (Stein), 1985, 25). Stein's photographs are valuable records of the site, but the forts would have been recorded in more detail if the camera had been aimed from an angle nearer to the vertical. Despite the suspiciously large size and curious appearance of the other fort, Ain Sinu I, the so-called 'Barracks' (Fig. 167), excavation has now proven the

Roman origin of both (Oates and Oates, 1959; Oates, 1968, 80-92).

Ain Sinu II covers an irregular rectangle measuring *c.* 220 × 180 m./720 × 590 ft (3.7 ha./9.2 acres), which makes it one of the largest Roman

FIGURE 113 Ain Sinu II, Neineva, Iraq (36°37′N 42°11′E): oblique view looking north-west from a height of 600 ft (c. 200 m.). *Photograph: Royal Air Force (13.10; 31 March 1938). Stein Archive (Institute of Archaeology, London, inv. no. AP 1703).*

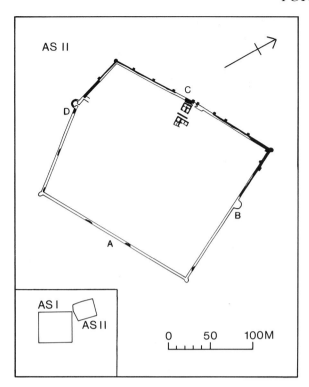

AS II

C

D

B

A

AS I

AS II

0   50   100M

FIGURE 114 Ain Sinu II, Neineva, Iraq (36°37′N 42°11′E): plan of the 'Castellum'. *Adapted from Oates, 1968, Fig. 3.*

forts in the East. The massive stone curtain wall, 3 m. (10 ft) thick, is of particular interest (cf. Fig. 117), as are the round projecting corner towers paired with square interval towers. In both cases the projection is fairly modest, 2–3 m. (7–10 ft), but the combination is highly unusual. On the middle of the west wall there was also a large semi-circular projecting tower which may have been duplicated on the east. Excavation of the gateway proved it to have had a brick built vault over limestone walls, and found possible evidence for a machicolation (Oates, 1968, 85ff). Two regular buildings just within the north gate were investigated, but the excavator was unable to make an intelligible ground plan by inspection of the ruins elsewhere in the interior. The explanation offered for the possible absence of a regular layout inside was that structures may have been sited and aligned to take advantage of natural rises in the ground (Oates, 1968, 82, 85). However, while the photograph is unclear in many respects, it appears to show the lines of at least

three long parallel structures running up to the eastern wall of the fort. They resemble barrack blocks.

In view of the presence of projecting towers, normally regarded as characteristic of the later third century onwards, it is of particular interest that the excavator plausibly dated construction of the fort to the early third century (stratified coins of Caracalla and Severus Alexander). It was occupied for a relatively short time. The location of Ain Sinu II on higher ground than its neighbour suggests that it is likely to have been the earlier of the two forts. This was confirmed by the excavations, which pointed to a slightly later date for its neighbour, Ain Sinu I.

The fort is sited to command passage through the Gaulat Pass, a route round the eastern end of the Jebel Sinjar from Nisibis towards either Hatra or the Tigris crossing at Eski Mosul.

AVDAT I, ISRAEL
(Figs. 115 and 116)

The vertical photograph, unfortunately not sharp because it has had to be greatly enlarged, shows one of the impressive military structures at Avdat, the ancient *Oboda*. The fort is also seen in the corner of a view of the ancient city which is printed below (Fig. 143).

The remains of the fort stand to a good height and have been known since 1902. Plans by both Brimer (apud Segul, 1981, fig. 2) and Cohen (1980, 44) have been published recently. While in broad agreement, they differ in important details. Brimer's plan, derived from the air photograph (Fig. 115), has been used as the basis of the plan given here (Fig.116); some further detail and proposed reconstruction was added.

Shadows and the rough 'texture' of the surface show the ruins of the defensive wall and of rows of buildings, all stone-built. The circuit wall encloses *c.* 100 × 100 m./325 × 325 ft (1 ha./2.47 acres). There were towers projecting at the corners, six towers on the curtain wall (two on each of three sides), and a large projection in the middle of the east wall. The towers were previously thought to be round and semicircular, but recent excavation has revealed that the intermediate towers on the south wall were square, and the south-east corner tower was rectangular

(Cohen, 1982, 245). It may be presumed that all were square or rectangular, but with the example of mixed square and semicircular at Ain Sinu II (Fig. 113), one must be cautious. The projection identified on the east wall might be either some elaborate structure at a gateway or, more probably, the *principia*.

The internal arrangement is intriguing. There were casemate walls, pierced by gates in the middle of the south side, and perhaps in the east also. Excavation on the south gate exposed the remains of the charred wooden doors and fragments of their bronze sheeting. Within the walls, the space is divided by a broad north–south road, on either side of which were disposed four barrack blocks occupying all of the available area. The internal partition walls of individual barracks still stand to 1.4 m ($4\frac{1}{2}$ ft) and excavation has revealed small rooms 5.2 × 3.7 m. (17 × 12 ft), in two rows of five for each block, giving a total of 80 rooms in the barracks (cf. the excellent oblique view published by Negev, 1983, 69). Rooms are broadly comparable in size with those at Ain Sinu I (Fig. 167), Da'ajaniya (Fig. 117) (a fort of similar size) and Lejjun (Figs. 76-7). The rooms around the perimeter may have been

stables, if so there is adequate space here for 200–300 men, as at Da'ajaniya.

Like Ain Sinu I and Tell Brak 2 (Fig. 169), there is no provision in the fort for the expected administration buildings. However, as noted above, the structure projecting from the middle of the east wall may have been the *principia*, a feature certainly identified at Azraq (Fig. 126), Bshir (Fig. 122) and Ad-Diyatheh (Fig. 141). Alternatively, as may have been the case at Ain Sinu I, the rooms set within the thickness of the casemate walls may have provided much of the necessary space, and Avdat I might better be classed with Ain Sinu I as a 'Barracks Fort' (see below, p. 213).

The expected reservoir in or near the fort is not visible on the photograph.

Few ceramic finds have been made at the fort and there is at present little evidence about its date, though the design suggests a late date, third century at least. The two excavators have differing opinions. Negev (1977, 624) views the fort as Nabataean. For Cohen, however, the finds were insufficient 'to determine whether the camp was occupied only during the first century C.E. or after the annexation of the Nabataean realm'

FIGURE 115 Avdat I, Hadarom Hanegev, Israel (30°48′N 34°46′E): vertical view. *Supplied by A.Segal.*

FIGURE 116 Avdat 1, Hadarom Hanegev, Israel (30°48′N 34°46′E): sketch plan of the fort. *Adapted from Brimer* apud *Segal, 1981, fig. 2 and from the air photographs.*

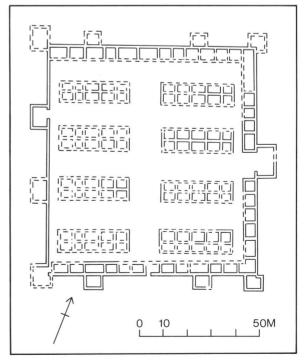

(i.e. into the second century) (Cohen, 1982, 245; cf. Cohen 1980). Constantinian coins were found amongst the robbed out debris but were interpreted by Negev (1977, 624) as dropped by the soldiers of a demolition gang seeking building material. They might more plausibly be associated with construction.

DA'AJANIYA, JORDAN
(Figs. 117, 118 and 119)

The distant oblique photograph gives a general impression of the fort and its surroundings on the desert's edge 40 km (25 miles) north-east of Petra in southern Jordan. The fortress at Udruh (Fig. 79) is 32 km (20 miles) to the south-west. The dark line of vegetation crossing the picture diagonally shows the course of a wadi, water from which was stored in the large reservoir (recently restored) seen on the left edge. A north-south road (not visible on the photograph) parallel to the *Via Nova Traiana* further west, and marked by milestones, ran by the site (Thomsen, 1917, 57f, nos. 176-84, no inscriptions preserved).

FIGURE 117 Da'ajaniya, Ma'an, Jordan (30°33′N 35°45′E): oblique view looking west. *Photograph: Royal Air Force (c.1938/9). Stein Archive (Bodleian Library, Oxford, Ms. Stein 331 fol. 43).*

The fort is relatively large, sub-square in shape, and measuring *c.* 100 × 100 m./325 × 325 ft (1 ha./2.47 acres). The massive basalt walls are interrupted by large square corner towers and smaller square towers between. Both sets of towers straddle the wall. Rooms are found built around the walls *and* across much of the interior. The barrack blocks are short and reminiscent of those at Lejjun (Fig. 77). There is no indication that the internal structures were two-storey and, judging by their characteristic appearance, most of the rooms seem to have been used either as

barracks (A on plan) or stabling (B) (Freeman, forth.). The provision of so much stabling within the fort would have seriously reduced the number of men who could be accommodated. Of the Early Empire regiments, half of a *cohors quingenaria equitata* could have been housed, i.e. three centuries of infantry and two *turmae* of horsemen (*c.*300 men).

No excavation has been done, no inscriptions are known, and the site has not been equated with any of those in the *Notitia Dignitatum*. During Parker's initial survey, collecting surface sherds, material ranging widely across five centuries of the Roman period was found, together with a coin of 308-10 (Parker, 1986, 94, 321). The design of the curtain wall has features in

FIGURE 118 Da'ajaniya, Ma'an, Jordan (30°33′N 35°45′E): ground view looking north across the restored reservoir. *Photograph: D.L. Kennedy.*

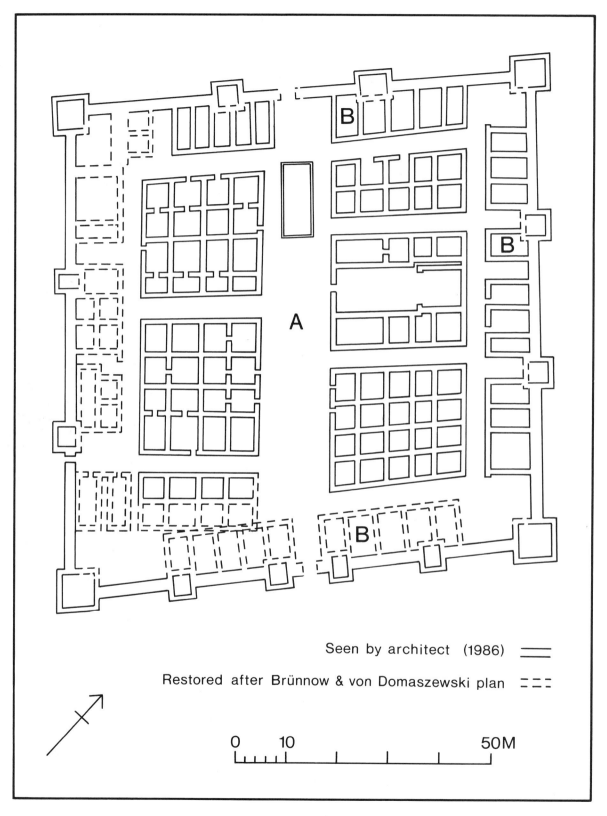

Seen by architect (1986) ————

Restored after Brünnow & von Domaszewski plan – – –

0   10   50M

FIGURE 119 Da'ajaniya, Ma'an, Jordan (30°33′N 35°45′E): plan of the fort. *After Freeman, forth.*

common with other forts in Arabia, notably Muhattet el-Hajj (0.26 ha./0.63 acres) (Parker, 1986, fig. 23) and Ad-Diyatheh (Fig. 141) (Lander, 1984, 144f), to which we might add the much larger fort at Umm er-Resas (Fig. 137). Lander regarded the type as transitional and suspected a Severan date (1984, 143–8), but a late third/early fourth century date seems more probable and would accord with the evidence from Umm el-Jemal (Fig. 130), where the internal layout of the early fourth century *castellum* was similar.

KHIRBET EL-FITYAN, JORDAN
(Figs. 120 and 121)

The site is 16 km (10 miles) north-east of Kerak and about 1.3 km (0.8 miles) north-west of el-Lejjun (cf. Fig. 76, a vertical view showing both fortress and fort). It stands on the northern rim

FIGURE 120 Khirbet el-Fityan, Al-Kerak, Jordan (31°14′N 35°48′E): oblique view looking north; height given as 200 ft (60 m). *Photograph: Royal Air Force (08.30; 25 May 1937). Crawford Collection (Institute of Archaeology, London RAF no. 12742).*

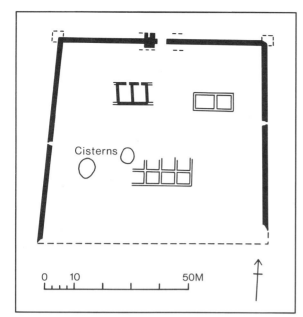

FIGURE 121   Khirbet el-Fityan, Al-Kerak, Jordan (31°14′N 35°51′E): plan of the fort. *After Parker, 1986, fig. 33. The alignments of the west and (restored) south walls have been altered slightly to accord with their appearance on the vertical photograph (Fig. 76).*

of the deep Wadi Lejjun into which some of the south wall and two corner towers have slipped.

The shape is sub-rectangular, 78.8 × 76.8 m./ 258 × 252 ft (0.6 ha./1.48 acres), with square corner towers and gates in three walls. Excavation has revealed Roman re-occupation of an Iron Age and possible Nabataean site (Parker, 1987, 434–7). The Roman fort included barrack blocks in the interior and produced a construction date of late third/early fourth century, closely contemporary with the fortress nearby. Occupation does not seem to have lasted long into the fourth century. It might be seen as the short-lived forerunner of the fortress, perhaps continuing in use briefly as a watch post. The nearest reliable water supply is the spring in the wadi below, which would always have been a difficulty for anything more than a modest garrison, even if there were a cistern inside the fort.

QASR BSHIR, JORDAN
(Figs. 122 and 123)

Figure 122, a high-level vertical view, is one of the few known air photographs (cf. Cover plate and Parker, 1987, 470, pl. 73) of the fort, which

FIGURE 122   Qasr Bshir, Al-Kerak, Jordan (31°20′N 35°58′E): composite vertical view from a height of 8000 ft (2500 m.). *Photograph: Royal Air Force (13.35; 17 July 1931). Crawford Collection (Institute of Archaeology, London, no inv. no., prints only).*

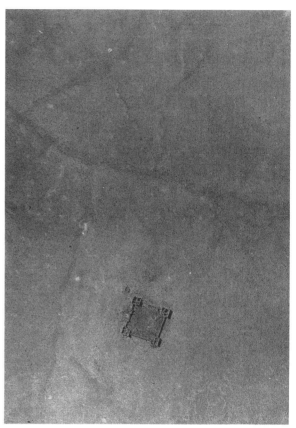

is located on a barren stone covered hill slope, about 18 km (11 miles) north–east of the legionary fortress at el-Lejjun (Fig. 76). Almost 0.5 km (c.500 yards) to the south-west is a large reservoir fed by channels, and there are five cisterns inside and outside the fort. Several watch towers are located on the hills within a few kilometres (cf. Fig. 175). A Roman road passed by, linking the site with Umm er-Resas (Fig. 135) and Lejjun.

The fort is small but massive in its build and is of special importance because it is closely dated. Walls several metres high enclose a trapezoidal area, c.56 m./185 ft (0.31 ha./0.78 acres). Towers

FIGURE 123   Qasr Bshir, Al-Kerak, Jordan (31°20′N 35°58′E): plan of the fort. *After Parker, 1986, 643, fig. 36.5.*

three storeys high, *c.* 12 × 12 m. (40 × 40 ft), partly project at the angles; slit windows are found in the upper levels. Internally, rooms two storeys high line the walls around a courtyard. Most of the ground-floor rooms (23 of 26) were used as stables, sufficient for 69 horses, and living

accommodation would have been in the towers and upper-floor rooms. Two smaller towers project 3 m. (10 ft) on either side of the gateway.

The earliest occupation on the site may have been a tower of Nabataean date, the foundations of which have been identified just outside the

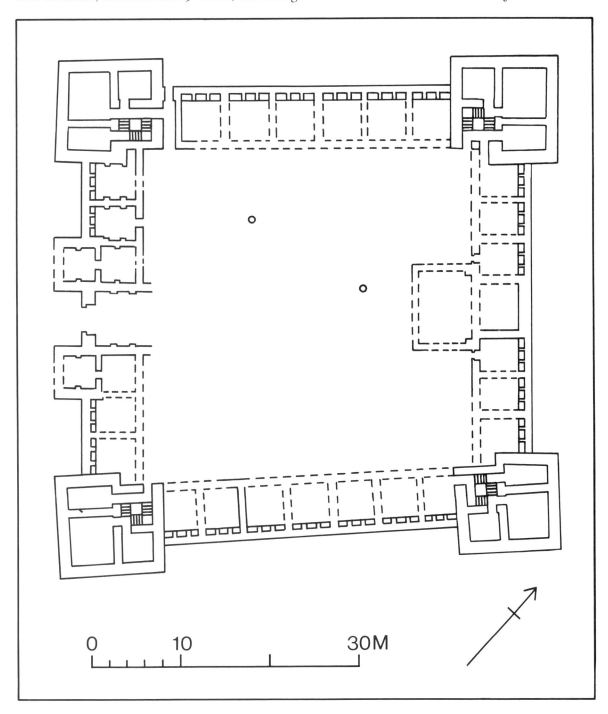

0   10   30M

FIGURE 124   Deir el-Kahf, Irbid, Jordan (32°17′N 36°50′E): vertical view. *Photograph: de Boysson (n.d.). From Poidebard, 1934, Pl.XLV.2.*

north-west wall. As for the structure visible today, a Latin inscription, still in place above the gate, records that in the period 293-305, *Castra Praetorii Mobeni* was built from the ground up (*a fundamentis*) by Aurelius Asclepiades, governor of Arabia. The recent excavations have supported this dating with their conclusion that the fort was built in the late third/early fourth centuries, occupied in the fourth century, and perhaps a little in the fifth century, then abandoned until it was re-occupied in the eighth century (Vincent *apud* Parker, 1987, 457-95; cf. Parker, 1986, 53ff). The fort is not named in the *Notitia Dignitatum* and on the basis of the name in the inscription it is suggested by Isaac (forth.) that it was not built to accomodate an army unit but as a fortified residence for a peripatetic governor.

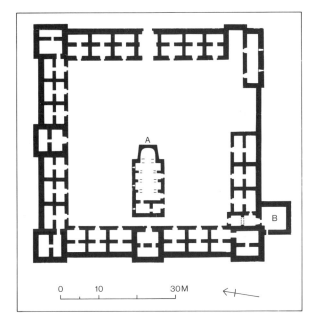

FIGURE 125   Deir el-Kahf, Irbid, Jordan (32°17'N 36°50'E): plan of the fort. *After Butler, 1909, 146, Ill. 127.*

DEIR EL-KAHF, JORDAN
(Figs. 124 and 125)

The photograph shows the well-preserved walls of the fort, seen with the sun in the east, and many surrounding stone walled corrals for animals, built by later bedouin visitors to the area. The site lies on the south-eastern edge of the Hauran, about 45 km (28 miles) south-east of the legionary fortress at Bostra (Fig. 71) and almost the same distance north of the fort at Azraq. Passing by, just to the west, is the major frontier road down to the Azraq Oasis, probably dateable to 208-10 (Fig. 28). Vertical photographs made in 1953 shows abundant traces of ancient agriculture to the north and west, and the land is again being farmed by a population now settled in a large village built round the fort.

The structure is some 60 × 60 m./200 × 200 ft (0.36 ha./0.89 acres). The walls are 1.5 m. (5 ft) thick and still rise in places to some 7.5 m. (25 ft). Square corner towers three storeys high project only slightly and there are intermediate towers on two adjacent walls. The ruins of rooms, c. 6 × 4.5 m. (19 × 14 ft), and two storeys high surround an internal courtyard.

Water was stored in a cistern (B) just outside the south-west corner (the work of a prefect called Agrippa, according to an undated Greek inscription) and accessible through a postern. There is also an internal cistern, and other cisterns and pools are found in the neighbourhood. Structure A is a later church.

Latin inscriptions (unfortunately no longer to be found) date construction to 306 with a repair, probably in the south-east corner, in the period 367-75. With a probable Severan date for the road running past it, it is possible that initial occupation of the site was at least a century earlier. In Arabic, '*kahf*' means cave; it has seemed attractive, therefore, to equate the fort with the otherwise unlocated *Speluncae* ('caves' in Latin) in the *Notitia Dignitatum* where we are told the *Equites Promoti Indigenae* were based (*Or.* XXXVII.18). Caves are, however, not uncommon in this region or indeed in Arabia (Gregory and Kennedy (Stein), 1985, 253-9; Parker, 1986, 21-4).

Though covering a modest ground area, the double storeys permitted a substantial garrison. The ground floors of the three northern towers at least are said to have been stables. With adequate space in rooms for 8 or 10 men, there was accommodation for 400-500 infantry plus some horses.

QASR EL-AZRAQ, JORDAN
(Figs. 126 and 127)

At the time when this early Royal Air Force photograph was taken, the Azraq Oasis was still the lonely and deserted spot described (as the 'Azraq Castle') by T. E. Lawrence in *Seven Pillars of Wisdom*, frequented only by occasional travellers and nomads with their camels or flocks (note the shepherds and their flock in the foreground). As described above (pp. 81-4), the oasis lies some 80 km (50 miles) east of Amman, a little less south-east of Bostra, and is the most important perennial source of water in the Syrian Desert after that at Palmyra.

The photograph shows in the foreground the marshy areas and mud-flats near the pools. In the upper right corner is a clump of palm trees, behind which is the fort. A short stretch of the wall of the supposed camp (Fig. 56) is visible behind the fort. From this direction of view we are looking at the sunlit side of the walls, which do not show well because of the absence of shadows.

The 'Castle' is a medieval reconstruction of what seems clearly to have been a Roman *castellum* with slightly projecting square towers

FIGURE 126 Qasr el-Azraq, Al-Asimah, Jordan (31°53′N 36°50′E): oblique view looking west from a height of 300 ft (100 m.). *Photograph: Royal Air Force (07.40; 24 June 1926). Institute of Archaeology, London, inv. no. AP 1035.*

at the corners and others on the curtain wall. There is also a projection (often called the '*Praetorium*', but more correctly *principia*) in the centre of the north-west wall, which may be compared with a similar construction at Khan Aneybeh (Fig. 155), Qasr Bshir (Fig. 122), Avdat 1 (Fig. 115) and, more closely, with that of Bourada in

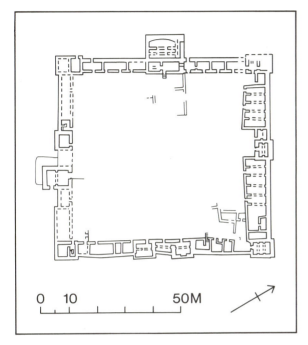

FIGURE 127 Qasr el-Azraq, Al-Asimah, Jordan (31°53′N 36°50′E): plan of the fort. *After Kennedy, 1982, fig 14.*

North Africa (Lander, 1984, fig. 189). The fort is almost square: 79 × 72 m./260 × 236 ft (0.57 ha./1.4 acres), and its appearance is still impressive. In design it is very close to the slightly smaller fort 43 km (26 miles) to the north at Deir el-Kahf (Fig. 124). Like Deir el-Kahf (and Qasr el-Hallabat: Fig. 147), it almost certainly had rooms of two storeys, towers of three. The internal layout of rooms visible today has been considerably modified, but is probably a close reflection of the original disposition. The large ranges on the north side were for stabling. The building seen set obliquely inside the courtyard is a later mosque.

The Severan milestones on the road into Azraq (Fig. 28) and the Severan building inscriptions from the dependent fort at Uweinid (Fig. 105)

give the earliest certain date for Roman occupation at the oasis, though there are no remains of a fort attributable to that period. The *castellum* is datable from inscriptions found on the site, in particular an altar of Diocletian and Maximian (287-305) and two building inscriptions (326/333; 333) (Kennedy, 1982, 69-96; Gregory and Kennedy (Stein), 1985, 261-68, 415ff; Kennedy and MacAdam, 1985; idem., 1986; cf. Parker, 1986, 19ff). A few Roman potsherds of the third and the early and middle fourth centuries have been found on the surface (Parker, 1986, 20).

The ancient name seems to have been *Dasianis* (Kennedy and MacAdam, 1985, 100–4; cf. Speidel, 1987, 215-19), but this does not appear in the *Notitia Dignitatum*. Perhaps the fort was abandoned before that document was compiled at the end of the century.

KHAN EL-MANQOURA, SYRIA (Figs. 128 and 129)

A very clear vertical view, taken with the sun in the south-east, shows the ruins of the walls and towers of the fort, around which are the remains of corrals for sheep or goats, built by later bedouin visitors to the site. The ruins, still standing to a good height in spite of stone robbing (cf. Poidebard, 1934, Pls XX.2 and XXII), are not obscured by any later deposits. The site is on the *Strata Diocletiana*, the great highway linking Damascus to Palmyra, and some 120 km (75 miles) from each.

The fort is some 90 × 90 m./295 × 295 ft (0.81 ha./2 acres) in area, has projecting 'fan-shaped' corner towers and intermediate rectangular towers with a semicircular end. A recent study (Lander 1984: *passim*, esp. 246ff) of Roman fortifications has examined this peculiar 'small fan-shaped' type of angle towers. The type is reported elsewhere in the Empire in contexts which point to the late third/early fourth centuries. In Syria, the closest parallels are also on the *Strata Diocletiana*, at Khan el-Hallabat (Fig. 151), Khan el-Qattar (Fig. 153), Dumeir (Musil, 1928, 131-4) and Khan el-Abyad (Poidebard, 1934, Pl. XXXIX).

If the rooms stood two storeys high behind the tall curtain walls, the fort could have accommodated a unit of about 500 men. This would

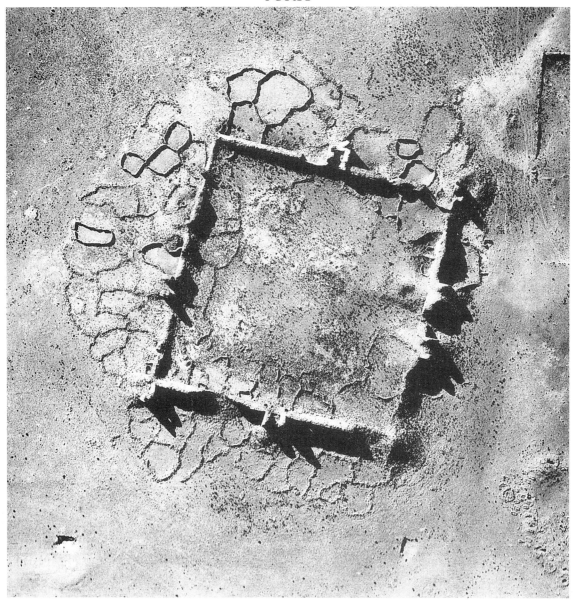

FIGURE 128 Khan el-Manqoura, Damascus, Syria (33°52′N 37°22′E): vertical view. *Photograph: de Boysson (November 1930). From Poidebard, 1934, Pl. XX.1.*

have been normal for an auxiliary unit of the early Principate but several times larger than the corresponding unit commonly found at this late period. Even without two storeys it would be relatively large. According to the *Notitia Dignitatum* (Or. XXXII.42) the garrison was the *Cohors I Iulia Lectorum*. Manqoura clearly housed a major garrison on the *Strata Diocletiana*, policing

not only traffic on the road but, like most of the similarly located units in the system, controlling movement over the Jebel Rawaq by means of the pass to the rear of the fort.

The fort lies at the centre of an elaborate system of water collection and has a substantial reservoir outside the south-west corner, fed by a canal drawing water from a barrage on the wadi to the north-west. There are several watch towers in the vicinity as well as the clear trace of the *Strata Diocletiana* (Poidebard, 1934, 45f; Pls. XXIII–XXIV). Milestone evidence which includes place names has pointed to this being

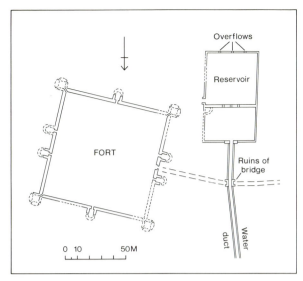

FIGURE 129   Khan el-Manqoura, Damascus, Syria
(33° 52'N 37° 22'E): plan of the fort. *After
Poidebard, 1934, Pl. XXI.*

the *Vallis Alba[na?]* listed in the late fourth
century *Notitia Dignitatum* (*Or.* XXXII.42)
(Dunand 1931). The milestones themselves are
Diocletianic, the road on which they are found
being the *Strata Diocletiana.*

UMM EL-JEMAL, JORDAN
(Figs. 130 and 131)

This photograph of Umm el-Jemal, like that of
Umm el-Quttein (Fig. 86), has been taken from
the Hunting vertical survey of 1953. Despite
the importance of the site, no good low-level
photographs are available. A few good oblique
views taken by the Royal Air Force were published many years ago (Horsfield, 1937), but the
whereabouts of the original prints and negatives
is not known; two prints of 1930 in the Institute
of Archaeology, London, are different and of
poorer quality.

Located 25 km (16 miles) south-south-west of
Bostra, this is easily the best-preserved of the
ancient towns of the Hauran. Well-built structures still stand up to the second and third stories.
Most were civilian, often ecclesiastical, of the
period *c.*250-700, but the place clearly had a
significant military history. Among the houses
are the ruins of a fort (A on Fig. 131a), partly
covered by later buildings. The town was

defended by a wall (B on Fig. 131a), which, as
the photograph shows, in some areas joined the
outer walls of buildings, including one wall of
the fort, and elsewhere crossed open land. A large
modern village has now grown at the site but it
is fortunate that the inhabitants have been allowed
little scope to encroach on the ruins of the ancient
town. The ancient buildings have, therefore, not
been drastically modified for modern use in the
way that has unfortunately taken place elsewhere,
e.g. Umm el-Quttein (Fig. 86).

Excavations made in 1981 supplied valuable
information about the chronology of the site,
dating the town to the period 250-700 and the
fort to the early fourth century. Recent work
has also established that the town we see today
did not occupy the same site as its Nabataean and
early Roman predecessor. This, surprisingly, was
several hundred metres to the east, just appearing
on the edge of the photograph as enclosures and
an area of uneven ground (C) (De Vriess 1986;
cf. Parker, 1986, 26–9).

It is possible that there was a fort at Jemal as
early as the second century. A Latin inscription
of 177-80, referring to *opus valli* ('rampart work')
is commonly taken to refer to the walling (B) of
the town itself, since it came from beside the
West Gate (D). However, the previous view that
this wall was built in the late 170s must now be
questioned in the light of the dating for the town
and the discovery on a different site of its
predecessor of the second century and earlier.
An alternative explanation may be that the
inscription came from a now vanished fort, and
was simply re-used on a new site.

The fort seen on the photograph, the early
fourth century *castellum* (A), which was first
recognized in 1981, is an irregular rectangle with
sides of 95-112 m./310-365 ft (*c.*1 ha./2.47 acres)
(Fig. 131b). There are projecting towers at the
corners and at three of the four gates. One is
immediately struck by the similarity in design
with Khirbet es-Samra, 40 km (25 miles) away,
though the latter is much smaller (Fig. 144).
Excavation has revealed ranges of rooms built
against the walls as well as what are plainly
barrack blocks in the middle. The centre of
the northern half is dominated by a structure
identified as the *principia*, the courtyard of which
can be seen on the air photograph. The buildings

appear to have been single storeyed.

The next military structure appears to have been a *burgus*, the building of which in the year 371 by the *Equites Nona Dalmatae* is recorded by a Latin inscription. It is not known when this unit arrived, and certainly it soon left, being found in the imperial field army soon afterwards (Speidel, 1978, 718ff). No traces of the structure have been identified.

Finally, in the southern part of the town is the building usually known as the 'Barracks' (E), to which epigraphy, confirmed by excavation, gives a date of *c.* 412. Its military character is suggested by the tall walls and two towers and a general similarity to the nearby fort at Qasr el-Baiq, dated epigraphically to 411 (Parker, 1986, 24-6). It may have been the successor to the castellum.

FIGURE 130   Umm el-Jemal, Irbid, Jordan (32°19'N 36°22'E): vertical view. *Photograph: Hunting (September 1953). Copyright: Royal Jordanian Geographic Centre. From Aerial Photographic Archive for Archaeology in the Middle East, inv. no. HAS 56.063.*

FIGURE 131   Umm el-Jemal, Irbid, Jordan (32°19'N 36°22'E): plan of the 'city' and castellum. *Adapted from De Vries, 1986, fig. 10.1.*

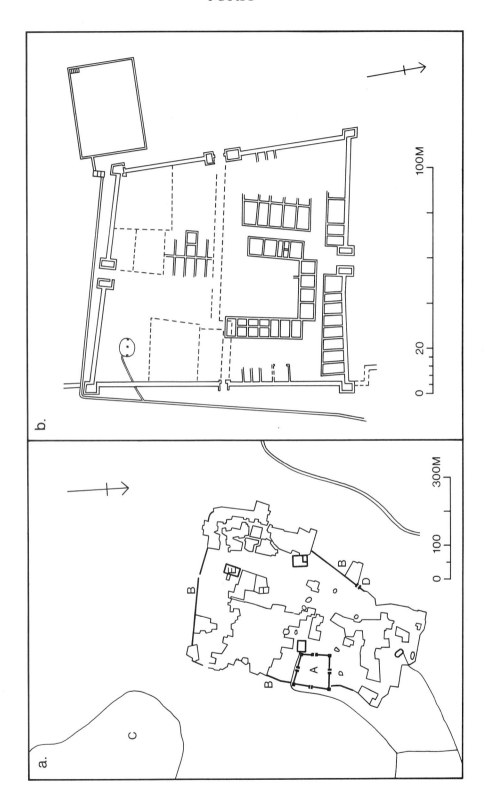

FIGURE 132   Qasr Tell Brak I, Al-Hasakeh, Syria   *David (1927-8). From Poidebard, 1934, X; cf CXXIV.*
(36°40′N 41°4′E): vertical view. *Photograph:* G.

FIGURE 133 Qasr Tell Brak I, Al-Hasakeh, Syria (36°40′N 41°4′E): ground view of parts of the site after excavation revealing the depth of cover over the ruins and the extensive nature of the buried remains. *Photograph: A. Poidebard (1927-8). From Poidebard, 1934, Pl. CXXVII.2.*

FIGURE 134 Qasr Tell Brak, Al-Hasakeh, Syria (36°40′N 41°4′E): plan of the fort. *After Poidebard, 1934, Pl.CXXV.*

QASR TELL BRAK I, SYRIA
(Figs. 132, 133 and 134)

On the vertical view, shadows outline the square mound, under which the ruins of the fort were buried, and the trenches of Poidebard's excavations, then in progress. The fort lies within a ditch, which shows as a vegetation mark. The buried remains were discovered from the air in the aftermath of the first rains of autumn, when

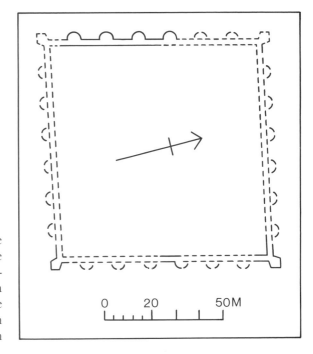

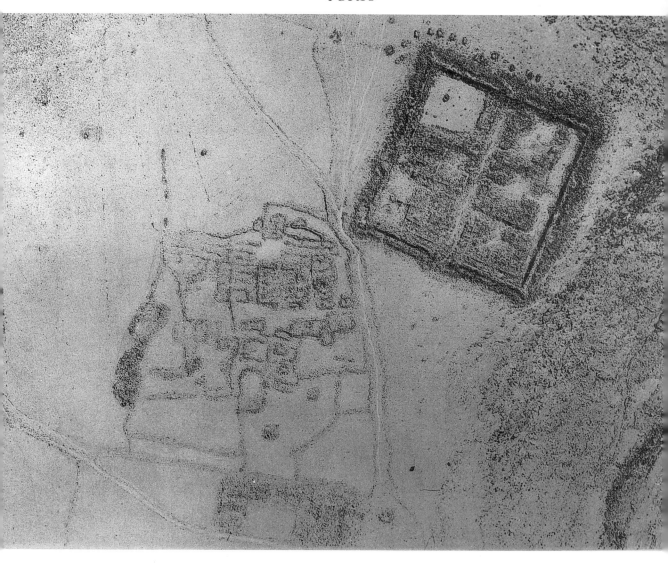

FIGURE 135 Sa'neh, Suweida, Syria (32°41′N 36°4′E): vertical view. *Photograph: de Boysson (1925/32). From Poidebard, 1934, Pl.XLIX (cf. XLVIII).*

the sun had begun to dry out the ground, causing the positions of the angle towers to appear as light-toned vegetation marks (above p. 67). The excavation, made with a work-force of soldiers from the Assyro-Chaldean Battalion, recovered walls at a depth of 1 m. (*c.* 3 ft) under wind blown soil (above, p. 57 and Poidebard, 1934, 144), the thickness of which is demonstrated by Figure 133.

The fort is 91 × 91 m./300 × 300 ft (0.83 ha./2.05 acres), with walls 2.35 m. (7 ft 8 in.) thick. The most striking feature is the series of projecting 'towers'. On the corners are diamond-shaped towers and along each of the walls six semi-circular towers. No evidence of internal buildings was reported and none is visible on these photographs.

In the absence of any artefacts which he could date, Poidebard fell back on the construction technique for diagnostic signs. From that he concluded that the work was Justinianic, paralleled by buildings with brick stamps of that Emperor at Circesium (1934, 144ff). A more recent informed visitor to the site prefers a fourth century date (D. Oates, pers comm. 24 July, 1987). The towers, however, are unusual and more reminiscent of the buttresses on the retaining walls of Early Islamic reservoirs and gardens (Grabar, 1978, photo 181; Kennedy, 1982, 96–107).

SA'NEH, SYRIA
(Figs. 135 and 136)

The well-preserved ruins of a fort and an adjacent civil settlement, unobscured by any later wind-blown deposits, stand out very clearly on the bare surface of the *hamada*. The ground carried very little vegetation when the photograph was taken, but the land beyond the fort must have

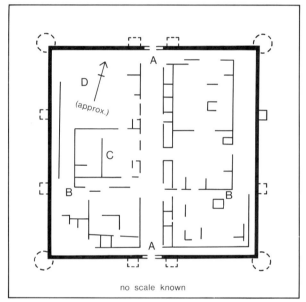

no scale known

FIGURE 136 Sa'neh, Suweida, Syria (32°41′N 36°54′E): sketch plan of the site. *Drawn by D.N.Riley from the air photograph.*

been used in the past to grow crops, because another photograph (Poidebard, 1934, Pl. XLVIII) shows in the background banks and heaps of stones cleared from the land when it was being cultivated. Similar banks and heaps give the plan of ancient fields elsewhere and also may be seen at the edges of modern fields in parts of Syria and Jordan where stony ground has been taken into plough recently. The site lies almost 48 km (30 miles) north-east of Bostra on the route to Nemara and was regarded by

Poidebard as the point beyond which the Bostra to Palmyra road constituted the *limes* (1934, 60). It is perhaps the ancient *Sounva*, which is known from a Greek inscription (Dussaud, 1927, 367).

Poidebard gave no dimensions or plan for this fort; Dumand (1931) said it was '100 paces'. He noted that it was one of his '*types d'après Dioclétien*' (i.e. round towers on the angles and at intervals along the walls), but that the internal layout was of the old style in which buildings stand along streets and not grouped around a central court-yard. He suggested, therefore, that an old fort was reconstructed in the Diocletianic period as one of a series guarding approaches from the south-east (1934, 67ff). Lander (1984, 145) contrasted the layout with that at Da'ajaniya (Fig. 117).

The plan shows a main street (AA) bisecting the camp and flanked by a regular series of rooms on either side, of a style which might be stables. The halves are apparently subdivided by a road (BB) meeting AA at right angles. Near the intersection, there seems to be a large rectangular structure (C). One corner (D), is largely empty. Outside the fort, lines of stones framing tracks, enclosures and modest structures are clustered around the remains of a large square building.

UMM ER-RESAS, JORDAN
(Figs. 137 and 138)

The good quality vertical photograph shows a remarkably interesting rectangular fort and adjacent settlement of irregular plan some 55 km (35 miles) south of Amman (cf. back jacket photograph). The ruins are shown by a combination of shadows and differences of 'texture' – rough where there are the stony ruins of fallen walls and smooth on the surrounding land. Structures may be divided into three categories: the fort and internal ruins, the ruined buildings outside the fort walls, and a scattering of modern houses. The wall of the fort may be drawn with some confidence, but the other ruins are much more difficult and have only been tentatively sketched on the plan (Fig. 138). Recent fieldwork has clarified some details, particularly the plans of numerous churches, which have been incorporated in the drawing.

The site is dominated by the ruins of the large

FIGURE 137 Umm er-Resas, Al-Asimah, Jordan (31°30′N 35°54′E): vertical view. *Photograph: Institut Géographique National (1978). Copyright: Royal Jordanian Geographic Centre. Supplied by Studium Biblicum Archive, Jerusalem IGN-78-JOR, no. 1731.*

FIGURE 138 Umm er-Resas, Al-Asimah, Jordan (31°30′N 35°54′E): plan of the fort. *Drawn by D.N.Riley after Piccirillo, 1986a, 8, fig. 5 and the air photograph.*

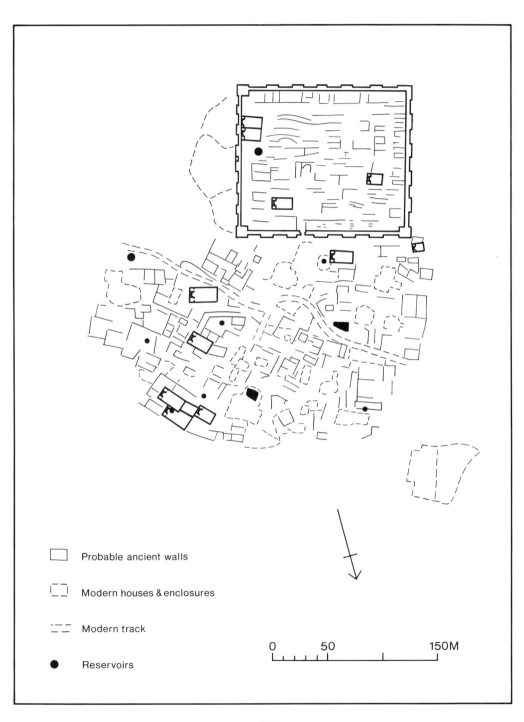

Probable ancient walls

Modern houses & enclosures

Modern track

Reservoirs

0   50   150M

FIGURE 139 Tell al-Ghail, Neineva, Iraq (35°52′N 41°38′E): oblique view looking south-west from a height of 800 ft (250 m.). *Photograph: Royal Air Force (10.17; 22 March 1938). Stein Archive (Institute of Archaeology, London, inv. no. AP. 1791).*

fort, which measures 158 × 139 m./515 × 455 ft (2.2 ha./5.4 acres), and has projecting rectangular towers on the angles. There are also projections on the curtain walls, but these are perhaps more aptly described as buttresses than towers. They resemble the towers spanning the external wall at Da'ajaniya, but lack the internal parts. Whether the latter were never built or were removed in later re-modelling will only be determined by further work on the site.

The interior of the fort is a mass of collapsed stonework. When the photograph was taken the sun was in the south, and its light showed much of the lines of walls running from east-to-west, but little of those running north to south. Figure 136 therefore shows little but east to west walls. Only the positions of the four later churches, recorded on the ground, can be planned accurately. However, the buildings of the fort appear to have been arranged regularly. This is especially noticeable along the north and south sides, where rooms may be seen built against the walls, and along the west wall, where a succession of parallel walls at right angles to the curtain are plainly visible (cf. Brünnow and von Domaszewski, 1904–9, II, 63–72; Saller and Bagati, 1949, 245–51).

While details are lacking, it seems clear that the fort had an arrangement rather like that at Da'ajaniya (Fig. 117) and Umm el-Jemal (Fig. 130) with rooms both in the interior and against the external wall. It could comfortably have accommodated a large cavalry regiment, with men in barracks in the interior and horses in stables against the curtain wall.

Although a very suggestive Royal Air Force air photograph was published by Glueck long ago (1939, Fig. 67; 1970, Fig. 78), it has passed unnoticed that the ruins were those of a Roman fort, even recently by Parker (1986, 37, 45, 48). The revelation has come from the discovery of a mosaic of AD 785 in one of the churches, naming the site as *Kastron Mephaa* (Piccirillo, 1989, 1986b; cf. Saller and Bagati, 1949). To find such a name (given in Greek) lingering a century and half into the Islamic period is interesting enough, but it also allows us to locate an important place name found in two literary sources that provide evidence about the Roman army. The first was Eusebius (*Onom.* 128.21–3; 129.20f), who wrote in the fourth century and named '*Mephaath/Mefaath ... trans Iordanem in qua praesidium Romanorum militum sedet propter vicinam solitudinem*' ('Mefaath ... the other side of Jordan in which there is situated a fort of Roman soldiers beside a neighbouring desert place'). Later, the name occurred in the *Notitia Dignitatum (Or.* XXXVII.19), where *Equites Promoti Indigenae, Mefa* were mentioned.

An adjoining photograph of the area to the north of the ancient town, shows several wadis with clear evidence of a succession of cross walls, while the intervening slopes are dotted with the stone heaps like those made to facilitate ancient water harvesting in the Negev Desert (Evenari *et al.*, 1981). These are most likely to be associated with the town which developed around the fort and continued in existence even after churches had begun to be erected inside its presumably deserted walls.

TELL AL-GHAIL, IRAQ (Fig. 139)

This substantial fort, located in a remote desert area 60 km (38 miles) south of Singara, was first noted by Poidebard (1934, 128) on information from a '*mission aérienne*' which flew during the delimitation of the frontier between Syria and Iraq after the First World War. Poidebard recorded no other details, but marked it on his map of the *limes*. This photograph, one of Stein's, shows the site well, with the ditch and bank visible as vegetation marks.

The fort measures some 116 × 116 m./380 × 380 ft (1.35 ha./3.3 acres). Stein recorded that the remains of the walls, which were apparently built of mud brick, were 5–5.5 m. (16–18 ft) high, and had decayed into banks *c*.8 m. (26 ft) wide. There seem to have been corner towers and perhaps a tall (square?) tower in the north-west angle (the corner near the lower edge of the photograph). There is no dating evidence.

A few kilometres to the north is another small post, which Stein considered to be earlier. (For both sites see Gregory and Kennedy (Stein), 1985, 48–55.)

· Small Forts With ·
External Towers

The dividing line between large and small forts in this category is placed at 0.40 ha. (*c.* 1 acre). This line is not entirely arbitrary, as there is a significant group of forts at or below that size, particularly 0.14-0.22 ha. (0.34-0.54 acres), in contrast to the more widely spread size distribution of the forts larger than 0.40 ha. (1 acre). However, the division cannot be made too rigidly. As mentioned earlier (p. 167), two 'small' forts, Qasr Bshir (Fig. 122) and Deir el-Kahf (Fig. 124), with ground areas of 0.36 and 0.31 ha. (0.89 and 0.77 acres) respectively, were included with the 'large' forts because the buildings inside them were double storeyed and therefore provided much more accommodation. A different kind of exception, the fortlet at Upper Zohar (Fig. 149), is so small (0.034 ha./0.08 acres) that it might well go into the chapter on towers, but it is included here because its disproportionately large corner towers make it a miniature fort.

There are 14 forts described, of which six are

in Syria, four in Jordan, two in Iraq and two in Israel. The Syrian examples include three from the notable series of forts – all with external towers – that stand at intervals along the *Voie des Hans* ('Road of the Caravanserai'), the part of the *Strata Diocletiana* that links Damascus with Palmyra (cf. Fig. 128).

At only four of these forts has a Roman date been firmly established by fieldwork or excavation (Ad-Diyatheh, Avdat 2, Khirbet es-Samra, Qasr el-Hallabat and Upper Zohar – Figs. 141, 143, 144, 147 and 149). This reduced amount of secure dating evidence in comparison with the previous category of large forts is mainly because so many of the small forts are in Syria, a country from which relatively little new information has come since the Second World War. However, three Syrian forts (Khan el-Hallabat, Khan el-Qattar and Khan Aneybeh – Figs. 151, 153 and 155) on the *Strata Diocletiana* can be identified confidently as Roman by milestone citations and inclusion in the *Notitia Dignitatum*. Likewise, two in the Wadi Araba in Jordan (Et-Telah and Gharandal – Figs 157 and 159) can also be identified plausibly with forts in the *Notitia*. Little is known about the dates of the remaining two forts in Syria (Figs. 162 and 163) and the two in Iraq (Figs. 164 and 165).

The forts illustrated are all stone-built. Towers are nearly always square and are almost entirely on corners alone. Interval towers are rare because they were not needed on the short curtain walls, but there are exceptions at Ad-Diyatheh, Avdat 2 and Khirbet es-Samra (Figs. 141, 143, 144), which have both angle and interval towers. Round towers are found on two, perhaps three, forts – Khan el-Hallabat, Khan el-Qattar, and perhaps El-Qdeyr (Figs. 151, 153, 162). In Iraq, Jaddalah 1 (Fig. 164) is a possible Roman fort with U-shaped towers. Qasr Khabbaz (Fig. 165), also in Iraq, with circular corner and interval

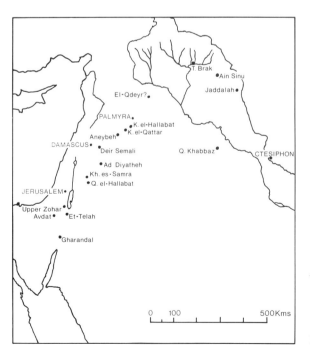

FIGURE 140   Location map.

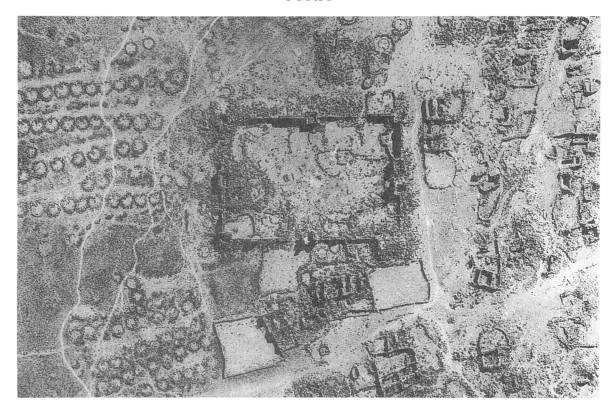

FIGURE 141   Ad-Diyatheh, Suweida, Syria
(32°48′N 36°53′E): vertical view. *Photograph: de
Boysson (1926/32). From Poidebard, 1934, Pl.L.1.*

towers, has never had any informed study made
of it and is included solely on the basis of its
location and Stein's instinct.

Plainly, even the largest of these forts could
have housed only a modest number of people,
but no estimates of troop numbers can be made
because little is known about the internal buildings. There is no suggestion of buildings of
more than one storey in these forts, except for
the two floors in towers. In some instances
this lack of information is because the available
photograph reveals nothing in the interior and
the site has not been surveyed on the ground. In
a number of cases, however, there seem not to
have been internal structures. Thus, Ad-Diyatheh
and Advat 2 (Figs. 141, 143) could have accommodated soldiers in the towers, but the large empty
courtyard may have been intended to provide
refuge or safe camping for travellers. Similarly,
Khan el-Qattar and Khan Aneybeh may not have
had barracks for soldiers. Until more of these

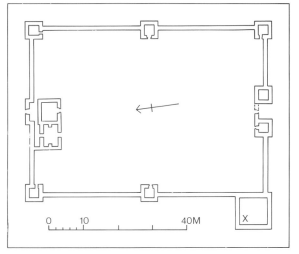

FIGURE 142   Ad-Diyatheh, Suweida, Syria
(32°48′N 36°53′E); plan of the fort. *From Villeneuve,
1986, Fig. 39.3.*

forts have been excavated, the picture will remain
obscure. At the moment we must be prepared to
accept that some of the forts in this category may
simply have provided safe camping under the
protection of a very modest garrison.

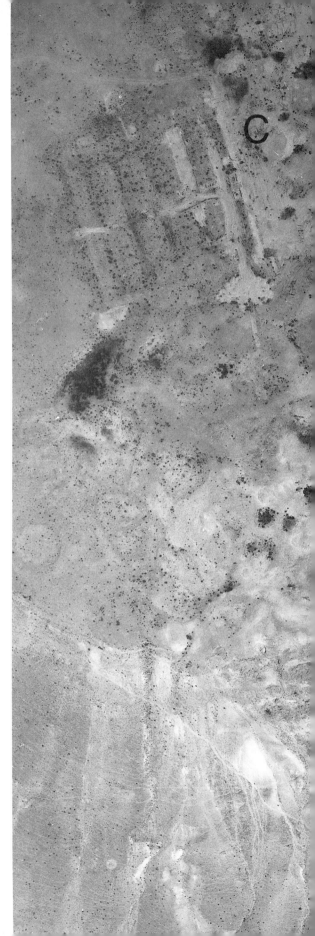

FIGURE 143   Avdat 2, Hadarom Hanegev, Israel (30°45′N 34°46′E): vertical view. *Photograph: Pantomap (1988). Inv. no. 469/88*

AD-DIYATHEH, SYRIA
(Figs. 141 and 142)

The view shows the well-preserved walls of the fort and, to the right, many ancient houses and other buildings. The rows of stone rings seen on the left of the picture were made when a French army unit camped there in the time of the Mandate, not long before the photograph was taken (information from T. Bauzou). Various crudely walled enclosures are probably also recent.

The fort is located some 55 km (35 miles) north-east of Bostra, on the eastern edge of the Jebel Druze, and on the very edge of the region of cultivation. The enclosure measures 71.7 × 51.7 m./235 × 170 ft (0.37 ha./0.92 acres), and has large square towers straddling the corners and at intervals on the walls. Against the middle of the north wall are the remains of what may have been a *principia* in the style of those at Qasr Bshir (Fig. 122) and Qasr el-Azraq (Fig. 126). No other buildings have been identified inside; excavation may reveal if they ever existed.

The building sequence is known as a result of the recent excavations and a tentative chronology has been proposed, though no dated building inscriptions or even coins were found. Occupation began in the first century AD, and a tower (X) was erected in, perhaps, the second century. At the end of the third century, the rectangular walled enclosure with towers was built. This is in line with Poidebard's dating but is at variance with the proposed Severan date for other similar sites in Arabia (Lander, 1984, 144-9; cf. above, p. 175 and Fig. 117). The fort continued in occupation throughout the fourth, fifth and, perhaps, sixth centuries. By the end of this period a considerable village had grown up nearby and it continued to exist into the Ommayad period (Villeneuve, 1986).

AVDAT 2, ISRAEL (Fig. 143)

Two important fortifications and the site of the ancient town of *Oboda* are shown by this photograph. Because there are few shadows to

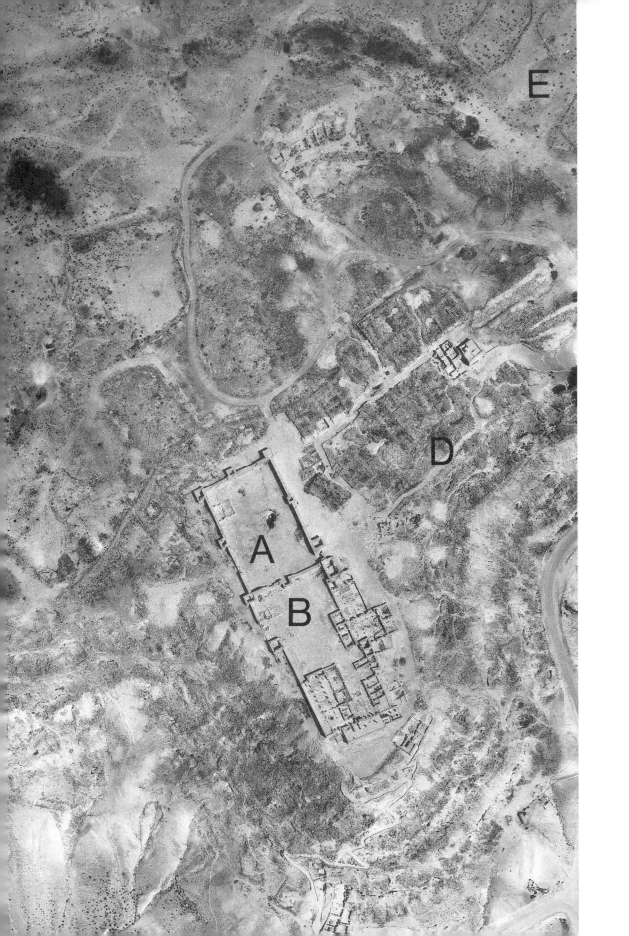

emphasize the lines of walls – and perhaps also because the walls are built of limestone, light in colour and presenting insufficient contrast with the surrounding ground, the only structures to appear prominently are those that have been excavated and partially rebuilt. Outstanding is the citadel – the two large walled compounds in the upper right of the picture. One compound (A) has strong walls measuring *c.*60 × 40 m./ 195 × 130 ft (0.24 ha./0.6 acres), with rectangular angle towers and square interval towers, but its interior is virtually empty. Apart from a chapel and a small room, no internal structures were reported by the excavator, who has conjectured that it was not a fort but a place of refuge, in which the essential water supply for the townspeople would have been provided by the two underground cisterns (Negev, 1986, 287). A dark spot on the photograph gives the position of a large hole within compound A where the roof of a cistern has collapsed. Many such tanks at Oboda were used to collect and store rainwater. The second (larger) compound (B) incorporated two churches and a monastery, which stand above the cliff forming the western side of the hill top occupied by the ancient town. Excavation has revealed that the acropolis area was remodelled in the second half of the fourth century, and at this time the citadel was constructed.

At the lower left corner can be seen the ruins (C) of the square fort, Avdat 1, discussed above (Fig. 115). It shows rather indistinctly by slightly darker tones on the surface, emphasized by black spots indicating small clumps of vegetation that manage to exist in this barren desert region. Four broad bands crossing the interior give the positions of the collapsed buildings of barrack blocks. Pale-toned areas show where fallen debris has recently been cleared from the outer surface of the southern wall, its central gateway, the road inside it and part of the road between two of the barrack blocks. The outside of one of the square corner towers is just visible.

Ruins of the houses of Oboda occur in many places and show quite well in the area marked D, as do small fields in area E.

FIGURE 144   Khirbet es-Samra, Irbid, Jordan (32°11′N 36°10′E): vertical view. *Photograph: Hunting (1953). Copyright: Royal Jordanian Geographic Centre. Supplied from Aerial Photographic Archive for Archaeology in the Middle East, inv. no. HAS 54.058.*

KHIRBET ES-SAMRA, JORDAN
(Figs. 144, 145 and 146)

The site is located beside the *Via Nova Traiana* 37 km (23 miles) south-south-west of Bostra, 48 km (30 miles) from Philadelphia (Amman). While the report of the Princeton Expedition (Butler, 1919, II.A.2, p.XV) has for long indicated that there was a fort here, only the fieldwork of the last few years by Desreumaux and Humbert made the site comprehensible. A very rich harvest has been gathered: a walled town, in and near which are a fort, two fortlets and two towers.

Stone robbing caused a great deal of damage during the last century. The gangs building the

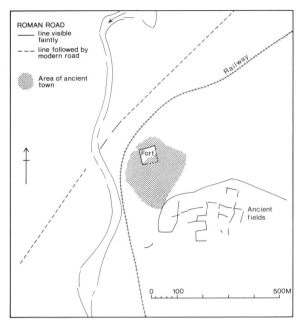

```
ROMAN ROAD
——— line visible
      faintly
- - - line followed by
      modern road

      Area of ancient
      town
```

Railway

Fort

Ancient
fields

0   100   500M

FIGURE 145 *Khirbet es-Samra, Irbid, Jordan (32°11′N 36°10′E): sketch map of the area. Drawn by D.N.Riley from the air photograph and after the plan of the town and* castellum *given in Humbert, 1986, 77, fig. 1.*

Hedjaz Railway found these ruins an attractive quarry and, if one compares the accompanying photograph of 1953 (Fig. 144) with one taken more recently by the IGN, it is plain that the process has continued. Despite the loss of sharpness through enlargement, the north wall, the northern stretches of the west and east walls, and traces of the rest of the circuit of the *castellum* inside the town can be traced on the photograph. Like Jemal (Fig. 130), the town itself had a defensive wall, though here it also had towers – on the east side at least.

A strange complex of walled enclosures, clearly of recent date, may be noted at the top left hand corner of the photograph. By the time of the later IGN survey photograph they had been removed.

The fort is reminiscent in design to that at Jemal, 26 km (16 miles) away, but it covers less than half the area: 60 × 65 m./195 × 212 ft (0.39 ha./0.95 acres). Rectangular, though dissimilar, towers project from each corner; square interval towers straddle each of the walls – one on each side except the east where a pair flank a

gate. This is plainly the fort mentioned by the Princeton Expedition (p. 198).

Many structures can be detected inside the walls and some have been planned by the excavators. One (A on Fig. 146) is certainly a church, which had an unusually broad ground plan, attributed by the excavators to its use of the foundations of an earlier structure. It is located where the *principia* might have been expected. Most of the other buildings are very irregular. Only on the southern part of the west wall, and built against it, is there a hint of what might be original chambers. Elsewhere in the town, the investigators have identified a number of other churches (B) and a reservoir (R).

The excavators have suggested that the fort was constructed in the Diocletianic period, albeit in a location which had seen earlier Roman and Nabataean occupation, perhaps military. They note the possibility that the final phase of occupation – as evidenced by the church in the middle of the *castellum* – may have been monastic. The church itself was deserted in the seventh century (Humbert, 1981-1986).

A consensus now favours identifying Khirbet es-Samra with the *Hatita* of the Peutinger Table and the *Adtitha/Aditttha* of the *Notitia Dignitatum* (*Or.* XXXVII.30; 31) (Kennedy, 1982, 148-52; Desreumaux and Humbert, 1982, 241). The latter attributes to the town the *Cohors Prima Miliaria Thracum* and, *apud Aditttha*, mentions the *Ala Secunda Felix Valentiniana*.

QASR EL-HALLABAT, JORDAN (Figs. 147 and 148)

The fort as we see it is the ruins of an Ommayad desert castle, but like Qasr el-Azraq (Fig. 126) it was Roman in origin. As may be seen, it has suffered a good deal, including the removal of stone for use in the bedouin graveyard stretching from near the mosque (left foreground on Fig. 147, just beyond the south-east tower) across the east face of the fort. From examination of the construction techniques and the building materials (yellow limestone was used at first, giving way to black basalt in the final stages), the fort can be seen to have gone through several phases of development, at least two of which were fundamental. The earliest surviving defended element is a fortlet, 17.5 × 17.5 m. (57 × 57 ft) (A on Fig. 148), 0.03 ha. (0.07 acres), built of limestone. In the next phase, this was incorpor-

ated into a fort, 38 × 38 m./124 × 124 ft (0.14 ha./0.36 acres) again probably of limestone. It is arguable that the semi-projecting towers were a still later addition, part of a scheme in which the curtain wall was heightened (Kennedy, 1982, 19-29), and basalt stones were brought on the site for the first time, though that is doubted by recent

FIGURE 146 Khirbet es-Samra, Irbid, Jordan (32°11'N 36°10'E): plan of the castellum and its surroundings. *After Humbert, 1986, 77, fig. 2.*

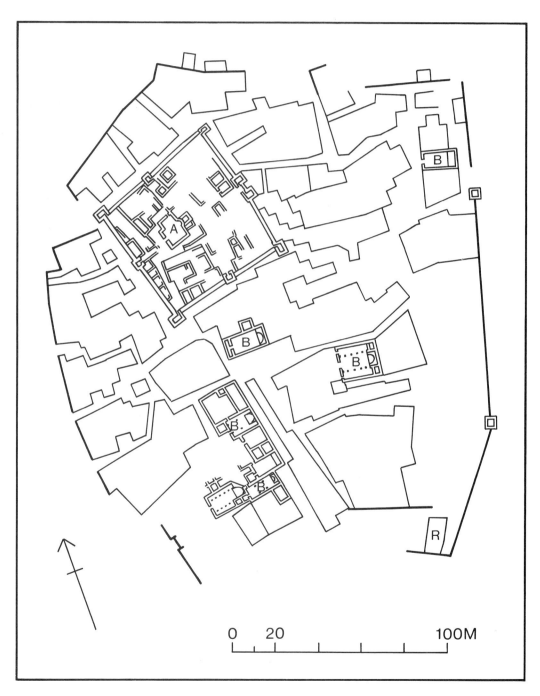

FIGURE 147 Qasr el-Hallabat, Al-Asimah, Jordan (32°06′N 36°20′E): oblique view looking south-west across the fort and towards the reservoir in the distance. *Photograph: Royal Air Force (c.1939). Stein Archive (Bodleian Library, Oxford, inv. no. Ms Stein 331 fol.7).*

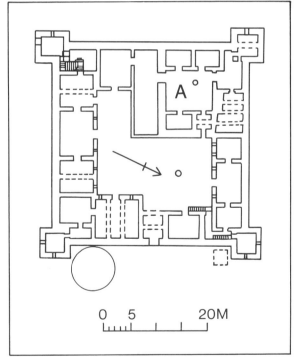

FIGURE 148 Qasr el-Hallabat, Al-Asimah, Jordan (32°06′N 36°20′E): plan of the fort. *After Kennedy, 1982, 61, fig. 10.*

commentators (Bisheh, forth; Parker, 1986, 32).

Building in 212-4 and 529 is recorded by inscribed basalt blocks re-used within the fort. The tendency to assign them to two of the recognizable building phases (Kennedy, 1982, 50; Parker, 1986, 30-2), must be treated with great caution. It has recently been suggested, not implausibly, that these texts, together with all of the basalt blocks including the dozens bearing a great edict of Anastasius, *might* have been imported as building material in the Ommayad period from another site, perhaps Khirbet es-Samra (west-north-west) (Fig. 144), or Umm el-Jemal (north) (Fig. 130) (Bisheh, forth). Certainly, worked stone taken from buildings has regularly been moved from one place to another for re-use, both in ancient and recent times.

The final phase of occupation and development

was Ommayad (AD 650-740). The mosque was built, a bath building constructed a mile away at Hammam as-Sarakh, the agricultural complex in the wadi to the west (3 on Fig. 21) laid out, and elaborate mosaics put down in the rooms of the fort (Bisheh, 1980; 1982; forth).

UPPER ZOHAR, ISRAEL
(Figs. 149 and 150)

Shadows cast by the sun shining from the south-west emphasize every unevenness of a flat barren landscape in which there are few man-made features to be found. Atop the ridge is a Roman fortlet; the rough 'texture' on the photograph suggests the lumps of rock from which its walls were built – large blocks of flint gathered from the surrounding area. The heaps of stone at the corners of the fortlet give the positions of corner towers, which appear to have been square, a conclusion verified by the excavations mentioned below. On the same ridge was a police post of

FIGURE 149 Upper Zohar, Hadarom Hanegev, Israel (31°14′N 35°14′E): plan of the fortlet. *From Harper, 1986, Fig.17.1.*

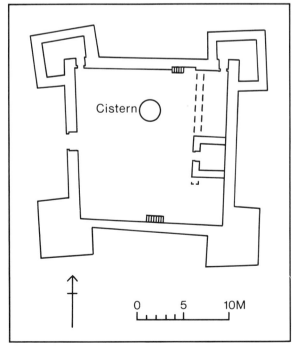

FIGURE 150 Upper Zohar, Hadarom Hanegev, Israel (31°14′N 35°14′E): vertical view. *Photograph: Pantomap (1982), inv. no. 3420/82.*

the British Mandate period, suggesting that both the Roman and British forces stationed here may have had somewhat similar functions. The fortlet stands near an old road, which runs mainly along the ridges, whereas the modern road follows the valleys.

The site is well understood as a result of recent excavation. As may be seen from the plan, the little fort is sub-square in shape. It measures 19.2 × 18.6 × 17.7 × 18 m./63 × 61 × 58 × 59 ft (0.034 ha./0.08 acres). Large square towers mark the angles and there is a gate in the middle of the west side. Inside, a room was built against the

FIGURE 151 Khan el-Hallabat, Homs, Syria (34°22′N 38°4′E): vertical view. *Photograph: de Boysson (November 1930). From Poidebard, 1934, Pl. XL.*

wall opposite the gate, stairs led up to the north and south walls and there seems to have been a cistern below the courtyard. Pottery and coins go back no earlier than the fifth century, though the structure is of a type which would not be out of place in the fourth century. There seems to have been repair and reconstruction in the Justinianic period (Harper, 1986).

KHAN EL-HALLABAT, SYRIA
(Figs. 151 and 152)

The site is 31 km. (19 miles) from Palmyra at the north-eastern end of the valley through which

the *Strata Diocletiana* runs. Like Khan el-Manqoura (Fig. 128), Khan el-Qattar and Khan Aneybeh (Figs. 153, 155), the fort is one of a series along the '*Voie des Hans*', which is well marked between Dumeir and Palmyra along the south of the Jebel Rawaq (Poidebard, 1934, 49ff; Dunand, 1931). The vertical photograph provides an excellent record of the plan of the fort, with the walls highlighted by the sun and given emphasis by deep shadows. The water course running diagonally across the photograph, though dry when it was taken, had clearly held running water during the rains of the previous winter. The area is a centre of pasturage – though the vegetation is sparse, to judge from the photograph – and has a perennial water supply. There is a well inside the south-west tower and three more are outside the fort. Its appearance, especially that of the towers, is similar to other forts along this route (Figs. 128, 153) (Poidebard, 1934, 48f). The fort is relatively small, measuring 47 m. (153 ft) square, 0.22 ha. (0.55 acres), but it has massive double walls, 3.5 m. (11.5 ft) thick. The towers are 7.5 m. (24.5 ft) in diameter, and

FIGURE 152 Khan el-Hallabat, Homs, Syria (34°22′N 38°4′E): plan of the fort. *From Poidebard, 1934, Pl. XLI.*

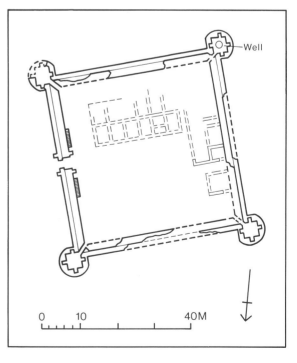

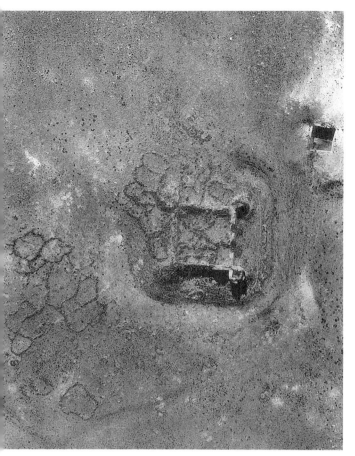

have an unexpected internal plan – square, with slots projecting from the centre of each side (cf. Fig. 155). Unusually, many of the internal buildings visible are set in from the walls and are thus reminiscent of Da'ajaniya (Fig. 117) rather than the numerous small forts with a central courtyard (e.g. Figs. 147, 155).

The site has been identified with *Veriaraca* of the *Notitia Dignitatum* (*Or.* XXXII. 34), base of the *Ala Nova Diocletiana*.

KHAN EL-QATTAR, SYRIA
(Figs. 153 and 154)

On this photograph the walls and towers of the fort, high-lighted by a late morning sun, are outlined by deep shadows on their north-west side. Likewise the west side of the ditch at the bottom of the picture is highlighted in contrast with that on the right. Tumble from the walls on the north and east has been used to construct bedouin enclosures outside.

Though rather smaller, 41 × 41 m./135 × 135 ft (0.17 ha./0.42 acres), and without intermediate towers, the fort is very similar in design to Khan el-Manqoura, a square enclosure with 'fan-shaped' corner towers (Fig. 128). Towers with the 'fan-shaped' ground plan are also found, with slight variations, at Khan el-Hallabat (Fig. 151), Khan el-Abyad (Poidebard, 1934, Pl. XXXIX), and at the two legionary fortresses of Lejjun (Fig. 76) and Udruh (Fig. 79) (Poidebard, 1934, 48 and 52; Lander, 1984, 246-57). There are no visible traces of internal structures other than the bedouin animal corrals (but cf. Fig. 155). Water supply was assured – as at Manqoura – by a reservoir fed from a canalized wadi course.

Qattar may be either *Carneia* or the *Cunna* of the *Notitia Dignitatum* (*Or.* XXXII.35), base of the *Ala Prima Francorum* (Dunand, 1931, 241; 247ff).

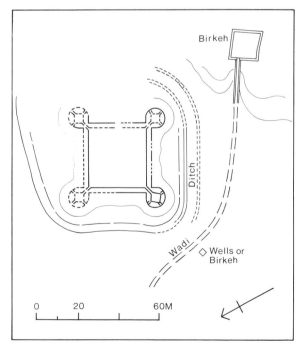

FIGURE 155 Khan Aneybeh, Homs, Syria (33°58′N 37°26′E): vertical view. *Photograph: de Boysson (November 1930). From Poidebard, 1934, Pl. XXVII.*

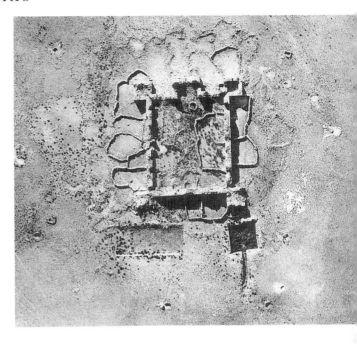

KHAN ANEYBEH, SYRIA
(Figs. 155 and 156)

This vertical view shows a fort, measuring 48.6 × 39 m./160 × 128 ft (0.19 ha./0.47 acres). It is of massive build, with walls 2-3 m. (6-10 ft) thick and large square towers, 9 m. (*c*.30 ft) on the side, projecting at the angles. The interior plan of the towers is like that at Khan el-Hallabat, though there they are 'fan-shaped' (Fig. 151). In the centre of the south wall, projecting as far as the towers, is a large rectangular structure reminiscent of that at Qasr Bshir and Qasr el-Azraq (Figs. 122, 126; cf. Fig. 141). Although on the photograph only irregular bedouin structures are visible inside the curtain wall, Poidebard's plan of the fort included traces of regular buildings. Water was provided by two reservoirs just beyond the north wall (Poidebard, 1934, 46ff). Poidebard dated the fort stylistically to the Diocletianic period (1934, 54).

The fort lies on the *Strata Diocletiana* between Manqoura and Basiri, just at the point where a road runs off to the north-north-west over the Jebel Rawaq towards Qaryateyn. A watch tower is located nearby and the road is well defined. The place has been identified as *Oneuatha* (or *Anab[atha]*) of the *Notitia Dignitatum* (Or. XXXII.41), base of the *Cohors V Pacata Alamannorum* (Dunand, 1931).

ET-TELAH, JORDAN
(Figs. 157 and 158)

The remote desert site of Et-Telah lies some 25 km. (16 miles) south of the Dead Sea, on the eastern side of the Wadi Araba, the deep and wide valley connecting the Dead Sea with the Gulf of Aqaba, 65 km (40 miles) to the south. Early visitors, who saw the site at ground level or from the vantage of a neighbouring slope, were struck by the extensive decayed remains. It

FIGURE 156 Khan Aneybeh, Homs, Syria (33°58′N 37°26′E): plan of the fort. *After Poidebard, 1934, Pl.XXVIII.*

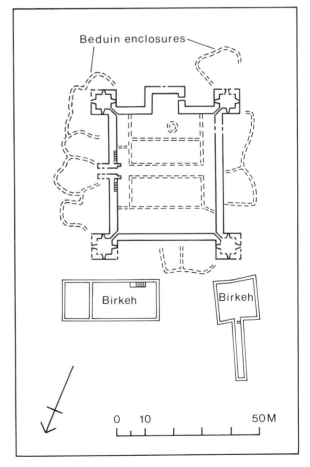

Beduin enclosures

Birkeh

Birkeh

0 10 50M

FIGURE 157 Et–Telah, Al-Kerak, Jordan (30°49′N 35°24′E): oblique view looking west from a height of 200 ft (60 m). *Photograph: Royal Air Force (07.45; 25 May 1937). Crawford Collection (Institute of Archaeology, London, RAF no. 12735).*

was subsequently recorded by the Royal Air Force in 1937 on several good oblique air photographs, one of which is reproduced here. This photograph shows a small fort (A on Fig. 158), its walls outlined by shadows, a reservoir (B) fed by an aqueduct, and in the background a very regular system of ditches. This is the view that was seen from the air by Glueck and Traill (cf. above p. 52). Only approximate dimensions are available for the fort, which is about 40 × 40 m./130 × 130 ft (0.16 ha./0.39 acres). The walls are 2 m. (6.5 ft) thick, and there are remains of square corner towers.

The extensive grid of ditches (Fig. 158) was

presumably dug for irrigation purposes. When the photographs were taken the sun was high in the sky, so the relief of the ground is not shown by shadows, but the ditches can be followed very well by the vegetation growing in them, which is seen particularly clearly on one of the unpublished Royal Air Force photographs. The remains of various walls are also visible; in some cases two walls running close together in parallel may have been conduits for water. The site is between the tributary valleys of the Wadi et-Telah and the Wadi es-Sidre and the complex has been partly washed away by torrents from the hills.

Although Glueck identified no Roman pottery amongst the large number of almost exclusively Nabataean sherds he reported, Et-Telah has been identified convincingly with *Toloha*, base of the *Ala Constantiana* in the *Notitia Dignitatum* (Or. XXXIV.34). The fort is small, but is almost identical in size to that at Khan el-Qattar (0.17

ha. (0.42 acres); cf. above, Fig. 153), which was likewise intended to accommodate an *ala* (Musil, 1907-8, 209-14; Frank, 1934, 214f; Alt, 1935, 14; Glueck, 1935, 11-17; *idem.*, 1939, 149f).

GHARANDAL, JORDAN
(Figs. 159, 160 and 161)

The old Royal Air Force vertical photograph (Fig. 159) gives a good impression of this small

FIGURE 158 Et-Telah, Al-Kerak, Jordan (30°49′N 35°24′E): plan of the site. *Drawn by D.N.Riley from a vertical air photograph of 1953 (Aerial Photographic Archive for Archaelogy in the Middle East HAS 24.079).*

fort, which lies in the lower half of the Wadi Araba. The fort is at the mouth of a minor tributary wadi which flows from the hills rising on its east, and is located beside a road which runs over the hills to the fort at Sadaqa *(Zadacatha)* and then north to Petra. The dark spots are patches of vegetation also seen on the ground view (Fig. 160), which shows the nature of surface in this desolate area. Wind blown sand and silt has covered the remains of the fort walls, which now only show as broad stony banks, as also may be seen in the ground view; the figure is standing on the west wall and the south-west corner tower is in the left centre of the photograph. The hills in the background are

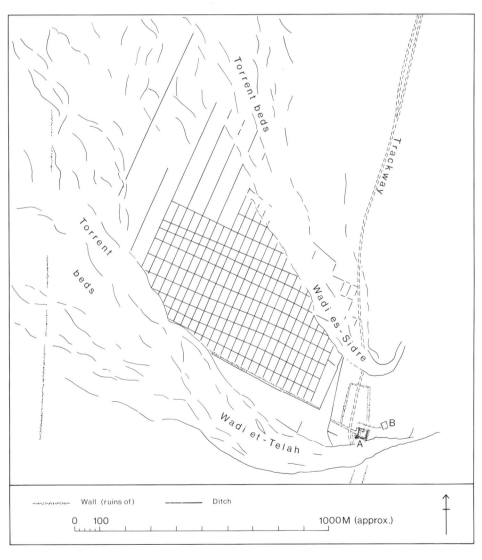

those along the west side of the wadi, the breadth and flatness of which is brought out in this view.

The fort measures 37 × 37 m./120 × 120 ft (0.14 ha./0.34 acres), with remains of projecting corner towers: according to Musil (1907–08, 193–7), two are small and square and two, very elongated. Musil also observed two other structures: a reservoir (A) fed by a channel coming in

from the hills to the east and part of a straight sided structure (B). Neither can be seen on the photograph, perhaps because in the generation after Musil's visit, they were washed away or buried deeper by the changed flow pattern in this wadi fan. A watch tower on one of the hills to the east would have made sense, but none has been reported.

Dating the fort to the Roman period is dependent partly on its appearance and location. More important, on the basis of its place on the list and the name itself, it is identified with the *Arieldela* of the *Notitia Dignitatum*, base of the *Cohors Secunda Galatarum* (Or. XXXIV.44).

FIGURE 159 Gharandal, Ma'an, Jordan (30°05′N 35°12′E): vertical view from a height of 4000 ft (1200 m.). *Photograph: Royal Air Force (16.00; 14 March 1938). Stein Archive (Bodleian Library, Ms Stein 331, fol. 50).*

FIGURE 160 Gharandal, Ma'an, Jordan (30°05'N 35°12'E):.ground view of the fort looking north-west. *Photograph: D.L.Kennedy (c.14.00; 29 May 1985).*

EL-QDEYR(?), SYRIA
(Fig. 162)

The brilliance of Poidebard's results, so early in the history of aerial archaeology, tends to divert attention from many frustrating gaps in the information he published. Technically, this photograph is a good record of an extensive field of ruins, every detail of which is revealed by shadows thrown by morning sunlight. Unfortunately Poidebard was not sure of the exact location of this site, which he did not visit on the ground, and even the name El-Qdeyr is uncertain (Poidebard, 1934, 81). Its approximate position is about 70 km (44 miles) south of the Euphrates on the route from Palmyra to Sura. Musil noted what seem to be the same ruins, but without comment (1928, 71). It must be included here because of the good state of preservation of the fort and the buildings surrounding it, the rediscovery of which is very desirable.

The site consists of two elements. There are ruins of many buildings apparently partly covered by wind-blown material, and a square fort with (square?) corner towers, also mantled by silt. It is not clear whether the settlement grew up around an existing fort or the fort was built within an existing settlement. The nature of the

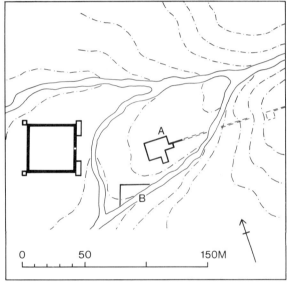

FIGURE 161 Gharandal, Ma'an, Jordan (30°05'N 35°12'E): plan of the fort. *From Musil 1907-08, fig. 142.*

large settlement is of interest, and the traces of planning might suggest a military character for it too. Some buildings at least are plainly square or rectangular and what seems to be a street runs across the site just north of the fort. The whole is surrounded by a wall, at least on the top and left sides of this photograph. Regrettably Poidebard gives no dimensions and there is nothing in the photograph that allows us to calculate them even approximately.

FIGURE 162 El-Qdeyr(?), Damascus, Syria (35°20'N 38°50'E): vertical view taken from a height of 3800 ft (1250 m.). *Photograph: de Boysson (10.00; 23 October 1930). From Poidebard, 1934, Pl. LXXIV.1.*

DEIR-SEMALI, SYRIA (Fig. 163)

This low level photograph, taken with the sun ahead and a little to the left, was selected by Poidebard to illustrate his *contre-jour* technique (see above p. 60). It shows the fort and the rocky slopes near it outlined by short shadows and the intersection of two Roman roads seen as a highlight.

The fort is one of a group close to the crossing of the important roads from Damascus to the Jebel Seys and from Dumeir to Shaqqa (Poidebard, 1934, 169). It is situated on an eminence overlooking the crossroads. Square with projecting square towers at the angles, it is described by Poidebard (1934, 194) as of Diocletianic type. No dimensions are given, but 40 to 50 m./130 to

FIGURE 163 Deir Semali, Damascus, Syria (33°26'N 36°44'E): oblique view looking south from a height of 300 ft (c.100 m.). *Photograph: A. Poidebard (08.00; 17 June, 1932). From Poidebard, 1934, Pl. IX.*

175 ft (0.16 to 0.25 ha./0.4 to 0.6 acres) might be estimated very approximately from the road widths. There is nothing known about the date of the fort.

JADDALAH 1, IRAQ (Fig. 164)

This structure, identified by Stein as a *castellum*, stands just across a wadi from the Parthian structure described below (Fig. 186). A rectangle of light-toned vegetation marks, inside which is a dark mark, give the general plan. On its east (the right-hand side) the remains of the curtain wall and at least two towers can be seen. The fort is *c*.47 × 47 m./154 × 154 ft (0.22 ha./0.55

FIGURE 164 Jaddalah 1, Neineva, Iraq (35°47′N 43°08′E): looking west from a height of 150 ft (c. 50 m.). *Photograph: Royal Air Force (10.45; 10 November 1938). Stein Archive (The British Museum, Department of Western Asiatic Antiquities, Small Archive, Air Photographs—Stein-Iraq, RAF no. 13842).*

acres), with walls of cemented rubble. Small semi-circular towers project from the curtain wall and there are circular towers on the corners. The plan resembles those of the forts at Khirbet el-Khan and Mujaiyir (Poidebard, 1934, Pl. CXLIX.1 and 2), which had circular corner towers and two semi-circular interval towers on each wall (see Gregory and Kennedy (Stein), 1985, fig. 7).

Stein saw this fort as part of a series marking the route linking Hatra to Tell Afar on the main road from Singara to the Tigris (Gregory and Kennedy (Stein), 1985, 72ff). Even if his identification of the whole of that route northwards is open to challenge, the first stage, across open flat terrain to the end of a chain of hills, is plausible. As such, he is probably correct in identifying the locale as the *Ad Herculem* of the *Peutinger Table*, the *Herakleous Bomoi*, 'Altars of Heracles', of Ptolemy (*Geog*. V.18.1) (Gregory and Kennedy (Stein), 1985, 67-9, 81ff, 399, 400). There is a water supply in the wadi, as may be seen in the photograph by the approaching column of sheep.

FIGURE 165 Qasr Khabbaz, Al-Anbar, Iraq (33°33′N; 42°15′E): oblique view looking west from a height of 200 ft (60 m.). *Photograph: Royal Air Force (5 January 1939). Stein Archive (The British Museum, Department of Western Asiatic Antiquities, Small Archive, Air Photographs – Stein-Iraq, RAF no. 05708).*

QASR KHABBAZ, IRAQ
(Figs. 165 and 166)

The ruins of this fort are some 50 km. (31 miles) west of Hit on the Euphrates. Like Umm es-Selabikh and Qasr es-Swab, it served as a stage post on the caravan route across the desert from Hit to Palmyra and Damascus. It is *c*.29 × 29 m./96 × 96 ft (0.084 ha./0.21 acres) with round corner towers and semi-circular interval towers that still stand to almost 5 m. (15 ft). Internal rooms face onto a courtyard. The fort is above a deep wadi which has been dammed to create a large reservoir, now silted up.

The site is illustrated well by this air photograph, which makes good use of shadows to emphasize the walls of the fort and the steep edge of the wadi. It also shows the flat ground on both sides of the wadi, on which Stein's pilot had evidently landed the Vincent aircraft (seen in the distance on a ground view). The pale-toned areas on the right side of the wadi are presumably deposits of wind-blown material.

Stein was in no doubt about the Roman date of the fort. Though this remains to be proved (and is rejected by Bell, 1911, 121), the location of Qasr Khabbaz conforms well with the growing corpus of evidence for Roman occupation in the region, coming from Kifrin, Bijan Island, Telbis Island and Ana (Fig. 62) on the Euphrates 80–100 km (50–60 miles) to the north (Gregory and Kennedy (Stein), 1985, 185–95). Its position on a known Palmyrene trade route (Teixidor, 1984, 20–3) is also suggestive.

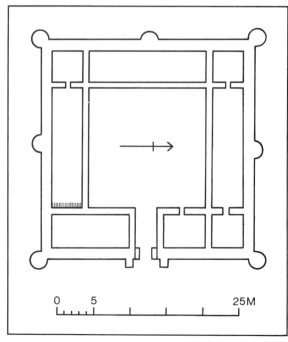

FIGURE 166 Qasr Khabbaz, Al-Anbar, Iraq (33°33′N 42°15′E): sketch plan of the fort. *Prepared from air photographs and Stein's description (Gregory and Kennedy (Stein), 1985, fig. 16; cf. Bell, 1911, 120, fig. 65).*

As one would expect, the interiors of Roman forts are largely taken up with accommodation for the soldiers and, where appropriate, their mounts. The two sites illustrated below, and a third at Tell Bati (Poidebard, 1934, Pl. CXXXIX), are unusual in seemingly consisting *only* of such accommodation. As such they are unparalleled anywhere else in the Empire.

Caution is necessary, however. At Ain Sinu I (Fig. 167) there is evidence of rooms set within

FIGURE 167 Ain Sinu I, Neineva, Iraq (36°37′N 42°11′E): oblique view looking north-east from a height of 600 ft (200 m.). *Photograph: Royal Air Force (13.05; 31 March 1938). Stein Archive (Institute of Archaeology, London, inv. no. AP 1701).*

the thickness of wide double walls, which may have supplied some of the space necessary for administrative functions and for storage. Alternatively, it has been suggested that the unusual layout might be explained by the provision of many of the administrative functions from the adjoining fort, Ain Sinu II (Fig. 113). A similar suggestion might be made about the other Roman fort discussed, Tell Brak 2 (Fig. 169), which is not far from the fort of Tell Brak 1 (Fig. 132). In addition, we should compare the plan of Avdat 1 (Fig. 115), which on the photograph is a seeming 'barracks fort', but on excavation proved to have had rows of additional chambers around three of the curtain walls.

While both forts at Ain Sinu have been

excavated and dated to the Severan period, there
is no evidence of date from the fort at Tell Bati
and no close date within the Roman period from
that at Tell Brak 2 (Fig. 169).

FIGURE 168 Ain Sinu I, Neineva, Iraq (36°37′N
42°11′E): plan of the 'Barracks'. *From Oates, 1968,
Fig. 6.*

AIN SINU I, IRAQ
(Figs. 167 and 168)

This very interesting photograph records the plan
of a large fort, Ain Sinu I, which was dubbed
the 'Barracks' by the excavator (Oates, 1968, 82-
5). Light and dark marks, presumably caused by
differences in the vegetation, give the positions
of the rampart of the fort and of six strips of

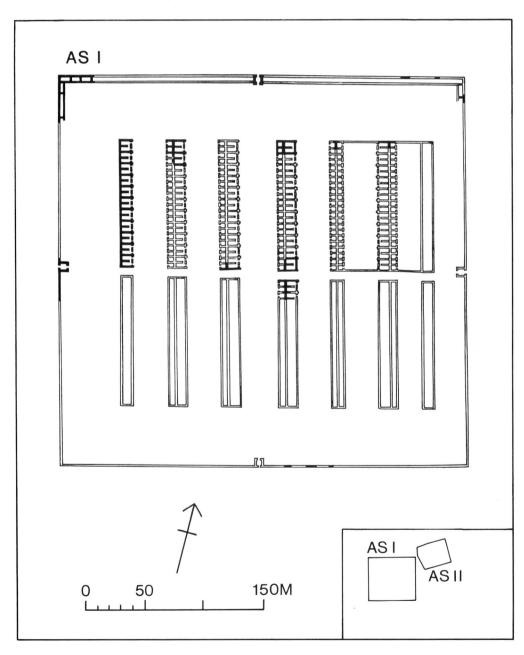

raised ground inside (Gregory and Kennedy (Stein), 1985, 25). On the left edge of the picture, near the north-eastern angle of Ain Sinu I, is the site of the adjacent fort, Ain Sinu II (the 'Castellum'), which can be seen only indistinctly.

The 'Barracks' is one of the largest forts known in the East: 342 × 310 m./1220 × 1013 ft (10.6 ha./26.2 acres). It is also one of the strangest: none of the expected administrative buildings were found, only rows of rooms of two sizes (Fig. 168). A possible interpretation is that the fort was built to house two newly formed large cavalry regiments (*alae milliariae*, each of 720 men) which were to be trained and administered under the eyes of the neighbouring garrison. The 14 blocks form 12 sets of courtyards each flanked by a row of large rooms (stables?) and a row of small (barracks?) rooms laid out symmetrically. Casemate walls enclose rooms identified as 'magazines' (Gregory and Kennedy, 1985 (Stein), 391-3). Excavation by Professor D. Oates has dated the 'Barracks', like the 'Castellum', to the early third century (Oates, 1968, 82-5). In contrast to long standing practice in the Early Empire (Lander, 1984, ch. III), the corners meet at sharp angles rather than being rounded.

TELL BRAK 2, SYRIA
(Fig. 169)

A sub-square fort, 197 m. (644 ft) across, which Poidebard called '*camp tête du pont*' (bridgehead fort), is shown well by vegetation marks. The fort has an exterior ditch 20 m. (65 ft) wide and a wall or rampart, probably covered by wind blown silt; inside are four parallel ridges, two of which are apparently divided at mid-point. At the upper right of the picture is the River Jaghjagh, and between this and the fort is a '*tell observatoire*' (cf. Fig. 100).

A trial excavation was made (by French colonial legionnaires of the Assyro-Chaldean battalion, who had also been employed in the excavations at Tell Brak 1) in 1927, which apparently confirmed that the site was Roman (Poidebard, 1934, 144). As the site is very similar in appearance to Ain Sinu 1, it may have served the same

FIGURE 169 Tell Brak 2, Al-Hasakeh, Syria (36°40′N 41°04′E): vertical view from a height of 8000 ft (2500 m.). *Photograph: Favriau (15.00; 24 October, 1927). From Poidebard, 1934, Pl. CXXII.*

purpose. Though only a little over one third the size of the latter, it is still large (4 ha./ 9.88 acres). On the analogy of Ain Sinu, the '*strigae*' may be reconstructed as three long – or perhaps six short – sets of opposing rooms and stables. The size would suit a normal cavalry regiment, an *ala quingenaria* of 480 men, or, if less generously laid out than Ain Sinu 1, an *ala milliaria* of 720.

· CHAPTER ELEVEN ·

Towers

Towers are frequent throughout the region, but have very seldom been recorded well by air photographs. They appear only incidentally on Poidebard's published photographs, are seen on none of Stein's surviving material, and the high-level verticals are too small in scale to show such small features adequately. It is possible that some of the lost Poidebard photographs showed towers better, in support of which suggestion it may be noted that his map (1934, Pl. XXIV) of the surroundings of the fort at Khan el-Manqoura (Fig. 128) included five towers. These deficiencies in the air photographs have not been made good

FIGURE 170 Location map.

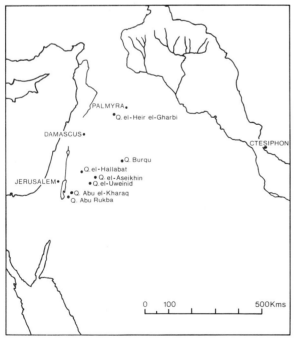

to any extent by field work and survey on the ground, though the recent work at Lejjun by Parker must be mentioned.

In some instances towers were the 'eyes' of a fortress or fort (cf. Kennedy, 1988), perched on surrounding hilltops. An experiment by Parker has shown that the towers around Lejjun could be in visual communication with each other and the Late Empire fortress at Lejjun, especially after dark by beacon lights (Parker, 1986, 79-84). Elsewhere, they were links between forts, as along the *Strata Diocletiana* (see Poidebard's map).

In north-eastern Syria, where the valley of the River Khabur and its tributaries have numerous ancient tells, the Romans were believed by Poidebard to have made use of such elevated positions for the sites of '*tells observatoires*' (1934, 129 *et seq.*). The theory has merit, though in practice none of his tell sites is known to have been used for a Roman watch tower. Since his time, however, excavations have supported the idea of Roman exploitation of tells; there were Roman forts on top of Tell el-Hajj, just above the Euphrates' bend (Stucky, 1973; 1975), and on Tel es-Seba (Fig. 107) in the Negev.

At Qasr Burqu (Fig. 172) the tower was plainly intended as an outpost rather than an observation point. Its dimensions are not much less than those of the smallest of the forts discussed previously. Similarly, from its hill top, the small fort which preceded the larger towered fort at Qasr el-Hallabat (Fig. 147) served a dual function of observation point and outpost; it provided more accommodation than a simple watch tower. The small hilltop post at Qasr Aseikhin (Fig. 176) on the edge of the Azraq oasis may be compared (Kennedy, 1982, 107-13).

Most towers were very simple in design (Fig. 176). The ground plan was normally square or rectangular, giving about 100 square metres (1000 square feet) of floor area, perhaps divided into two or three chambers. Their heights were often considerable. The tower at Qasr Abu Rukba was still standing 9 m. (*c.* 30 ft) high when Brünnow and von Domaszewski (1905, 43) passed in 1898, and there are several others still surviving to similar heights even now (Figs. 171, 172). Unfortunately, many other towers have become little more than heaps of rubble on hill tops or beside Roman roads.

The dates of towers are difficult to determine from the evidence at present available. Towers dating to the Nabataean period are common in Arabia, and many were re-used in the Roman period, though it is not certain how many for military purposes. Some continued in use during later periods. Pottery sherds from the surface near the towers around Lejjun collected by Parker, together with the results of similar surveys in Moab and around the Wadi el-Hesa will produce useful if very broad evidence of dates, though sherds unfortunately prove nothing about the person who broke the vessel, whether it was a soldier on duty or a shepherd taking shelter at a deserted site.

QASR EL-HEIR EL-GHARBI, SYRIA (Fig. 171 and 176)

The photograph shows the tower as it appeared shortly before Schlumberger commenced excavation in 1936. With the exception of the partially collapsed masonry of the tower, the buildings on

FIGURE 171 Qasr el-Heir el-Gharbi, Homs, Syria (34°23′N 37°37′E): oblique view looking north. *Photograph: de Boysson (n.d.). From Poidebard, 1934, Pl. XXXV.2.*

FIGURE 172 Qasr Burqu, Irbid, Jordan (32°36'N 38°02'E): oblique view looking north-west. *Photograph: Matson (1931/33). Matson Collection (Library of Congress, inv. no. LC-M33-4523).*

the site have gradually been reduced to mounds of debris.

The site lies 65 km (40 miles) west–south-west of Palmyra at the crossing of two great routes, one from Damascus to Palmyra via Qaryateyn, and that from Emesa to Jauf. At Qasr el-Heir water was supplied by wells, but the site forms part of the major scheme of water harvesting, agriculture and settlement which was described above in connection with the dam at Harbaqa (Fig. 17).

Poidebard interpreted the remains at this place as a Roman *castellum* to which a tower had been added. Excavations, however, have demonstrated

that the tower is the earlier, its relatively good state of preservation being due to the good stone of which it was made. Its outer dimensions are 15.6 × 12.5 m. (51 × 41 ft), and it still reaches to a height of 16.75 m. (55 ft). The attached structure was an elaborate Ommayad edifice with central courtyard (Schlumberger, 1986, 9 and pl. 22), built of stone, burnt brick and semi-dried brick, with stucco decoration. Its decay produced the ruin which Poidebard interpreted as a *castellum*. The sequence of occupation on the site gives a probable Roman road station in the fourth and fifth centuries, a Byzantine monastery in the sixth century, then an Early Islamic desert castle. The monastery, firmly attested by inscriptions, included, as was common with such structures, the strong tower which was later incorporated into the Ommayad castle.

The Roman name appears to have been *Heliara-*

FIGURE 173 Qasr Burqu, Irbid, Jordan (32°36′N 38°02′E): ground view looking east across the ghadir towards the tower. *Photograph: G. Bisheh.*

mia, which is on the Peutinger road map but not, significantly, in the *Notitia Dignitatum* (Schlumberger, 1986, 24ff).

QASR BURQU, JORDAN
(Figs. 172, 173, 174 and 176)

This near oblique view of Qasr Burqu (Fig. 172) supplements the distant view given previously (Fig. 18). The well-preserved walls of the tower and the outer enclosure are emphasized by shadows of the midday sun. In the foreground are numerous corrals built for the animals of bedouin tribesmen who were probably attracted to the site by the water supply. At the time the air photograph was taken the water level in the reservoir was evidently low, but some water can be seen beyond the tower.

As noted above, the tower is of a different build and certainly earlier than the circuit wall and its chambers. It is massive – as may be seen in the ground view with its human scales (Fig. 173) – measuring 11.3 × 8.2 m. (37 × 27 ft), with walls 1.17 m. (3 ft 10 in.) thick, which, at the time of Stein's visit in 1939, still stood over 9 m. (30 ft) high (Poidebard, 1934, 97-101, 121-4, Pl.XCII.2,3; Field, 1960, 94-9, 150-8; Gregory and Kennedy (Stein), 1985, 240-7; Gaube, 1974a).

The outer circuit of enclosure wall and rooms has been dated to the Early Islamic period by an inscription of 700 (Field, 1960, 161-4). The tower is of a different build; Christian crosses and Greek inscriptions (one perhaps of the third century) on its stones point to the Roman period.

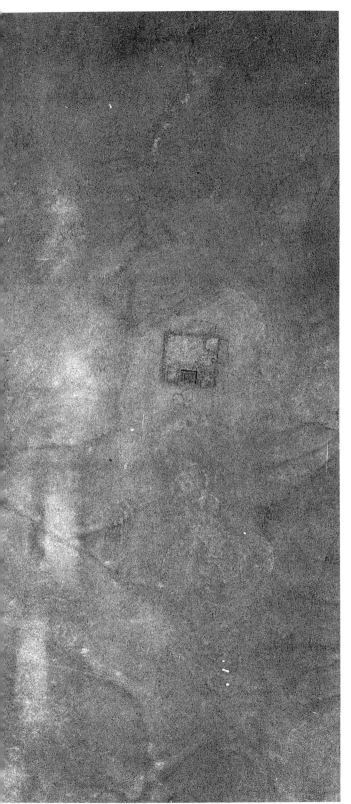

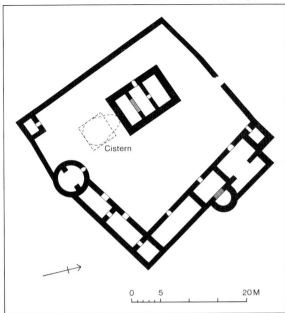

FIGURE 174 Qasr Burqu, Irbid, Jordan (32°36′N 38°02′E): plan of the tower and outer circuit. *After Gaube, 1974a, fig. 1.*

QASR ABU EL-KHARAQ
(Fig. 175)

The site is some 3 km (2 miles) north-west of Qasr Bshir (Fig. 122). A tall tower (cf. Glueck, 1970, 169 and fig. 81) measuring 18 × 22 m. (59 × 72 ft) was set inside and against the north wall of an earlier, larger enclosure, *c.* 60 × 60 m. (195 × 195 ft). Sherding on the site produced evidence from the Iron Age to modern times, with the great majority of sherds divided fairly evenly between Iron Age II and the Nabataean/Early Roman periods (Koucky *apud* Parker, 1987, 59 and 82f, Site 105).

FIGURE 175 Qasr Abu el-Kharaq, Al-Kerak, Jordan (31°18′N 35°57′E): vertical view from a height of 8000 ft (2400 m.) of the tower and earlier (?) enclosure. *Photograph: Royal Air Force (13.25; 17 July 1931). Crawford Archive (Institute of Archaeology, London; no inv. no.).*

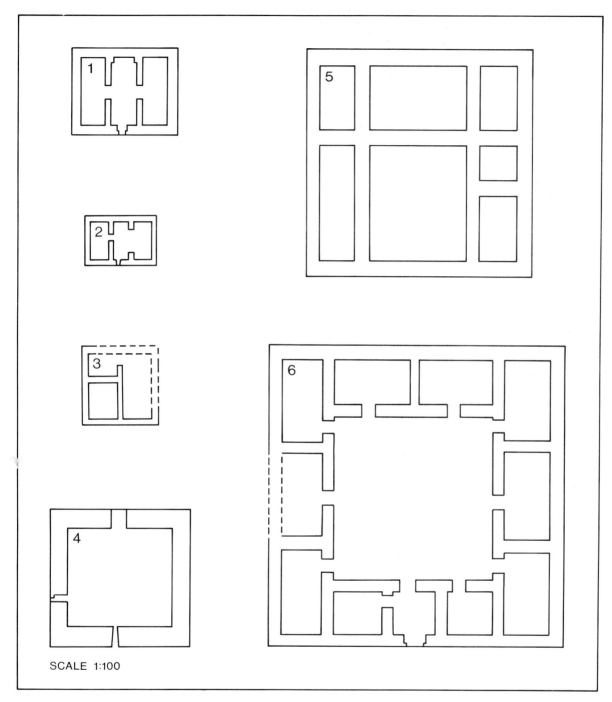

SCALE 1:100

FIGURE 176 Plans of Roman towers. 1. Qasr el-Heir el-Gharbi; 2. Qasr Burqu; 3. Qasr Uweinid (wadi tower); 4. Qasr Abu Rukba. Cf. 5. Hallabat fortlet and 6. Qasr Aseikhin.

· CHAPTER TWELVE ·

Miscellaneous

A handful of sites are added here which for various reasons cannot be placed in one of the earlier chapters, but which are nevertheless of interest.

The Roman practice of utilizing for military purposes the abandoned fortifications of an earlier period is now familiar in Britain and Gaul (Todd, 1985; cf. Agache, 1978, 218). The recently discovered camp at Umm Ubtulah (Fig. 178) may be the closest parallel to this practice yet found in the East.

At the Roman 'promontory fort' at Ertaje there is no suggestion that the site of an earlier fortification had been occupied, but it is an example of Roman use of a site which was presumably chosen as the best strategic location on that part of the bank of the Euphrates, although it did not allow the construction of a regular fort of conventional type (Fig. 180). A similar situation may have obtained at Khatuni-yeh (Fig. 181).

The tell at Marqada (Fig. 182) is only a possible Roman site, but Poidebard's suggestion that it was the location of one of a series of Roman posts built on the top of large artificial mounds is not implausible (cf. Fig. 107), and the photograph emphasizes the potential of such prehistoric tells.

Finally, Kurnub (Fig. 183) is included in token recognition of all those garrisoned towns which do not belong to the 'fortress towns' category but for which we can assert a Roman military presence, even if no military base can be detected. As we have seen, Dura Europos is the sole instance where the site is known of the military encampment established within a town's walls. Units are attested, usually epigraphically, at several other urban centres of the East, particularly

in the Early Empire. Thus, the inscriptions attesting a Thracian cavalry regiment at Gerasa in the first century AD (Welles *apud* Kraeling, 1938, 446ff, nos. 199-201); those naming regiments at Palmyra in the second century (Fig. 82); and the mention in a papyrus of the Babatha Archive, of a Roman military officer (and hence his troops presumably) in the city of Rabbathmoab/Areopolis in Arabia (Polotsky, 1962, 260; Yadin, 1963, 239). At Kurnub not only is there epigraphic evidence for a garrison, but excavation has recovered a cemetery in which soldiers were buried.

For interest, we have included two forts which

FIGURE 177 Location map.

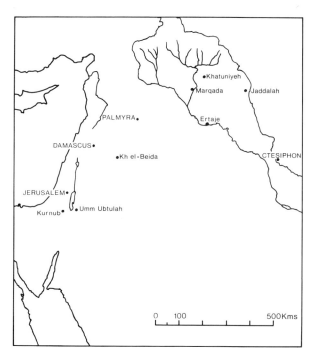

were not Roman. The Arab allies of Rome in the Late Empire are not generally associated with complex military architecture, but the Ghassanids were an exception, and at Khirbet el–Beida (Fig. 184) is what appears to have been a substantial and elaborate fort of one of their princes, though it was perhaps designed by Roman architects. Very little is known about Parthian or Persian forts on Rome's eastern frontier. The Parthian site at Jaddalah 2 (Fig. 186) is therefore important because part of it at least is dated. It lies opposite a fort that Stein identified as a Roman *castellum* (Fig. 164). Its inclusion helps to bring out something of the tradition of military architecture of Rome's principal opponents.

FIGURE 178 Umm Ubtulah, Al-Kerak, Jordan (30°53′N 35°53′E): view taken from the ground looking north. *Photograph: B. MacDonald (16-17 May 1983). Copyright: B. MacDonald (Wadi el-Hasa Survey, inv. no. 16–17 May 1986, frame 6).*

UMM UBTULAH, JORDAN
(Figs. 178 and 179)

The photograph illustrates the spectacular location of this very unusual site. Umm Ubtulah lies on a loop of the deeply cut Wadi el-Hesa, 14 km. (9 miles) south-east of Kerak and 11 km (7 miles) east of Rujm el-Faridiyyeh (Fig. 34). The oblique 'air' photograph, is actually a ground view taken from the opposite side of the valley.

The photographs show a large irregular enclosure, *c.*520 × 250 m. (1700 × 820 ft), 13 ha. (32 acres), stretching up the side of the wadi and along the top of the crest beyond. The enclosure is in two parts, in both of which are rows of regularly planned structures resembling barrack blocks. Those in the upper part differ from the lower, being wider, with two rows of rooms lengthwise.

More interesting, perhaps, is the difference noted (Eadie, 1986, 246) between the identified

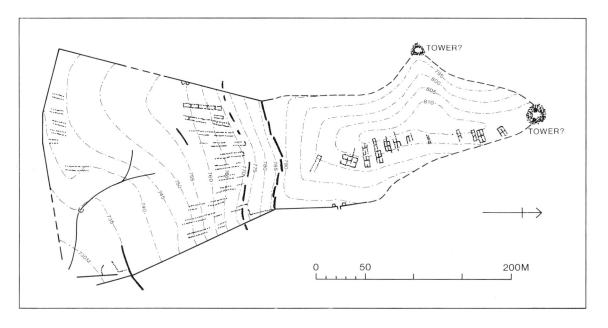

FIGURE 179 Umm Ubtulah, Al-Kerak, Jordan (30°53′N 35°53′E): plan of the site. *After MacDonald et al., forthcoming (original drawing by S. Balderstone).*

sherds from each part: in the upper area they are exclusively Early Bronze Age, but in the lower they range from Early Bronze to recent times, with Nabataean, Nabataean/Roman and Byzantine (i.e. Late Roman) predominant. This may be an Early Bronze Age defended site re-used and extended in the Nabataean and Roman periods (MacDonald, 1984, 230f; MacDonald *et al.*, forth.; cf. Gregory and Kennedy (Stein), 1985, 437ff). It is tempting to think of it as a temporary camp belonging to one of the attested Roman expeditions into the Nabataean kingdom in the period between Pompey and the annexation of 106.

ERTAJE, IRAQ
(Fig. 180)

Two fortifications appear in the centre of this rather distant view, a square mud-brick fort with projecting towers, and a stone-built fort on the steep sided crag jutting out over the Euphrates. Both occupy a commanding position on the high bank (45 m./150 ft) of the river between Dura-Europos and Ana just before it began a great loop. That one of the sites ought to be Roman was deduced by Stein from Musil's plausible

equation (1927, 230) of Ertaje with ancient *Belesi Biblada*. The latter is named by the Augustan writer, Isidorus of Charax (*Mansiones Parthicae* 1), as a staging post on the route down the Euphrates, 17 *schoeni* below the fortress city of Dura-Europos (Figs. 58, 60). More importantly, one of the Dura papyri (*P.Dura* 60B) of *c*.208, names a *Biblada* as the first of two outposts downstream of Dura through which a Parthian envoy was to pass on his journey into the Roman Empire.

Stein confidently interpreted the square fort as a Roman *castellum* (Gregory and Kennedy (Stein), 1985, 173-9; 408). Although that explanation has superficial attractions, and mud-brick forts were built by the Romans (Procopius, *Buildings* II.viii, 4-6 and cf. Figs. 109, 139, 167), he was certainly wrong in his identification in this instance. On the basis both of similarities of building technique and of ceramic parallels with the Severan fortress at Kifrin, a recent visitor to the site, familiar with the pottery of the region, has concluded that it is the small crag fort which is Roman; the mud brick fort is certainly not Roman and is probably later in date (Invernizzi, 1986, 375f). Part of the crag fort has been eroded into the river, but Stein reported apparently solidly built stone 'quarters' and 'careful stucco plaster' on the walls (Gregory and Kennedy (Stein), 1985, 176f).

FIGURE 180 Ertaje, Al-Anbar, Iraq (34°28′N 41°23′E): oblique view looking south-west from a height of 300 ft (100 m.). *Photograph: Royal Air Force (10.31; 3 January 1939). Stein Archive (British Museum, RAF no. illegible).*

It seems likely that the region was occupied by Rome at the same time as Dura itself in the 160s, and that this was one of a number of small posts designed to control movement along the river. The destruction of Dura by Shapur I *c.*252, would certainly have ended occupation at Biblada too, if it had not already been abandoned (cf. Fig. 62).

KHATUNIYEH, IRAQ
(Fig. 181)

The peninsula jutting out into Lake Khatuniyeh has probably been a strong point from early times. This photograph demonstrates the nature of the site and shows the wall which defends an area at the tip of the peninsula. The site lies just beyond the north-western end of the Jebel Sinjar, at the junction of several roads linking Thannouris, Nisibis, Singara and Eski Mosul. It is commonly identified with the *Lacus Beberaci* of the Peutinger Table (Dussaud, 1927, 488; 492), but however suggestive may be the network of roads, neighbouring forts and the defensive wall, it must be said that no Roman material has as yet been reported from the site (Poidebard, 1934, 157ff; cf. Gregory and Kennedy (Stein), 1985, 34).

FIGURE 181 Khatuniyeh, Al-Hasakeh, Iraq (36°23′N 41°13′E): oblique view looking northwest. *Photograph: Royal Air Force (11.23; 31 March 1938). Stein Archive (Institute of Archaeology, London, inv. no. AP 1700).*

MARQADA, SYRIA
(Fig. 182)

The great flat-topped mound of Marqada, here seen from the north-east, is undoubtedly of prehistoric origin, but the hummocks on its surface may mark the sites of Roman or early Islamic buildings comparable to those at Tell es-Seba (Fig. 107). The shadows of the morning sun reveal these remains and also outline the steep sides of the mound, which was defended by a strong wall and wide ditch (Poidebard, 1934, 135). Beside the River Khabur, which winds into the distance towards its confluence with the Euphrates, are irrigated fields. The landscape is flat, but not entirely so, because the edge of the basalt plateau of Al-Hammé is just off the right margin of the photograph.

Located 67 km (42 miles) north of Circesium, Poidebard saw this as one of a regular series of more ancient sites utilized in the Roman period

FIGURE 182 Marqada, Al-Hasakeh, Syria (35°45′N 40°44′E): oblique view looking south-west.
Photograph: Commandant Ruby (n.d.). From Poidebard 1934, PL.CIX.

for forts and watch-towers guarding the line of the River Khabur. While it is not at all unlikely that some, perhaps many, of these sites were garrisoned and used for just such a purpose, in practice we cannot identify a single one. Even *Suchere*, named as the garrison of the *Cohors III Augusta Thracum* in a papyrus from Dura-Europos (*P.Dura* 26), cannot be located more closely than on the lower River Khabur.

KURNUB, ISRAEL
(Fig. 183)

Kurnub, the ancient *Mampsis*, lies in the northern Negev Desert some 35 km (22 miles) west of the southern tip of the Dead Sea and about the same distance south-east of Beersheva. Its location was important as lying on a route linking Gaza with *Characmoab* (modern Kerak) on the eastern side of the Dead Sea, and on a north-south road leading deeper into the Negev to Avdat (Fig. 143). The settlement was established on high ground above the Wadi Kurnub, the waters of which were captured and exploited. Several dams ponded water and diverted it to potentially arable soils near the wadi mouth (Evenari *et al.*, 1982, 110-14).

The ruined town seen on the photograph, is largely of the second century AD. The wall was built towards the end of the third century, enclosing a settled area of some 4 ha. (10 acres). The majority of the buildings continued in use until the Moslem conquest of the region.

Latin inscriptions from one of the cemeteries (just off the photograph) attest the presence of the *Cohors I Augusta Thracum*, one of whose personnel was buried there in the early second century (Mann, 1969), and there was, perhaps, also a detachment of the *Legio III Cyrenaica* (Negev, 1977, 658). Both presumably were stationed in the town only in the early years of the newly created province. No quarters have been identified for soldiers; presumably they were simply billeted in existing houses. In the cemetery there is a contrast between the native practice of inhumation in wooden coffins, and that of the Roman soldiers, cremated on a pyre at the site and the ashes interred under a funerary pyramid or heap of stones.

The site regained its importance as a security point in the early twentieth century. The long white roofed building on the right, just above the large aisled church, is a British police station of the time of the Mandate.

KHIRBET EL-BEIDA, SYRIA
(Figs. 184 and 185)

The site (called Qasr al-Abyad by Poidebard) lies on the eastern edge of the Safa, one of the great masses of tortuous rock left by former lava flows in this region. The fort and adjacent buildings are in a good state of preservation, and their plans are recorded well by this photograph.

This is one of the larger fortifications in the region, measuring 62 × 62 m./202 × 202 ft (0.38 ha./0.95 acres), with walls 1 m. (3 ft) thick. The towers circular at the corners and semi-circular at the middle points of walls, have a diameter of 3.6 m. (*c.* 12 ft). Internally, rooms around a central courtyard are arranged almost symmetrically on either side of an east-west axis.

Poidebard considered it to be a Roman fort, dating it on stylistic grounds to his fourth century 'Post-Diocletianic' type (1934, 55). Recent investigation, however, illuminated by comparison with other and better-known similar structures, has convincingly shown that it was a major palace-fortress of the allied Ghassanid tribal federation of the Late Empire (above, p. 39f). It is probably best interpreted as one of the seasonal desert palaces (cf. Fig. 64) of the Ghassanid princes (Gaube 1974b).

JADDALAH 2, IRAQ
(Figs. 186 and 187)

The conspicuous debris-covered ruins at this site known as Jaddalah 2 were visited by Stein on the ground on 6 March 1938 and after that must have been very easily identified from the air. A small stream (foreground) flows past the ruins, dividing them from Jaddalah 1 (Fig. 164).

The two sites at Jaddalah lie some 35 km (22 miles) north-east of Hatra. Stein identified this, the more prominent of the two, as Parthian. His

FIGURE 183 Kurnub, Hadarom Hanegev, Israel (31°03′N 35°02′E): vertical view of the town. *Photograph: Survey of Israel. Supplied by A. Segal.*

FIGURE 184 Khirbet el-Beida, Damascus, Syria
(33°2′N 37°17′E): vertical view from a height of
3300 ft (1000 m.). *Photograph: de Boysson (08.00; 20
October 1930). From Poidebard, 1934, Pl.LIII.*

FIGURE 185 Khirbet el-Beida, Damascus, Syria
(33°2′N 37°17′E): plan of the fort. *After Gaube
1974b, fig. 7.*

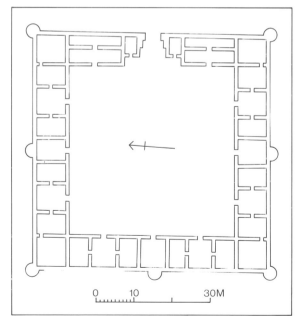

date was based on the columns and moulded
bases on the structure in the centre of the site,
which appeared to be a Parthian temple in
Hellenistic style. Excavation in recent years has
proven his dating (Ibrahim, 1980; 1983). The
central structure has produced two Aramaic lintel
inscriptions bearing the construction date AD
141/2. The outer circuit, c.105 × 105 m. (345 ×
345 ft), has curious towers and there were ranges
of rooms against three walls.

As already noted, there are grounds for identify-

FIGURE 186 Jaddalah 2, Neineva, Iraq (35°50′N 43°06′E): oblique view of the Parthian site looking east from a height of 200 ft (60 m.). *Photograph:* *Royal Air Force (12.22; 14 November 1938). Stein Archive (British Museum, Department of Western Asiatic Antiquities, RAF no. 13861).*

ing the settlement here as the *Ad Herculem* of the Peutinger Table and the *Herakleous Bomoi*, 'Altars of Heracles', of Ptolemy (*Geog.* V.18.1) (Fig. 164).

If the outer circuit also is Parthian, the site is of particular interest as a rare example of a Parthian fortification. Moreover, it would seem

that the site was ignored years later when a Roman garrison arrived and constructed its own encampment on the other side of the wadi.

FIGURE 187 Jaddalah, Neineva, Iraq (35°50′N 43°06′E): plan of the Parthian site. *After Ibrahim, 1983, 220, pl.5.*

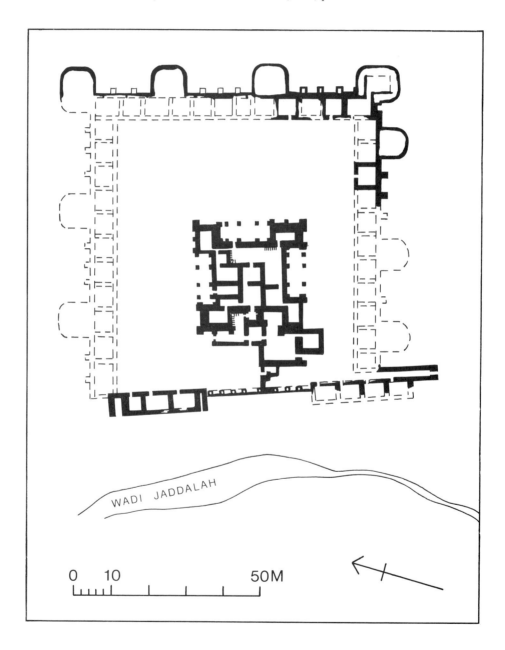

WADI JADDALAH

0   10   50M

· PART D ·
Conclusion

· CHAPTER THIRTEEN ·

Bones Of The Red Horse

The purpose of this final chapter is to summarize briefly the important conclusions derived from the study of the sites discussed in Part C, to relate these findings to the techniques of aerial archaeology outlined in Part B and to place the sites in the context of the geographical and historical surveys of Part A. A final section looks to the future.

· Summary and Lessons ·

1 THE SITES In the preface to this book, the opportunities open to the archaeologist working on the eastern desert frontier were suggested by the dramatic words of Sir Mortimer Wheeler, who quoted from a passage in *The Revelation*, here given in full on page 10. The air photographs reproduced in the present book show some of the 'bones of the red horse' to which he referred, the Roman military constructions which are still standing at many places on the desert margins. These photographs and the site descriptions accompanying them should have demonstrated that Wheeler's high-sounding words were justified, even though 40 years have passed since they were written and few of the opportunities have yet been taken.

In Part C (Chapters 5 to 12), the core of this book, we have covered a wide selection of Roman military sites, some of the 'bones' that Wheeler had in mind. They have been divided into eight broad categories, only two of which – water supply (Chapter 5) and fortress cities (Chapter 8) – may be unexpected to readers more familiar with Roman Europe. The arrangement of the material in this way is standard archaeolog-

ical practice, and it brings out the variety and the range of the elements in the Roman military network.

More thorough analysis and sub-division of the various types of sites can have important implications. Within the major categories, the number and range of examples are often sufficient to permit some refinement of the classification. In particular, the forts have been subdivided provisionally into five groups on the basis of their size and the presence or absence of external towers, features which are certainly related to the period of construction. The provisional nature of this classification must be stressed, however; when so many of the sites are undated, there are limits to the reliance that can be placed on the results of a study of their typology. Although the legionary fortresses are much fewer in number, they may be divided into early and late groups on the basis of their size and design, rather similarly to the forts.

Few temporary camps are known in relation to the vast territory dealt with in the book, and their number is too small to allow any attempt at classification, though if more camps come to light in the future, the plans of their entrances may yield clues about their dates, as they have done in the West. In view of the success of aerial reconnaissance in finding the sites of hundreds of previously unknown temporary camps in Britain and along the Rhine-Danube frontier, perhaps there may be many to be found by similar means in the East.

A group of fortress cities has been described, most of which are in or near the Euphrates valley (Chapter 8). Their impressive defensive walls and towers may be divided into two groups, the earlier dating from the early third century (Figs. 53-4, 60) and the later from the mid sixth century (Figs. 63-7). Other cities of great importance, such as Nisibis and Dara, were inevitably mentioned in the historical survey (Chapter 2), but have not been illustrated; they lie within the borders of Turkey, the area from which no air photographs are available.

The design of the installations that served the military network – the water supply (Chapter 5) and the roads (Chapter 6) – appears to have depended on their purpose rather than their date, though this is a view that may have to be modified when more is known about them. Roman roads which were surfaced and those which were cleared and marked should be considered less in respect of chronology than of their intended use and the kind of country that they crossed. The third type, the unmarked tracks across the desert, followed routes on which water could be found; they were no doubt used by eastern traders and travellers long before and after the Roman period. The vital water supply for military sites on the desert margins also appears to have been based on well established eastern practices. These installations, whether mentioned in the chapter dealing with water supply, or in the descriptions of forts and their facilities given in Chapter 10, have not been discussed in any detail. There would be little value in attempting to do this without also taking into account the much larger body of data about the supply of water to ancient towns and agricultural sites. This a subject which would fill an interesting book (cf. Evenari *et al.*,1982).

2 THE PHOTOGRAPHS The range of photographs selected displays some of the primary uses of aerial reconnaissance and photography. It is instructive to place them under some of the headings used by Bradford in his classic book *Ancient Landscapes* (1957, 11-13).

A *Graphic demonstrations of a known site in the context of its surroundings* are provided, for example, by Poidebard's oblique photographs of Dura Europos. The view reproduced here (Fig. 60) and the companion view from another direction given in *La Trace de Rome* (Poidebard, 1934, pl. LXXXVIII) show not only the city layout and defences, but its location - the narrow fertile strip on the right bank of the Euphrates and the outlook of the garrison over the river towards Parthian and Sasanian territory. Similarly, the oblique view of the siege works at Masada (Fig. 44), and the verticals of those at Machaerus (Fig. 47) and Battir (Fig. 49) supply very good impressions of the difficult terrain over which the Roman army operated at those places. Numerous other obliques are very striking, and the reader might turn back now to re-examine a few. Figures 17, 27, 33 , 64, 74, 82 and 139 may be taken as examples, but others could be cited. Many of the verticals are as good, for instance Figures 24, 53, 96, 100, 128, 135, 137 and 151.

B *The topographical study of areas of particular significance*, which Bradford said 'is intermediate between demonstration and discovery', is a subject with many facets. Some applications may be suggested by the vertical photographs of important areas that have not yet been fully explored, for example Figures 49, 68, 71 and 89. Again, the vertical mosaic of Azraq (Fig. 28) shows the black lava desert surrounding the site, on which may be seen many features, some ancient, others recent. The ancient sites that are still intact should be surveyed in detail on the ground; unfortunately many have already been lost in the area surrounding the Roman fort, which has now been engulfed by modern roads and buildings.

C *Discovery from the air*. Many of the sites illustrated in this book were aerial discoveries. Frequently there were standing remains, often well preserved, which would have been recognized by ground exploration. In practice the nature of the terrain made many of the sites inaccessible or far from the beaten track, so that they might have still been unknown if Poidebard and Stein had not made use of the mobility of the aeroplane to reconnoitre remote regions (see comments about Poidebard's work, page 62 above) and photographed what they saw. Indeed, many of the sites located by both these men are still known from their records alone. Sites easily recognizable only from the air by vegetation marks or slight lines of stones have been recorded less often, but examples may be seen on Figures 26, 27 (lines of stones), 98 and 101 (vegetation marks).

3 GEOGRAPHY A close relationship is often seen between geography and topography on the one hand and the location and character of sites on the other. Looking at the most important factors, the ability of the land to support human life is critically influenced in the Middle East by water. Parts of the great river valley of the Euphrates and the well-watered regions of northern Mesopotamia and Syria were relatively densely inhabited. It was only these areas which could be crossed in ancient times by invading armies, which had to live off food and other supplies obtained locally. In these fertile regions stood populous cities, vulnerable to attack, and which were therefore fortified; such fortress cities became bulwarks of the defence against invasion (Chapter 8).

Conversely, the lack of water on the desert margins becomes critical in areas where the rainfall is below a certain level. A comparison of Figure 2 with the sites shown on the location maps of forts (Figs. 85, 104, 112, 140) will stress the close relationship between the 200 m ($7\frac{1}{2}$ in.) rainfall isohyet and the distribution of military sites in the region. We may note that near these forts there are always water conservation works – reservoirs, cisterns and wells (see Chapter 5 and, for example, Figs. 129, 153, 155, 165). The forts are usually small and quite widely separated. It was unlikely that invading armies could have crossed such sparsely populated and dry regions, and it would have been considered necessary only to provide small forces for the policing of nomadic tribes and protection of travellers on the roads.

The nature of the country, its relief and the water supply exerted a great influence on the road system and on the tactical siting of forts. Much could be written about both questions, but a single example must suffice. The line of the Jebel Rawaq between Damascus and Palmyra determined the routes chosen for the roads along it, while the gaps and saddles across the range indicated where roads crossing it had to be built. Taking into account the positions of these cross roads, the choice of sites for forts (e.g. Figs. 128, 151, 153 and 155) along the principal road (the *Strata Diocletiana*) then had to be made at intervals of about 20-25 km (*c.* 12-15 miles) at places where a supply of water could be assured.

4 HISTORY There is much variation in the extent to which our present knowledge of the Roman military remains in the Middle East can be related to a broad historical survey and even extend or develop it. In some regions and some periods there is little yet to be learned, particularly as so few sites have been excavated, but in others there is important information already available, some of which enables suggestions to be made about the long-term strategy of the Roman Empire in the East.

To mention first two important subjects about which information is minimal: for the first two centuries of Roman rule there is virtually no archaeological evidence of a military nature from the region, and the fertile parts of Syria remain a near blank on the archaeological map of military installations at all times under Roman rule. There is also a lack of information about north-eastern Syria and in northern Iraq where many forts have been found, but little is known about them. There, the distribution of Poidebard's and Stein's sites would be very instructive if more of Poidebard's photographs were available and there was evidence about the dates of the forts, but it is not certain whether most of them even belong to the Roman period. The best that can be said is that their distribution suggests the nature of the Roman military position in Mesopotamia and underscores the important strategic change which took place in the late second and early third centuries and later. It can be seen from these gaps in our knowledge how far the study of Roman military affairs in the East lags behind the same subject in Europe. For the later periods and various other parts of the region, however, archaeology can supply valuable information; we must now turn to this and stress the positive aspects of the knowledge that is available.

Probably the most informative air photographs from the Middle East are those showing the contemporary siege works at Masada (Figs. 44 and 45) and Machaerus (Fig. 47) and the later, but again contemporary, works at Battir (Fig. 49). They give a remarkable picture of the works carried out during the sieges that ended the Jewish wars of the late first and early second centuries AD. Such information is an important supplement to the accounts that have survived in the literature.

Information from the Severan period is especially good because of the combination of types of evidence, including that from important fieldwork. The excavations at Dura Europos (Fig. 60) revealed in much detail the accommodation for troops in this fortress city and unearthed papyri which illuminated not only the composition of the garrison but something of the position at other less important stations further down the Euphrates. At the two Ain Sinu forts (Figs. 113 and 167) in northern Mesopotamia, a single season of excavation produced most useful information about the date and design of two forts, one of very unusual type. Little is yet widely available in detail about the Iraqi excavations at Hatra (Fig. 54), but they will certainly prove important when published.

The provisional classification of forts into five groups (Chapters 5) has yet to be amplified by much information about the dates of individual structures. Nevertheless, it is fairly clear that in the Late Roman period the forts were not only much more strongly defended, but were much smaller. The garrisons cannot have been large, and where it is known that a fort was occupied by a single unit, the normal situation, it is clear that the size of the unit was often very small. It seems that there was probably a change from large Early Empire forts with modest defences to smaller and heavily defended Late Empire forts, as in the Western Empire. This must mark a change in tactics, with the emphasis on defence in the later period.

Roman strategy is a question about which at present we can only make suggestions, but in reviewing the evidence, lines for future research may emerge. Luttwak has proposed three phases in the first four centuries of Roman rule – at first an external frontier guarded by client states and mobile armies, followed by a period of 'scientific' frontiers and defensive measures which precluded penetration by enemy forces, and finally by a period of defence in depth (1976; cf. Mann, 1974; 1979). Such an interpretation can only be supported by evidence drawn indiscriminately from different regions at different periods and by potentially misleading generalizations. It is, for example, not easy to discern evidence in the West for Luttwak's first phase. On the other hand, the second phase is persuasive when the considering the evidence from the long European frontier between the North Sea and the Black Sea in the second century. Finally, the evidence he cites for a change to defence in depth in the West is problematic. In the same way, one must have reservations about harmonizing his three phases with the evidence available in the East.

The scarcity of forts or other military stations in Syria, Jordan and Iraq dateable to the earlier centuries of Roman rule may well accord with a policy that relied much on the services of the forces of client kings. In the Roman provinces, it may be argued, there were at first Julio-Claudian mobile armies billeted in cities as circumstances required, while beyond them were client states, whose armies policed their territories and protected the frontier (Fig. 4). However, client kings had armies and may have needed forts – but where are they?

After Hadrian's withdrawal from Trajan's conquered territories in Mesopotamia, the legions may have begun to occupy permanent fortresses, such as that at Bostra (Fig. 71). A 'scientific', preclusive, frontier then might have been proposed along the Euphrates in the north, but of this there are at present only hints (cf. Crow, 1986). Perhaps no special arrangements may have been considered necessary along the desert margins to the south, because the desert was policed by Palmyrene forces.

In the last years of the second century, the campaigns of Septimius Severus advanced the frontier in northern Mesopotamia to the Middle Tigris and the Jebel Sinjar range. South of the latter stood the Ain Sinu forts (Figs. 113, 167), dated by excavation to the early third century. There is also Severan material from Dura Europos and from the Azraq oasis (Figs. 56, 105). The three places are hundreds of kilometres apart, however; an aggressive strategy and ambition to seize new territories may be inferred, but few useful conclusions can be drawn about the frontier (cf. Kennedy, 1980).

Nearly another century later, following the fall of the secessionist Palmyrene Empire, the desert frontier was reorganized under the Tetrarchy. There appears to have been much building, for example the forts along the *Strata Diocletiana*, several of which have been illustrated (e.g. Figs. 128, 151, 153 and 155). Although the evidence must be regarded with caution, because very few of the forts on the desert frontier have yet been dated by excavation, we can now see some sort of uniform system of forts along roads between Aqaba in the south and Souriya on the Euphrates (Fig. 188). The conventional wisdom that the roads *linked* forts whose purpose was to bar movement across their line is now, however, being persuasively challenged by the suggestion that the forts were intended to provide security for travellers and accomodation for small forces policing movement along the road itself (Isaac, forth.; cf. Graf, forth.)

Under the Tetrarchy in the early fourth century, therefore, for the first time there are indications of a carefully planned system in a frontier area, in this case the desert south-west of the Euphrates. The forts were almost all of the small type with external towers (pp. 194–212), suitable for small forces controlling local tribesmen and policing roads in a difficult border territory, but, as already suggested above, no more than this was likely to have been needed there.

The real danger area was further north in the fertile lands that would have been chosen as the route for large invading forces (Fig. 188). If a preclusive strategy was intended, the strong barrier should have crossed these more northern regions, that is north-western Syria and northern Iraq. Poidebard thought he had traced a line of forts up the Khabur (e.g. Fig. 182) and beyond to the Turkish border, and Stein photographed forts near the Jebel Sinjar. Their dates are unknown, but even if they were all of early fourth century date, it cannot be suggested that they formed any kind of formal barrier like that along the Rhine and Danube. A 'preclusive' scheme is unlikely. The real strength in this very important sector must have been in the fortress cities, which provided the defence in depth.

The accounts preserved by Ammianus Marcellinus of the mid and later fourth century and by Procopius of the sixth make it clear that defence by then *did* depend on a network of great strategically placed fortresses and fortress cities: Singara (Fig. 73), Bezabde, Nisibis, Dara and Amida all figure prominently in Mesopotamia and forced Sasanian armies to undertake lengthy and costly sieges. On the Syrian Euphrates, defence lay in the similar fortress cities of Halebiyeh, Resafa and Souriya (Figs 63–5), which blocked easy access to the rich interior of Syria. Even there, however, cities were provided with great walls now, reflecting the all too realistic fear that a Persian army would break through the border defences.

To summarize, we can at present suggest with any confidence only two major strategic stages. At first Roman policy relied considerably on client kings. The nature of the intermediate period in the second and early third centuries is unclear, though it is possible that gaps in our information about this phase may be filled by future excavations at some of the large forts without towers. During the later period there was defence in depth by fortress cities in the vulnerable north and a lightly policed frontier road along the desert margins in the south from the Euphrates to the Gulf of Aqaba. In the end, nothing availed, Syria and the provinces to the south all collapsed before an invader coming from a new direction – the desert.

· *The Future* ·

It has been possible to say a great deal about most of the sites discussed above, though a weakness in many instances has been the shortage of detailed information about their construction and internal layout, and their dates and building sequences. The consequence is the reliance that has had to be placed on the good series of aerial photographs. In many cases the photographs themselves were a source of important information because of the data they give about the plans and geographical locations of sites. But aerial reconnaissance is an initial stage of investigation, which must be supplemented adequately by work on the ground. Many current problems in the study of the eastern frontier are caused by the lack of evidence about the dates and detailed particulars of sites, which aerial survey cannot be expected to give, but which have not yet been provided by field work and excavation, as they have in the West. When considering this difficulty, it is necessary to take stock of the situation. Although far below the level of information that is taken for granted in the West, the amount that

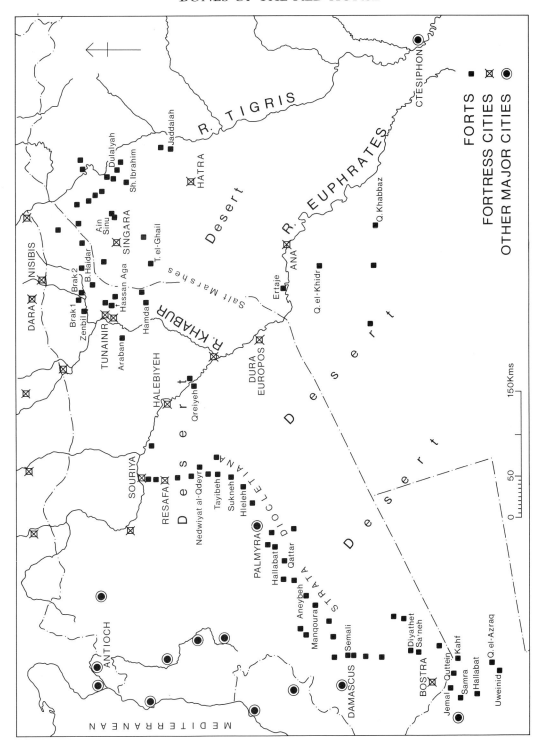

FIGURE 188 The northern part of the Desert Frontier showing forts in Syria mentioned in Poidebard's *La Trace de Rome*, in Iraq mentioned in Stein's *Limes Report* (Gregory and Kennedy (Stein), 1985), and a few others in Jordan, together with fortress cities and other cities of general importance. The map demonstrates the various concentrations of military structures in the eastern desert.

is known about sites in the East must not be under-rated.

For Poidebard, the key to his great programme of research lay in identifying and surveying the Roman roads. That approach would be no less valid for a renewed flying programme. The major roads are highly distinctive and much may yet be achieved by pursuing the search for roads and forts from the air and the milestones along the roads by ground survey.

A few of the recent results suggest lines of work which can be pursued by scrutinizing existing vertical photographs when available. The identification of temporary camps on verticals (Figs. 47, 49, 55) has been mentioned several times. Less has been said about the forts visible on photographs of settlement sites at Umm el-Quttein, Umm el-Jemal and Khirbet es-Samra (Figs. 86, 130, 144). The major gaps in archaeological knowledge of military affairs are obvious enough. If existing air photographs are made available or new flying is permitted, the following subjects should be matters of priority.

1. The military bases of the Late Republic and Early Empire in inner Syria and Judaea immediately come to mind. In view of the clearness of the legionary fortress on the old Royal Air Force vertical of Bostra (Fig. 71) it is probable that similar photographs would reveal the fortress at Raphanaea and perhaps those at Apamaea and Cyrrhus, all of which are in the modern country of Syria. Further scrutiny may yet reveal the military quarters within towns such as Caesarea, Ascalon and Samaria, all described as garrison cities by Josephus.

2. Part of Roman Syria lay in what is today south-eastern Turkey. The location of the legion-ary fortress at Samosata, one of the major cities of the East, is unknown; that at Zeugma, another important city, is a matter only of speculation. Air photographs might resolve both problems if ever the Turkish authorities release them.

3. Sites should be sought along the Rivers Khabur and Jaghjagh – some were established there at least as early as the late second century (Cassius Dio LXXV.1.2-4) and at least one specific fort (*Sachare*) on the Lower Khabur is named on a Dura papyrus of 227 (*P. Dura* 26).

4. Stein's sites on both sides of the Tigris require re-examination – there is now a Latin military inscription from the Tigris near Mosul (Kennedy, 1988) and Herodian's reference (VI.2.5) to the Persians 'laying siege to the Roman garrison camps on the banks of the rivers, the camps which defended the empire', may refer to both the Tigris and Khabur.

5. All of the sites located by Poidebard and Stein need to be looked at again both on other existing coverage and from new flying.

We have written of some of the more important initial objectives for the aerial archaeologist, but in doing so have not forgotten that the discovery and photography of a site is only the first step in its investigation. The sites that may be located in the future, no less than those already identified, will provide the basis for great programmes of field work, survey and excavation, vital to provide dates and details. It is the authors' earnest hope that this book will help to advance the time when this will occur and that it will encourage more general interest in the defences of the Roman East among archaeologists and historians.

· GLOSSARY ·

With the exception of the Arabic terms, a fuller definition of many of the words and expressions listed below can be found in N.G.L. Hammond and H.H. Scullard (eds.), *The Oxford Classical Dictionary*, 2nd edition, Oxford, 1970.
Ar. = Arabic; Gr. = Greek; Lat. = Latin.

AIN (Ar.) A spring, pool, well.

ALA (Lat.) Literally 'a wing', the standard military term for a regiment of auxiliary cavalry (see AUXILIA).

ARABIA PETRAEA One of two terms employed to designate the Nabataean kingdom, the other being Nabataea.

AUXILIA (Lat.) The collective term used to describe the non-citizen troops of the Roman army. Usually raised amongst subject provincials, they could, however, also be recruited from beyond the frontiers, a practice which became increasingly common from the third century onwards. In the very Early Empire, regiments were usually equipped in the fashion customary in their homeland. Some regions were renowned for their particular contributions: e.g. Balearic slingers, Syrian archers, Spanish and Gallic cavalry. Special conditions, as with the deserts of North Africa and the Near East, led to the formation of regiments of *dromedarii* or the allocation of a few camel mounted troops to regiments of infantry or cavalry.

Most regiments were one of three types: an *ala* (s.v.), a *cohors peditata* (q.v. COHORT), or a *cohors equitata* (q.v. COHORT). That is, cavalry, infantry, or mixed infantry and cavalry. Most were *quingenaria*, nominally '500 strong', but from the mid first century others are found described as *milliaria* (s.v.) (nominally '1000 strong' but probably with a strength nearer to 800).

In the Severan period there were probably some 400 auxiliary regiments Empire-wide, with a nominal strength of some quarter of a million men.

BIR (Ar.) A well.

BIRKEH (Ar.) Pool, cistern or reservoir.

BURGUS (Lat.) Usually a watch tower but found applied in contexts which suggest it might also be applied to a fort.

CANABAE (Lat.) Literally 'the booths', the settlement which grew up outside any military installation, usually along the approach road(s).

CASEMATE A chamber built within the thickness of the wall in a fortification.

CASTELLUM (Lat.) A fort or stronghold, a diminutive of *castrum*, in use from the time of the Roman Republic but commonly applied to the small, towered forts of the Late Empire.

CASTRA (Lat.) Military camp, commonly applied to a legionary fortress.

CASTRUM (Lat.) Fort or fortress, commonly applied today to a legionary fortress but used more loosely in antiquity.

CLAVICULA (Lat.) An internal or external extension of the rampart at the gateway of a camp or earth fort, usually in the form of a quarter circle.

CLIENT-KINGS The modern term applied to those rulers within or on the fringes of Roman provinces who had been recognized as 'Friend and Ally of the Roman People'. Their degree of independence varied but most could expect to have to provide troops in support of the Roman army in time of war.

COHORT (Lat.) A regiment of the *Auxilia* (s.v.), most commonly some 500 infantry or a mixture of three quarters infantry and the rest cavalry.

DEIR (Ar.) A monastery.

EARLY EMPIRE Here defined as 27 BC to AD 284.

FOGGARA (Ar.) Also called *qanat* or, in English, well-chains. This method of tapping groundwater is common from North Africa to Iran. It consists of a mother well(s) sunk vertically into the water table, a tunnel which then carries the water so tapped gradually to the surface by conducting it underground on a falling gradient but to a lower point on the landscape where it can emerge and flow into reservoirs. Construction of the tunnel and its subsequent maintenance was permitted by the chain of access shafts which mark out its course on the surface like a line of craters (Evenari, 1982, Ch. XI)

GHADIR (Ar.) Water hole.

GHASSANID CONFEDERATION In origin, a South Arabian tribe which established itself in the desert south-east of Damascus. By the end of the fifth century they had become Christian and allied to Rome. The peak of their power came in the sixth century with their defeat of the pro-Sasanian Lakhmids and the establishment by the Emperor Justinian of a Ghassanid overlordship of all the Arabs allied to Rome. These later Ghassanid rulers were cultivated men, patrons of towns in the desert fringes, and builders of churches, palaces and forts.

HAMADA (Ar.) Literally 'barren', the Syrian desert.

JEBEL (Ar.) Mountain.

KHAN or HAN (Ar.) Caravanserai.

KHIRBET or HIRBET (Ar.) Ruins.

LATE EMPIRE Here defined as AD 284 to 637.

LEGION A division of citizen soldiers in the Roman army. About 5000 strong and consisting almost entirely of heavy, well-disciplined infantry. They were expensive to maintain, recruits could be difficult to obtain, and the number of legions rose only slowly from the 25 at the death of Augustus (AD 14) to the 33 under Septimius Severus (AD 193-211). In the Late Empire, as a group they ceased to be the elite backbone of the Roman army, many of them fragmenting into two or more parts and many of the small rump forces which emerged declined into little more than a peasant militia (see LIMITANEI).

LIMES (Lat.) Derived from the agricultural term for a boundary, often a road or track, it came to be applied to the frontier zones of the Empire in which fortifications and strategic roads were intermixed.

LIMITANEI (Lat.) A term which appears in the third century to describe the frontier soldiers, those on the *limes* (s.v.). Increasingly in the Late Empire they declined in numbers, quality and status to end as little more than a peasant militia.

MILLIARY (Lat.) Literally '1000 strong' and applied, exaggeratedly, to the larger regiments of the *Auxilia* (q.v.).

NABATAEA See ARABIA PETRAEA.

OMMAYAD DYNASTY (661-750): Founded by the fifth caliph, Muawiyah (661-80). From their capital at Damascus this family ruled over an empire which ultimately stretched from Spain through North Africa and the Middle East to Afghanistan and northern India. The period was one of brilliant achievements in the arts, urban regeneration and remarkable desert palaces constructed by the caliphs and their supporters.

PRINCIPATE (Lat.) The name applied to the political system devised by Augustus to replace Rome's previous republican government and legitimize his own position. Derived from the Latin, *princeps*, 'First' or 'Most Distinguished Man', 'Leader'.

QASR (Ar.) Fort, castle.

QUADRIBURGIUM (Lat.) A fort with four towers.

REPUBLIC Defined here as the period down to 27 BC.

TELL (Ar.) An artificial mound formed by successive construction on the demolished site of earlier settlements.

TETRAPYRGIUM (Lat., from the Gr.) see QUADRIBURGIUM

TETRARCHY (Gr.) The form of government established by the Emperor Diocletian in which there were to be four emperors: two senior Augusti and two junior partners, Caesars, who were to replace them in due course and appoint new Augusti.

VEXILLATION (Lat.) A detachment.

VICUS (Lat.) The civil 'village' which often developed outside Roman forts.

WADI (Ar.) A water course, often dry for part of the year.

UMM (Ar.) Mother. Often employed as elements in place names, e.g. Umm el-Jemal = 'Mother of Camels'.

· BIBLIOGRAPHY ·

· Ancient Works and a · note on Ancient Authors

This is not a comprehensive list of all those authors with light to shed on military affairs in the Roman Near East, nor even of all those cited in the body of this book. Rather, it is a guide to the more important literary sources for the present subject; for a fuller discussion and bibliographical suggestions, the interested reader may consult the relevant entries in N. G. L. Hammond and H. H. Scullard (eds.), *The Oxford Classical Dictionary* (2nd ed.). All of these authors are available in English translation, some in Penguin, all in the Loeb Classical Library edition.

AMMIANUS MARCELLINUS (*c*.AD 330-95), *The History*. From Antioch in Syria. Ammianus served as an officer on the eastern frontier under the governor Ursicinus then later participated in the Persian expedition of the Emperor Julian. His *History* covered the period AD 96-378, but the surviving part spans only the years 353-78. His particular value is for the light it sheds on contemporary Roman military affairs in the East.

CASSIUS DIO (*c*.AD 163-230), *Roman History*. From Nicaea in Bithynia. Dio rose to high office under the Severan emperors, including two consulships and several provincial governorships. His voluminous *History*, from the origins of Rome to AD 229 in 80 books, is extant only in part. He provides a great deal of useful information on events in the East and is especially valuable for his accounts of Roman wars with Parthia and Sasanian Persia.

FLAVIUS JOSEPHUS (AD 37-*c*.95), *Jewish War* and *Jewish Antiquities*. Born into an aristocratic and priestly family, Josephus was initially one of the leading rebel commanders in the Jewish War of 66-70. After his capture by Vespasian, he accompanied the future emperor then his son Titus in their campaigns to end the rebellion. His two major surviving works are a vital source of information on the Roman Near East, informed by his personal experience of the Roman army as first opposing commander and then passive observer, and his subsequent access, while resident in Rome, to the *Commentaries* of Vespasian and Titus.

PLUTARCH (before AD 50-after 120), *The Parallel Lives*. From an aristocratic family of Chaeronaea in Achaea. There is a great deal of useful information on Roman military affairs in the East in the Late Republic to be found in the *Lives* of Sulla, Lucullus, Pompey, Crassus, Caesar and Antony.

PROCOPIUS (*c*.AD 500-after 562), *The History of the Wars, The Secret History* and *The Buildings* From Caesarea Palaestinae. An officer on the staff of Justinian's general Belisarius during his major campaigns, and later City Prefect of Constantinople. The account of the 'Persian War' and of the *Buildings* of Justinian are major sources of evidence for events and places, not least fortifications.

CORNELIUS TACITUS (*c*.AD 56-115), *Annals* and *Histories*. A senator of North Italian or Gallic family. Between them, these two works provide us with evidence of events in the East under the Julio-Claudian dynasty.

The Writer of the *Augustan History* (late fourth century). PLINY THE ELDER (AD 23/4-79), *Natural History*. STRABO (64/3 BC-AD 21), *Geography*. SUETONIUS TRANQUILLUS (*c*. AD 69-post-121/2), *Lives of the Caesars*. VELLEIUS PATERCULUS (*c*.19 BC-post AD 30), *The Roman History*. ZOSIMUS (late fourth/early fifth century), *The New History*.

Notitia Dignitatum: 'The List of Dignitaries' was compiled soon after AD 395 and covers the entire Empire. Its particular importance for military history is that it records, province by province, the title of the senior military officer then all of the units under his command together with their location. The text is only available in an old edition (Seeck, 1876); there is no English translation.

Papyri with information relevant to the eastern frontier come principally from two sites. The largest group, those from Dura Europos, have been fully published (Welles, 1959) though many have been revised and discussed elsewhere subsequently. Final publication of the more recently discovered group from caves above the Dead Sea is still in preparation and only brief reports are available (Polotsky, 1962; Yadin, 1971).

Inscriptions are scattered widely. Some are in *CIL* III, others in the reports of the German (Brünnow and von Domaszewski, 1904-9) and Princeton expeditions (Butler *et al.*, 1907-43). When the series is completed, most will be found in the various fascicles of *Inscriptions grecques et latines de la Syrie* and *Inscriptions grecques et latines de la Jordanie*.

·*Modern Works*·

The list which follows includes not only all of the works cited above in our text together with a handful of more general items, but all of the important relevant publications of Père Antoine Poidebard and of Sir Aurel Stein. A full list of the publications of Poidebard may be found in Mouterde, 1955-56, 325-8.

ADAMS, R.McC., (1981) *The Heartland of Cities*, Chicago.

ADAMS, R. McC. *et al.*, (1977) 'Saudi Arabian Archaeological Reconnaissance', *Atlal*, 1, 21-40.

AGACHE, R., (1978) *La Somme Pré-Romaine et Romaine*, Amiens.

AHARONI, Y. (ed.), (1973) *Beer-Sheba I. Excavations at Tel Beer-Sheba, 1969-1971 Seasons*, Tel Aviv.

ALT, A., (1927) 'Römerstrasse Jerusalem-Eleutheropolis. 4. Die Ausfluge (Beth-Ter)', *Palästina Jahrbuch*, 23, 9-15.
(1935) 'Aus der Araba II-IV', *Zeitschrift der Deutschen Palästinavereins*, 58, 1-78.

ANDRAE, W., (1908-12) *Hatra nach Aufnahmen von Mitgliedern der Expedition der Deutschen Orientgesselschaft*, Leipzig.

ANDREWS, F.H., (1944) 'Sir Aurel Stein: the Man', *Indian Arts and Letters*, 18, no.2 (May), 65-74.

APPLEBAUM, S., (1976) *Prolegomena to the Study of the Second Jewish Revolt* (AD 132-5), *Brit Archaeol Rep Int Ser 7*, Oxford.

AVI-YONAH, M., (1954) *The Madaba Mosaic Map*, Jerusalem.

BAATZ, D., (1978) 'Recent Finds of Ancient Artillery', *Britannia*, 9, 1-17.

BALTY, J.-CH., (1987) 'Apamée (1986): Nouvelles Donnés sur l'Armée Romaine d'Orient et les Raids Sassanides du Milieu du IIIᵉ Siècle', *Comptes Rendus de l'Académie des Inscriptions et Belles-Lettres*, 213-42.

BARADEZ, J., (1949) *Fossatum Africae*, Paris

BEAZELEY, G.A., (1919) 'Air Photography in Archaeology', *Geog J*, 53, 330-5.
(1920) 'Surveys in Mesopotamia During the War', *Geog J*, 55, 109-27.

BELL, G.L., (1911) *Amurath to Amurath*, London.

BIRLEY, A.R., (1981) 'The Economic Effects of Roman Frontier Policy', in *The Roman West in the Third Century. Contributions from Archaeology and History*, edited by A. King and M. Henig, *Brit Archaeol Rep Int Ser 109*, Oxford, 39-53.
(1988) *The African Emperor. Septimius Severus*, London.

BISHEH, G., (1980) 'Excavations at Qasr el-Hallabat, 1979', *Ann Dept Antiq Jordan*, 24, 69-77.
(1982) 'The Second Season of Excavations at Qasr el-Hallabat, 1980', *Ann Dept Antiq Jordan*, 26, 133-44.
(forth) 'Qasr el-Hallabat: a Summary of the 1984 and 1985 Excavations', *Ann Dept Antiq Jordan*.

BIVAR, A.D.H. (1983) 'The Political History of Iran under the Arsacids' in *The Cambridge History of Iran* 3 (i), edited by E.Yarshater, Cambridge, 21-99.

BOWERSOCK, G.W., (1971) 'A Report on Arabia Provincia', *J Roman Stud*, 61, 219-42.

BRADFORD, J., (1957) *Ancient Landscapes*, London.

BREASTED, J.H., (1924) *Oriental Forerunners of Byzantine Painting. First-Century Wall Paintings from the Fortress of Dura on the Middle Euphrates*, *The University of Chicago, Oriental Institute Publications Volume I*, Chicago.
(1933) *The Oriental Institute*, Chicago.

BREEZE, D.J., (forth.) *The Frontiers of the Principate*, London.

BRIMER, B., (1981) 'Archaeological Recognition Elements of Ancient Sites in the Negev', in A. Segal, *Shivta. Plan and Architecture of a Byzantine Town in the Negev*, Beersheva, 59-66.

BRULET, R., (1984) 'Estampilles de la IIIe Légion Cyrénaïque à Bostra', *Berytus*, 32, 175-9.

BRÜNNOW, R.E., and VON DOMASZEWSKI, A., (1904-09) *Die Provincia Arabia*, Strassburg.

BUTLER, H.C., LITTMANN, E. and PRENTICE, W.K., (1907-43) *The Publications of the Princeton*

University Archaeological Expeditions to Syria in 1904-5 and 1909, Leyden.

CAMPBELL, D.B., (1988) 'Dating the Siege of Masada', *Zeitschrift für Papyrologie und Epigraphik*, 73, 156-8.

CANTINEAU, J., (1933) 'L'Inscription de Umm es-Selabih', *Syria*, 14, 178-80.

CARROLL, W.D., (1923/4) 'Bittir and its Archaeological Remains', *Ann Amer Schools Oriental Res*, 5, 77-103.

CASKEL, W., (1954) 'The Bedouinization of Arabia' in *Studies in Islamic Cultural History* edited by G.E. von Grunebaum, *Memoirs of the American Anthropological Association 76*, Menshasha, WI, 36-46.

CHRISTLEIN, R., and BRAASCH, O., (1982) *Das Unterirdische Bayern*, Stuttgart.

COHEN, R., (1980) 'Excavations at Avdat, 1977', *Qadmoniot*, 49-50, (Hebrew).
(1982) 'New Light on the Petra-Gaza Road', *Biblical Archaeologist*, 45, 240-7.

COLLINGWOOD, R.G., and RICHMOND, I.A., (1969) *The Archaeology of Roman Britain*, London (2nd ed).

CORBO, V., (1978) 'La Fortezza di Macheronte', *Liber Annuus*, 28, 217-31.

COULSON, J.C., (1986) 'Roman, Parthian and Sassanid Tactical Developments', in *The Defence of the Roman and Byzantine East*, edited by P.Freeman and D.Kennedy, *Brit Archaeol Rep Int Ser 297*, Oxford, 59-75.

CRAWFORD, O.G.S., (1929) 'Air Photographs of the Middle East', *Geog J*, 73, 497-512.
(1954) 'A Century of Air Photography', *Antiquity*, 28, 206-10
(1955) *Said and Done*, London.

CRAWFORD, O.G.S., and KEILLER, A., (1928) *Wessex from the Air*, Oxford.

CRESWELL, K.A.C., (1969) *Early Muslim Architecture*, Oxford.

CROW, J., (1986) 'A Review of the Physical Remains of the Frontier of Cappadocia', in *The Defence of the Roman and Byzantine East*, edited by P.Freeman and D.Kennedy, *Brit Archaeol Rep Int Ser 297*, Oxford, 77-91.

DABROWA, E., (1986) 'The Frontier in Syria in the First Century AD', in *The Defence of the Roman and Byzantine East*, edited by P.Freeman and D.Kennedy, *Brit Archaeol Rep Int Ser 297*, Oxford, 93-108.

DEBEVOISE, N.C., (1938) *A Political History of Parthia*, Chicago.

DESREUMAUX, A., and HUMBERT, J.B., (1982) 'Exploration à Khirbet es-Samra: Une Question pour l'Histoire de la Jordanie', in *Studies in the History and Archaeology of Jordan*, I, 239-42, edited by A.Hadidi, Amman.

DEVIJVER, H., (1976-80) *Prosopographia Militiarium Equestrium Quae Fuerunt Ab Augusto Ad Gallienum*, Leuven.

DE VRIES, B., (1986) 'Umm el-Jimal in the First Three Centuries AD' in *The Defence of the Roman and Byzantine East*, edited by P.Freeman and D.Kennedy, *Brit Archaeol Rep Int Ser 297*, Oxford, 227-41.

DUNAND, M., (1931) 'A Propos de la Strata Diocletiana', *Revue Biblique*, 40, 227-48; 579-84.
(1933) 'La Voie Romain du Ledgâ', *Mémoires de L'Académie des Inscriptions et Belles-Lettres*, 13, 521-57.

DUNBABIN, T.J., (1955) 'Sir John Myers', *Proc Brit Acad*, 41, 349-65.

DUNCAN-JONES, R.P., (1978) 'Pay and Numbers in Diocletian's Army', *Chiron*, 8, 541-60.

DUSSAUD, R., (1927) *Topographie Historique de la Syrie Antique et Médiévale*, Paris.

DYSON, S.L., (1968) *Excavations at Dura-Europos. Final Report IV.I.3, The Common Pottery. The Brittle Ware*, New Haven, CN.

EADIE, J.W., (1984) 'Humayma 1983: the Regional Survey', *Ann. Dept Antiq Jordan*, 28, 211-24.
(1986) 'The Evolution of the Roman Frontier in Arabia', in *The Defence of the Roman and Byzantine East* edited by P.Freeman and D.Kennedy, *Brit Archaeol Rep Int Ser 297*, Oxford, 243-52.

ECK, W. (1970) *Senatoren von Vespasian bis Hadrian*, Munich.

ENGELBACH, R., (1929) 'The Aeroplane and Egyptian Archaeology', *Antiquity*, 3, 470-3.

EVENARI, M., SHANAN, L. and TADMOR, N. (1982) *The Negev. The Challenge of a Desert*, (2nd ed.), Harvard.

FIELD, H., (1960) *North Arabian Desert Archaeological Survey, 1925-50*, Coral Gables, FL.

FRANK, F. VON, (1934) 'Aus der Araba I', *Zeitschrift des Deutschen Palästinavereins*, 57, 191-280.

FREEMAN, P.W.M., (forth.) 'Recent Work on a Roman Fort in South Jordan', in *Proceedings of the XIVth Internationalen Limeskongressus Bad Deutsch-Altenberg/Carnuntum 1986*, edited by M. Kandler, Vienna.

FREEMAN, P.W.M., and KENNEDY, D.L., (eds.) (1986) *The Defence of the Roman and Byzantine East, Brit Archaeol Rep Int Ser, 297* (= British Institute of Archaeology at Ankara, Monograph

No. 8), Oxford.

FRERE, S.S., and ST. JOSEPH, J.K.S., (1983) *Roman Britain from the Air*, Cambridge

FRITZ, V., (1973) 'The Roman Fortress', in *Beer-Sheba I. Excavations at Tel Beer-Sheba, 1969-1971 Seasons*, edited by Y. Aharoni, Tel Aviv, 83-9.

FRYE, R.N., (1983) 'The Political History of Iran under the Sasanians' in *The Cambridge History of Iran 3 (i)*, edited by E.Yarshater, Cambridge, 116-80.

GAUBE, H., (1974a) 'An Examination of the Ruins of Qasr Burqu', *Ann Dept Antiq Jordan*, 19, 93-100.

(1974b) *Ein Arabischer Palast in Südsyrien. Hirbet el-Baida*, Beirut.

GAVISH, D., and BIGER, G., (1983) 'Innovative Cartography in Palestine of 1917-1918. Initial Use of Aerial Photography in Town Mapping', *Survey Review*, 27, 81-91.

GAWLIKOWSKI, M., (1984) *Palmyre VIII. Les Principia de Dioclétien ('Camp des Enseignes')*, Warsaw.

GICHON, M., (1986) 'Aspects of a Roman Army in War According to the *Bellum Iudaicum* of Josephus', in *The Defence of the Roman and Byzantine East*, edited by P.Freeman and D.Kennedy, *Brit Archaeol Rep Int Ser* 297, Oxford, 287-310.

GLUECK, N., (1935) *Explorations in Eastern Palestine, II, Ann Amer Schools Oriental Res* XV (1934-1935), New Haven, CN.

(1937) 'An Aerial Reconnaissance in Southern Transjordan', *Bull Amer Schools Oriental Res*, 66, 27f; 67, 19-26.

(1939) *Explorations in Eastern Palestine, III, Ann Amer Schools Oriental Res* XVIII-XIX (1937-1939), New Haven, CN.

(1970) *The Other Side of Jordan*, Cambridge, MA.

GOGUEY, R., (forth.) 'Recherches sur l'Archéologie Militaire Romaine: Mirebeau – Alésia', *Proceedings of the Second International Symposium on Aerial Photography and Geophysical Prospection in Archaeology, 1986*, Brussels.

GRABAR, O., *et al.*, (1978) *City in the Desert. Qasr al-Hayr East*, Cambridge, MA.

GRAF, D.F., (1978) 'Saracens and the Defense of the Arabian Frontier', *Bull Amer Schools Oriental Res*, 229, 1-26.

(1988) 'Qura Arabiyya and Provincia Arabia, in *Géographie historique au Proche-Orient, Notes et Monographies Techniques*, 23, 171-211, Paris.

(1989) 'Rome and the Saracens: Reassessing the Nomadic Menace' in *L'Arabie Préislamique et son Environement Historique et Culturelle*, edited by T. Fahd, Strasbourg, 341-400.

GRAF, D.F., and O'CONNOR, M., (1977) 'The Origin of the Term Saracen and the Rawwafah Inscriptions', *Byzantine Studies*, 4, 52-66.

GREGORY, S., (in progress) *Military Architecture on the Eastern Frontier of the Roman Empire*, Ph.D. thesis, Sheffield.

GREGORY, S., and KENNEDY, D.L., (1985) *Sir Aurel Stein's Limes Report*, *Brit Archaeol Rep Int Ser*, 272, Oxford.

HANSON, W.S., (1987) 'Elginhaugh', *Current Archaeology*, 104, 268-72.

HANSON, W.S., and CAMPBELL, D.B., (1986) 'The Brigantes: from Clientage to Conquest', *Britannia*, XVII, 73-89.

HARPER, R., (1986) 'Upper Zohar: a Preliminary Excavation Report', in *The Defence of the Roman and Byzantine East*, edited by P.Freeman and D.Kennedy, *Brit Archaeol Rep Int Ser* 297, Oxford, 329-36.

HASSALL, M., (1972) Review of S. Dyson, *Dura Europos Final Report, IV.1.3. The Common Ware Pottery, The Brittle Ware*, Locust Valley, NY, *Palestine Exploration Quarterly*, 104, 159-60.

(1983) 'The Internal Planning of Roman Auxiliary Forts', in *Rome And Her Northern Provinces*, edited by B. Hartley and J. Wacher, Gloucester, 96-131.

HAWKES, C. (1929) 'The Roman Siege of Masada', *Antiquity*, 3, 195-213.

HELMS, S., and BETTS, A., (1987) 'The Desert "Kites" of the Badiyat esh-Sham and North Arabia', *Paleorient*, 13, 41-67.

HONIGMANN, E., and MARICQ, A., (1953) *Recherches sur les Res Gestae Divi Saporis*, Bruxelles.

HOPKINS, C., (1979) *The Discovery of Dura Europos*, Yale

HOPKINS, K., (1980) 'Taxes and Trade in the Roman Empire', *J. Roman Stud.*, 70, 101-25.

HORSFIELD, G., (1937) 'Umm el-Jamal', *Antiquity*, 11, 456-60.

HOVANNISIAN, R.G., (1982) *The Republic of Armenia, Vol. 2 From Versailles to London 1919-1920*, Los Angeles.

HUMBERT, J.-B., (1981) 'Une Exploration à Khirbet es-Samra', *Ann Dept Antiq Jordan*, 26, 33-84, pls X-XX.

(1981-1986) 'Khirbet es-Samra', *Liber Annuus*, 347-9, pl. 108; 498-501, pls 122f; 416-20, pl. 74;

442-4, pl. 91; 432-34, pl. 111; 358-61, pls 76f.

HÜTTEROTH, W-D., and ABDULFATTAH, K., (1977) *Historical Geography of Palestine, Transjordan and Southern Syria in the Late 16th Century*, Erlangen.

IBRAHIM, J.K., (1980) 'The Excavation of Khirbet Jaddalah', *Sumer*, 36, 163-8
(1983) 'The Excavations at Khirbet Jaddalah 1977-1978', *Sumer*, 39, 217-34.

INVERNIZZI, A., (1986) 'Kifrin and the Euphrates Limes', in *The Defence of the Roman and Byzantine East*, edited by P.Freeman and D.Kennedy, *Brit Archaeol Rep Int Ser*, 297, Oxford, 357-81.

ISAAC, B., (1984) 'Bandits in Judaea and Arabia', *Harvard Studies in Classical Philology*, 88, 171-203.
'Reflections on the Roman Army in the East', in *The Defence of the Roman and Byzantine East*, edited by P.Freeman and D.Kennedy, *Brit Archaeol Rep Int Ser 297*, Oxford, 383-95.
(1988) 'The Meaning of the Terms Limes and Limitanei', *J Roman Stud*, 78, 125-47.
(1990) *The Limits of Empire: The Roman Army in the East*, Cambridge.

ISSERLIN, B.S.J., (1984) 'The Expedition of Aelius Gallus and other Aspects of Roman Penetration into Arabia: Some Suggestions for Future Research', in *Studies in the History of Arabia II. Pre-Islamic Arabia*, Riyadh.

JOHNSON, A., (1983) *Roman Forts*, London.

JOHNSON, S. (1983) *Late Roman Fortifications*, London.

JONES, A.H.M., (1964) *The Later Roman Empire 284-602*, Oxford.

JONES, G.D.B., (1989) 'The Development of Air Photography in North Africa', in *Into the Sun. Essays in Air Photography in Archaeology in Honour of Derrick Riley*, edited by D.Kennedy, Sheffield, 29-47.

KARNAPP, W., (1976) *Die Stadtmauer von Resafa in Syrien*, Berlin.

KEAVENEY, A., (1981) 'Roman Treaties with Parthia circa 95-circa 64 BC', *Amer Jnl Philology*, 102, 195-212.
(1982) 'The King and the War-Lords: Romano-Parthian Relations circa 64-53 BC', *Amer Jnl Philology*, 103, 412-28.
(1980) 'Deux Dates Contestées de la Carrière de Sylla', *Les Etudes Classiques*, 48, 149-59.

KENNEDY, A., (1925) '*Petra its History and Monuments*' London.

KENNEDY, D.L., (1980) 'The Frontier Policy of Septimius Severus: New Evidence from Arabia', in W.S. Hanson and L.J.F. Keppie (eds) *Roman Frontier Studies 1979, Brit Archaeol Rep Int Ser 71*, Oxford, 879-88.
(1982) *Archaeological Explorations on the Roman Frontier in North East Jordan, Brit Archaeol Rep Int Ser, 134*, Oxford.
(1987) 'The Frontiers: the East', in *The Roman World*, edited by J.A. Wacher, London, 266-308.
(1987), 'The Garrisoning of Mesopotamia in the Late Antonine and Early Severan Period', *Antichthon*, 21, 57-66.
(1988) 'A Lost Latin Inscription from the Banks of the Tigris', *Zeitschrift für Papyrologie und Epigraphik*, 73, 101-3.
(forth) 'The Eastern Frontier', in *The Frontiers of the Principate*, edited by D.J.Breeze, London.
(1989) 'An Analysis of Poidebard's Air Survey over Syria', in *Into the Sun, Essays in Air Photography in Archaeology in Honour of Derrick Riley*, edited by D. Kennedy, Sheffield, 48-50

KENNEDY, D.L., and MacADAM, H.I. (1985) 'Some Latin Inscriptions from the Azraq Oasis', *Zeitschrift für Papyrologie und Epigraphik*, 60, 97-107.
(1986) 'Latin Inscriptions from Jordan, 1985', *Zeitschrift für Papyrologie und Epigraphik*, 65, 231-6.

KENNEDY, D.L., MacADAM, H.I., and RILEY, D.N. (1986) 'Preliminary Report on the Southern Hauran Survey, 1985', *Ann Dept Antiq Jordan*, 30, 145-53.

KENNEDY, D.L., and NORTHEDGE, A., (1988) 'Ana in the Classical Sources', in *Ana, Excavations of the British Archaeological Expedition at Qal'a Island 1981-2*, edited by A. Northedge, A. Bamber, and M. Roaf, *British School of Archaeology in Iraq, Iraq Archaelogical Reports*, 1, Warminster, 6-8.

KEPPIE, L.J.F., (1986) 'Legions in the East from Augustus to Trajan', in *The Defence of the Roman and Byzantine East*, edited by P. Freeman and D. Kennedy, *Brit Archaeol Rep Int Ser 297*, Oxford, 411-29.

KHOURI, R.G., and WHITCOMB, D., (1988) *Aqaba. 'Port of Palestine on the China Sea'*, Amman.

KILLICK, A.C., (1983) 'Udruh – The Frontier of an Empire: 1980 and 1981 Seasons, A Preliminary Report', *Levant*, 15, 110-31.
(1986) 'Udruh and the Southern Frontier', in *The Defence of the Roman and Byzantine East*, edited by P.Freeman and D. Kennedy, *Brit Archaeol Rep Int Ser 297*, Oxford, 431-46.

(1987) *Udruh. Caravan City and Desert Oasis*, Romsey.

KNAUF, A. and BROOKER, C.H., (1988) (Review of Whitcomb, 1988), *Zeitschrift des Deutschen, Palästinavereins*, 104, 179-81.

KOCHAVI, M. (ed.), (1972) *Judaea, Samaria and the Golan: Archaeological Survey 1967-68*, Jerusalem (in Hebrew).

KRAELING, C., (1938) *Gerasa: City of the Decapolis*, New Haven, CN.

LANDER, J., (1984) *Roman Stone Fortifications*, Brit Archaeol Rep Int Ser 206, Oxford.

LAUFFRAY, J., (1983) *Halabiya-Zenobia. Place Forte du Limes Orientale et la Haute-Mésopotamie au VIe Siècle*, Paris.

LEWIS, N.N., (1987) *Nomads and Settlers in Syria and Jordan, 1800-1980*, Cambridge.

LUNT, J., (1984) *Glubb Pasha. A Biography*, London.

LUTTWAK, E.N., (1976) *The Grand Strategy of the Roman Empire*, Baltimore.

MacADAM, H.I., (1986) *Studies in the History of the Roman Province of Arabia. The Northern Sector*, Brit Archaeol Rep Int Ser, 295, Oxford.
(1989) 'Fragments of a Latin Building Inscription from Aqaba, Jordan', *Zeitschrift für Papyrologie und Epigraphik*, forthcoming.

MacDONALD, B., (1984) 'A Nabataean and/or Roman Military Monitoring Zone Along the South Bank of the Wadi el-Hesa in Southern Jordan', *Echos du Monde Classique/Classical Views*, 28, 219-34.

MacDONALD, B., *et al.* (1988) *The Wadi el-Hasa Archaeological Survey 1979-1983, West-Central Jordan*, Waterloo, Ont.

MacDONALD, D., (1986) 'Dating the Fall of Dura-Europos', *Historia*, 35, 45-68.

MacDONALD, G., (1934) 'Rome in the Middle East' (Review of Poidebard, 1934), *Antiquity*, 8, 373-80.

McEWAN, C.W. *et al.*, (1958) *Soundings at Tell Fakhariyah*, Chicago.

MacMULLEN, R., (1980) 'How Big was the Roman Imperial Army?', *Klio*, 62, 451-60.

MAITLAND, P.E., (1927) 'The "Works of the Old Men" in Arabia', *Antiquity*, 1, 197-203.

MANN, J.C., (1969) 'A Note on an Inscription from Kurnub', *Israel Explor J*, 19, 211-4.
(1974) 'The Frontiers of the Principate', in H. Temporini (ed.), *Aufstieg und Niedergang der Römischen Welt*, Berlin-New York, II.1, 508-33.
(1979) 'Power, Force and the Frontiers of the Principate', *J Roman Stud*, 69, 175-83.

MARICQ, A., (1958) 'Res Gestae Divi Saporis', *Syria*, 35, 295-360.

MARSDEN, E.W., (1969) *Greek and Roman Artillery*, Oxford.

MATTHEWS, J.F., (1984) 'The Tax Law of Palmyra', *J Roman Stud*, 74, 157-80.

MESHEL, Z., and ROLL, I., (1987) 'Yotvetah', *Eretz Israel*, 19, 249-62.

MIRSKY, J., (1977) *Aurel Stein*, London.

MITCHELL, S., (1983) *Armies and Frontiers in Roman and Byzantine Anatolia*, Brit. Archaeol. Rep. Int. Ser. 156, Oxford.

MOLE, E., (1984) *Happy Landings*, Shrewsbury.

MOUTERDE, R., (1930) 'La Strata Diocletiana et ses Bornes Milliaires', *Mélanges de l'Université Saint-Joseph de Beyrouth*, 15, 221-33, 339-40.
(1955-56) 'In Memoriam le Père Antoine Poidebard, S.J.', *Mélanges de l'Université Saint Joseph (de Beyrouth)*, 31, 317-28

MOUTERDE, R., and POIDEBARD, A., (1931) 'La Voie Antique des Caravanes entre Palmyre et Hit au IIème Siècle ap. J.C.', *Syria*, 12, 111-15.
(1945) *Le Limes de Chalcis. Organisation de la Steppe en Haute-Syrie Romaine*, Beyrouth-Paris.

MUSIL, A., (1907-8) *Arabia Petraea, III. Edom*, Vienna.
(1927) *The Middle Euphrates*, New York.
(1928) *Palmyrena*, New York

NEGEV, A., (1977) 'The Nabataeans and the Provincia Arabia', in *Aufstieg und Niedergang der Römischen Welt*, edited by H. Temporini and W. Haase, Berlin-New York, II. 8, 520-686.
(1983) *Tempel, Kirchen und Zisternen*, Stuttgart.
(1986) *The Archaeological Encyclopedia of the Holy Land*, Nashville, TN.

NORTHEDGE, A., BAMBER, A. and ROAF, M., (1988) *Ana, Excavations of the British Archaeological Expedition at Qal'a Island 1981-2 British School of Archaeology in Iraq, Iraq Archaelogical Reports*, 1 Warminster.

OATES, D., (1968) *Studies in the Ancient History of Northern Iraq*, London
(1982) 'Excavations at Tell Brak, 1978-81', *Iraq*, 44, 187-204.

OATES, D., and OATES, J., (1959) 'Ain Sinu: a Roman Frontier Post in Northern Iraq', *Iraq*, 21, 207-42.

OLDHAM, C.E.A.W., (1943) 'Sir Aurel Stein, 1862-1943', *Proc Brit Acad*, 29, 329-48.

OLESON, J.P., (1987) 'The Humayma Hydraulic Survey: Preliminary Report of the 1986 Season', *Echos du Monde Classique/Classical Views*, 31, 263-72.

OPPENHEIMER, A., (1983) *Babylonia Judaica in the*

Talmudic Period, Wiesbaden.

PARKER, S.T., (1975) 'The Decapolis Reviewed', *J Biblical Literature*, 94, 437-41.

(1976) 'Archaeological Survey of the Limes Arabicus: a Preliminary Report', *Ann Dept Antiq Jordan*, 21, 19-31.

(1986) *Romans and Saracens. A History of the Arabian Frontier*, Winona Lake, IN.

(1987) *Limes Arabicus Project 1980-85, Brit Archaeol Rep Int Ser*, 340, Oxford.

PENNACCHIETTI, F.A., (1986) 'Kifrin. Il Posto dei Cipri', *Mesopotamia*, 21, 85-95.

PICCIRILLO, M. and ATTIVAT, T., (1986) 'The Complex of Saint Stephen at Umm er-Resas-kastron Meffaa', *Ann. Dept. Antiq. Jordan*, 30, 341-51.

POIDEBARD, A., (1926) 'Les Routes Anciennes du Haute Djézireh, Rapport', *Comptes Rendu de l'Académie des Inscriptions et Belles-Lettres*, 236-8.

(1927a) 'La Haute Djézireh', *La Géographie*, 1-16, 314ff.

(1927b) 'Les Routes Anciennes du Haute Djézireh', *Syria*, 8, 55-65.

(1928a) 'Reconnaissances Aériennes au Ledja et au Safa', *Syria*, 9, 114-23.

(1928b) 'Mission Archéologique en Haute-Djézireh (Automne 1927)', *Syria*, 9, 216-223.

(1929a) 'Mission d'Automne (1928) en Haute Djézireh', *Comptes Rendu de l'Académie des Inscriptions et Belles-Lettres*, 91-4.

(1929b) 'Notes sur l'Organisation Romaine de la Palmyrène', *Comptes Rendu de l'Académie des Inscriptions et Belles-Lettres*, 155f.

(1929c) 'Reconnaissances Aériennes au Ledja et au Safa', *La Géographie*, 1-17.

(1929d) 'Les Révélations Archéologiques de la Photographie Aériennes. Une Nouvelle Méthode d'Observation en Région de Steppe', *L'Illustration*, 660-2.

(1929e) 'Diagonale Aérienne Au-dessus du Désert de Syrie', *Etudes*, XX, 54-69.

(1929f) 'L'Aviation Militaire du Levant et les Recherches Scientifiques', *Revue des Forces Aériennes*, 319-51.

(1930a) 'Mission Archéologique en Haute Djézireh', *Syria*, 11, 33-42.

(1930b) 'Rapport. Missions en Haute Djézireh et Chamiyé', *Comptes Rendu de l'Académie des Inscriptions et Belles-Lettres*, 203-6.

(1931a) 'Recherches sur le Limes Romaine (Campagne d'Automne 1930)', *Syria*, 274-81.

(1931b) 'Sur les Traces de Rome. Exploration Archéologique Aérienne en Syrie',

L'Illustration, 560-3.

(1932a) 'Méthode Aérienne de Recherches en Géographie Historique', *Terre, Mer, Air, La Géographie*, 1-16.

(1932b) 'Photographie Aérienne et Archéologie. Recherches en Steppe Syrienne (1925-1931)', *Bulletin de Photogrammetrie*, 35-48.

(1933) 'La Photographie Aérienne dans la Lumière Eblouissante du Désert', *L'Illustration*, 312-4.

(1934) *La Trace de Rome dans le Désert de Syrie. Le Limes de Trajan à la Conquête Arabe. Recherches Aériennes (1925-1932)*, 2 vols., Paris.

(1937) 'La Trace de Rome dans le Désert de Syrie (Conférence)', *Mélanges d'Archéologie et d'Histoire*, 54, Paris, 1-24.

(1938) *Il Limes Romano in Siria, Quaderni dell'Impero, Il Limes Romano*, VI, Rome.

(1939a) 'La Route Septentrionale Antioche-Chalcis-Palmyre', *Mélanges Syriens Offerts à M. R. Dussaud*, 2, 761-71, Paris.

(1939b) 'Une Récente Exploration en Transjordanie' (Review of Stein, 1938; 1940), *Comptes Rendu de l'Académie des Inscriptions et Belles-Lettres*, 262-8.

(1939c) *Un grand port disparu. Tyr*, Paris.

POIDEBARD, A., and MOUTERDE, R., (1949) 'A Propos de S. Serge; Aviation et Epigraphie', *Analecta Bollandiana*, 67, 109-16.

POLOTSKY, H.J., (1962) 'The Greek Papyri from the Cave of the Letters', *Israel Exploration J*, 12, 258-62.

REES, L.W.B., (1929a) 'Ancient Reservoirs Near Kasr Azraq', *Antiquity*, 1, 89-92.

(1929b) 'The Transjordan Desert', *Antiquity* 3, 389-406.

REIFENBERG, A., (1950) 'Archaeological Discoveries by Air Photography in Israel', *Archaeology*, 40-6.

REY, L., (1917-19) *Observations sur les Premiers Habitats de la Macédoine Recueillies par le Service Archéologique de l'Armée d'Orient 1916-1919, Bull Corr Hell*, 41-3, Paris.

RICHMOND, I.A., (1962) 'The Roman Siege-Works of Masada, Israel', *J Roman Stud*, 52, 142-55.

(1963) 'Palmyra under the Aegis of Rome', *J Roman Stud*, 53, 43-54.

RILEY, D.N., (1982) 'Antiquities Recorded by Old Photographs taken by the Royal Air Force of the Desert near Azraq Duruz', in D.L. Kennedy, *Archaeological Explorations on the Roman Frontier in North East Jordan, Brit Archaeol Rep Int Ser*, 134, 345-55, Oxford.

(1986) 'Archaeological Air Photography and the Eastern Limes', in *The Defence of the Roman and Byzantine East*, edited by P.Freeman and D.Kennedy, *Brit Archaeol Rep Int Ser*, 297, Oxford, 661-76.

(1987) *Air Photography And Archaeology*, London.

ROGERSON, J., (1985) *The New Atlas of the Bible*, London.

ROTHENBERG, B., (1971) 'The Arabah in Roman and Byzantine Times in the Light of New Research', *Roman Frontier Studies, 1967*, edited by S. Applebaum, Tel Aviv.

SALLER, S, J. and BAGATI, B., (1949) *The Town of Nebo*, Jerusalem.

SARRE, F., and HERZFELD, E., (1911-20) *Archäologische Reise im Euphrat- und Tigris-Gebiet*, Berlin.

SARTRE, M., (1982) *Trois Etudes sur l'Arabie Romaine et Byzantine, Collection Latomus 178*, Bruxelles.

(1985) *Bostra. Des Origines à l'Islam*, Paris

SAUVAGET, J., (1939a) 'Les Ghassanides et Sergiopolis', *Byzantion*, 14, 115-30.

(1939b) 'Remarques sur les Monuments Omeyyades', *Journal Asiatique*, XX, 1-59.

(1939c) 'Les Ruines Omeyyades du Djebel Seis', 20, 239-56.

SAXER, R., (1967) *Untersuchungen zu den Vexillationen der Römischen Kaiserheeres von Augustus bis Diokletian, Epigraphische Studien 1*, Köln.

SCHLUMBERGER, D., (1939) 'Les Fouilles de Qasr el-Heir el-Gharbi (1936-1938). Rapport Préliminaire', *Syria*, 20, 195-238.

(1986) *Qasr el-Heir el-Gharbi*, Paris.

SCHULTEN, A., (1933) 'Masada die Burg des Herodes und die Römische Lager', *Zeitschrift des Deutschen Palästinavereins*, 56, 1-179.

SEECK, O. (ed.), (1962; reprint of 1876 edition) *Notitia Dignitatum*, Frankfurt

SEGAL, A., (1981a) 'Roman Cities in the Province of Arabia', *J Soc Architectural Historians*, 40, 108-21.

(1981b) *Shivta. Plan and Architecture of a Byzantine Town in the Negev*, Beersheva.

SHAHID, I. (1984) *Rome and the Arabs*, Washington, DC.

(1984) *Byzantium and the Arabs in the Fourth Century*, Washington, DC.

SMALLWOOD, E.M., (1976) *The Jews Under Roman Rule*, Leiden.

SPEIDEL, M.P., (1972) 'Numerus où ala Vocontiorum', *Syria*, 49, 495-7.

(1978) 'The Roman Army in Arabia', in *Aufstieg und Niedergang der Römischen Welt*, edited by H.Temporini and W.Haase, Berlin-New York, II.8, 687-730.

(1979) 'A Tile Stamp of Cohors I Thracum Milliaria from Hebron/Palestine', *Zeitschrift für Papyrologie und Epigraphik*, 35, 170-2.

(1987) 'The Roman Road to Dumata (Jawf in Saudi Arabia) and the Frontier Strategy of *Praetensione Colligare*', *Historia*, 36, 211-21.

SPEIDEL, M.P., and FRENCH, D., (1985a) 'Bithynian Troops in the Kingdom of the Bosporus', *Epigraphica Anatolica*, 6, 97-102.

SPEIDEL, M.P. and REYNOLDS, J., (1985b) 'A Veteran of Legio I Parthica from Carian Aphrodisias', *Zeitschrift für Papyrologie und Epigraphik*, 5, 31-5.

STEIN, M.A., (1919) 'Air photography of Ancient Sites', *Geogr J*, 54, 200

(1936) 'The Roman Limes in Syria' (Review of Poidebard, 1934), *Geogr J*, 87, 66-76.

(1938) 'Note on the Remains of the Roman Limes in North Western Iraq', *Geogr J*, 95, 428-38.

(1940) 'Surveys on the Roman Frontier in Iraq and Transjordan', *Geogr J*, 95, 428-38.

(1941) 'The Ancient Trade Route Past Hatra and the Roman Posts', *J Royal Asiatic Soc*, 9, 299-316.

(n.d.) *Personal Narrative [1938-39]*, Ms Stein, Bodleian Library, Oxford.

STROBEL, A., (1974a) 'Observations About the Roman Installations at Mukawer', *Ann Dept Antiq Jordan*, 19, 101-27 (+ plates)

(1974b) 'Das Römische Belagerungswerke um Machaerus: Topographische Untersuchung', *Zeitschrift der Deutschen Palästinavereins*, 90, 128-84.

STUCKY, R., (1973) 'Erster Vorläufiger Bericht über die auf Tell el-Hajj Durchgeführten Schweizerischen Archäologischen Ausgrabungen' *Annales Archéologiques Arabes Syriens*, 23, 161-200

(1975) 'Tell el-Hajj 1972', *Annales Archéologiques Arabes Syriens*, 25, 165-81.

TEIXIDOR, J., (1984) *Un Port Romain du Désert: Palmyre et son Commerce d'Auguste à Caracalla*, Paris.

THOMSEN, P. (1917) 'Die Römischen Meilensteine der Provinzen Syria, Arabia und Palaestina', *Zeitschrift des Deutschen Palästinavereins*, 40, 1-103.

TODD, M., (1985) 'Oppida and the Roman Army: a Review of Recent Evidence', *Oxford J Archaeol*, 4, 187-99

TOLL, N., (1946) *The Excavations at Dura-Europos: Preliminary Reports.* IX.ii, *The Necropolis,* edited by M.I.Rostovtzeff *et al.*, New Haven, CN.

USSISHKIN, D., (1986-7) 'Betar: The Last Stronghold of Bar-Kochba', *Bull Anglo-Israel Archaeol Soc,* 6, 49-50.

VAN LIÈRE, W.J., and LAUFFRAY, J. (1954-5) 'Nouvelles Prospection Archéologique dans le Haute Jezireh Syrienne', *Les Annales Archéologiques de Syrie,* 4-5, 129-48.

VARDAMAN, (1968) *Preliminary Report on the Results of the 1968 Excavations at Machaerus,* Louisville, KY.

VILLENEUVE, F., (1985) 'L'Economie Rurale et la Vie des Campagnes dans le Hauran Antique (Ier siècle av. J.-C. – VIIe Siècle ap. J.-C.). Une approche', in *Hauran I,* 63-136, edited by J.M. Dentzer, Paris
(1986) 'Ad-Diyatheh: Village et Castellum Romains et Byzantins à l'Est de Jebel Druze (Syrie)', in *The Defence of the Roman and Byzantine East,* edited by P.Freeman and D.Kennedy, *Brit Archaeol Rep Int Ser,* 297, Oxford, 697-715.

WELLES, C.B., (1959) *Excavations at Dura-Europos. Final Report V.1, Parchments and Papyri,* New Haven, CN.

WHITBY, M., (1986) 'Procopius and the Development of Roman Defences in Upper Mesopotamia', in *The Defence of the Roman and Byzantine East,* edited by P.Freeman and D.Kennedy, *Brit Archaeol Rep Int Ser* 297, Oxford, 717-35.

WHITCOMB, D., (forth) ' "Diocletian's " *misr* at Aqaba', *Zeitschrift des Deutschen Palästiravereins.*

WIEGAND, T., (1920) *Sinai. Wissenschaftlichen Veröffentlichen des Deutsch-Türkischen Denkmalschutzkommandos,* Berlin.

WILLIAMS, W. A., (1989) *Against the Odds: The Life of Group Captain L. W. B. Rees,* Wrexham.

WILSON, D., (1982) *Air Photo Interpretation for Archaeologists,* London.

YADIN, Y., (1963) 'The Nabataean Kingdom, Provincia Arabia, Petra and En-Geddi in the Documents from Nahal Hever', *Ex Oriente Lux,* 17, 227-41.
(1967) 'Masada and the Limes', *Israel Explor J,* 17, 43-5.
(1966) *Masada: Herod's Fortress and the Zealots' Last Stand,* London.
(1971) *Bar-Kokhba,* London.

·APPENDIX: THE ROMAN EMPERORS·

Augustus		31 BC–AD14
Tiberius	Julio-Claudian dynasty	14-37
Gaius (Caligula)	Julio-Claudian dynasty	37-41
Claudius		41-54
Nero		54-68
Galba		68-69
Otho		69
Vitellius		69
Vespasian	Flavian dynasty	69-79
Titus	Flavian dynasty	79-81
Domitian		81-96
Nerva		96-98
Trajan		98-117
Hadrian		117-138
Antoninus Pius		138-161
Marcus Aurelius (and Lucius Verus)		161-169
Marcus Aurelius	Antonine dynasty	169-177
Marcus Aurelius (and Commodus)		177-180
Commodus		180-192
Pertinax		193
Didius Julianus		193
Septimius Severus	Severan dynasty	193-211
Caracalla	Severan dynasty	211-218
Macrinus		218-219
Elagabalus	Severan dynasty	219-222
Severus Alexander	Severan dynasty	222-235
Maximinus Thrax		235-238
Gordian I and Gordian II		238
Balbinus and Pupienus		238
Gordian III		238-244
Philip		244-249
Decius		249-251
Trebonianus Gallus		251-253
Aemilianus		235
Valerian and Gallienus		253-260
Gallienus		260-268
Claudius II		268-270
Quintillus		270
Aurelian		270-275
Tacitus		275-276
Florianus		276
Probus		276-282

·INDEX·

This index gives the more important references to subjects and proper names, most of which are place names. In order to keep the index at a reasonable length, the page numbers given against proper names cover only the instances where the text provides information, not the frequent geographical references, lists of sites or other brief mentions. An exception has been made in the case of army units, all references to which have been included.